ID768727

WAR, THE ARMY AND VICTORIAN LITERATURE

War, the Army and Victorian Literature

John Peck
Senior Lecturer in English
University of Wales, Cardiff

First published in Great Britain 1998 by
MACMILLAN PRESS LTD
Houndmills, Basingstoke, Hampshire RG21 6XS and London
Companies and representatives throughout the world

A catalogue record for this book is available from the British Library.

ISBN 0–333–69852–5

First published in the United States of America 1998 by
ST. MARTIN'S PRESS, INC.,
Scholarly and Reference Division,
175 Fifth Avenue, New York, N.Y. 10010

ISBN 0–312–21298–4

Library of Congress Cataloging-in-Publication Data
Peck, John, 1947–
War, the army and Victorian literature / John Peck.
p.   cm.
Includes bibliographical references (p.   ) and index.
ISBN 0–312–21298–4
1. English literature—19th century—History and criticism.
2. War and literature—Great Britain—History—19th century.
3. Literature and society—Great Britain—History—19th century.
4. Great Britain—History, Military—19th century.   5. Great
Britain—History—Victoria, 1837–1901.   6. Great Britain. Army-
-History—19th century.   7. Military history in literature.
8. Social change in literature.   9. Imperialism in literature.
10. Colonies in literature.   11. Soldiers in literature.
PR468.W37P43 1998
820.9'358—dc21   97–32315
                                                              CIP

This book is printed on paper suitable for recycling and made from fully managed and
sustained forest sources.

10   9   8   7   6   5   4   3   2   1
07   06   05   04   03   02   01   00   99   98

Printed and bound in Great Britain by
Antony Rowe Ltd, Chippenham, Wiltshire

For Alison

Contents

Preface

This book has its origins in a problem I was trying to resolve about Thackeray. The more I read his novels, the more it struck me that he was out of step with his contemporaries, but I found it hard to pinpoint a clear idea of how Thackeray differs from novelists such as Dickens, the Brontës, Gaskell and Eliot. Then I began to pay attention to the number of soldiers and military scenes that appear in his works. Four of the novels in particular, *Barry Lyndon*, *Vanity Fair*, *Henry Esmond* and *The Virginians*, deal respectively with the Seven Years War, the Battle of Waterloo, the War of the Spanish Succession and the American War of Independence. This struck me as interesting in itself, but what is also significant is that his contemporaries seldom refer to war at all and are unlikely to include military figures in their novels in any kind of featured role. Indeed, the vast majority of Victorian novelists, especially before the 1890s, do not make any reference at all to soldiers, the army or military matters.

This might not be so surprising were it not for the fact that in every year of Victoria's reign British soldiers were fighting somewhere in the world. This led me to start considering an apparent paradox, that Britain appeared to maintain the warlike stance it had developed in the century leading up to 1815 and the Battle of Waterloo, but simultaneously seemed to ignore the existence of war. The contrast with the Renaissance period here is striking: Shakespeare's plays are saturated with war, to the extent that even in the comedies issues of war are often in the background. In most Victorian novels, on the other hand, military conflict does not seem to exist at all despite historical evidence to the contrary. My first objective was to consider how this odd state of affairs came about. What I focus upon in the opening chapter of this book, therefore, is how and why the country that had been victorious at Waterloo turned its back on militarism. There are novelists, such as Charles Lever, who continued to produce military novels, novels that, almost without exception, return to the Napoleonic Wars. But from early on in the Victorian period most novelists chose to concentrate upon domestic issues. This change of direction was partly a matter of form. The realistic novel as it developed in

the nineteenth century seemed ideally equipped to deal with
domestic routine, whereas epic and romance are probably more
appropriate narrative forms for tackling the subject of war. This
shift away from militarism, however, extends beyond the novel as
a genre: in the second chapter, I look at reports from and memoirs
of the Crimean War, showing how the manner and values of
realistic fiction find an echo in these accounts. The change of
attitude towards war is, indeed, so pervasive that a novelist such
as Charles Kingsley, who, inspired by the Crimean War, writes a
novel about heroism, seems totally at odds with the spirit of his
age.

By the end of Chapter 2 it should be apparent just how fundamental a shift of values and attitude there is as we pass from the
era of the Napoleonic Wars to the 1850s, the decade of the Crimean
War and the Indian Mutiny. Britain moves from a view of life in
which military concerns are central to a view of life in which they
are side-lined (military conflict increasingly taking the form of, and
being viewed as, small wars in far-away places). At the same time,
the country moves from an aristocratic, military dispensation to a
middle-class, liberal culture. In line with this, an approach to
politics that is based upon confrontation yields to a politics of
negotiation and compromise. These changes are so obvious, and
perhaps so inevitable, that we are inclined to overlook them. If we
consider writers such as Tennyson and Thackeray, however, we
can see just how difficult it was for some Victorians to disentangle
themselves from a view of social relations based upon military
assumptions. This is most apparent in Thackeray's novels in the
way that he finds it almost impossible to devise a plot that does not
involve a duel; he can see the absurdity of duelling, but at the same
time finds it hard to work out a way in which social behaviour,
particularly between men, can be conducted on a basis of peaceful
compromise rather than armed confrontation.

Unlike Thackeray (the writer I focus on in Chapter 3), other mid-
Victorian novelists not only shun the subject of war, but also seem
to have absorbed, and to express, the new social, cultural and
political assumptions of the Victorian period almost instinctively.
I illustrate this most fully in Chapter 5, 'The Army at Home', which
focuses upon a whole range of well-known Victorian novelists
who, for the most part, have little interest in military matters;
their position is made particularly clear in novels that raise the
possibility of, or deal with the fact of, military intervention in

industrial or political disputes within Britain. Before this, however, I examine in Chapter 4, 'The Army Abroad', the literary response to India and the Indian Mutiny, showing how the assumptions of the new liberal code tend to be exposed as myopic the moment the reality of imperial aggression is considered in fiction. As I suggest in the chapter, Christian militarism, which developed largely in response to the Indian Mutiny, was an attempt to bridge the gap between military activity abroad and the moral standards taken for granted at home, but it provided only a temporary, and possibly inherently suspect, solution.

Indeed, it could be argued that Christian militarism serves merely to draw our attention to the fundamental split between a military impulse, which lauds aggression and heroism, and which finds its natural focus in the form of epic or romance, and a domestic impulse, which praises compromise and individual integrity, and for which the ideal form is the realistic novel. There are some writers who maintain a consistent commitment to the military virtues, but the traditional military virtues seem to mean very little to the vast majority of mid-Victorian writers and readers. In the last twenty years of the century, however, there is an extraordinary resurgence of militarism. While, therefore, the first half of this book concentrates on the decline of militarism in Britain in the years after 1815, the second half concentrates on how literature both reflects and contributes to a revival of militarism in the years after 1880. Chapter 5 starts with Gaskell and Eliot's lack of interest in military questions, something that is even more pronounced in Dickens's novels, but by the end I focus upon Hardy's renewed interest in the figure of the soldier. Chapter 6 starts with Ouida, Carlyle and Kingsley as isolated voices in support of the army, but the second half of the chapter deals with a different kind of militarism at the end of the century. This second major shift in attitudes in the nineteenth century, reflected in such phenomena as the rise of Jingoism, widespread enthusiasm for the army and popular interest in, and newspaper, magazine and book coverage of, its exploits, is part and parcel of a new politics of race, nation and empire which sees the virtual canonisation of General Gordon as the hero of the Sudan.

The more perceptive writers in the later years of the nineteenth century seem, however, to be aware of a deep division within the national character between aggressive, military impulses and peaceful, domestic impulses. It is a tension that Hardy, specifically in *Far From the Madding Crowd* and *The Trumpet-Major*, is perhaps the first to detect and explore. The problem, in essence, is how does the country reconcile its new-found enthusiasm for militarism with its, by now well-established, liberal tradition? How can the inward-looking insularity of the latter be combined with the outward-looking aggression of the former? It is against this background that the special significance of Kipling, and the scale of his achievement and impact, becomes clear. In the twentieth century there has been a great deal of hostile criticism of Kipling, but, probably more than with any other writer, it seems essential to abandon the wisdom of hindsight in order to attempt to grasp the quite unprecedented impression he made on his first audience. Kipling, as I discuss in Chapter 7, for a brief moment at the start of the 1890s, in the first wave of his short stories, seems to reconcile the inconsistencies in Britain's national identity. The early short stories amount to far more than a simple assertion of imperialist warmongering; on the contrary, they engage in a complex consideration of the nature of a revived militarism and its place in the nation's life.

The task Kipling sets himself in his stories is, then, ambitious, and it is, consequently, perhaps not all that surprising that by the end of the century they are buckling under the strain. This is particularly apparent in his Boer War stories. Kipling is, without doubt, the greatest writer on military matters in the Victorian period, but the moment he is confronted by a real war he seems to have nothing to say. Kipling, though, is not alone in this respect. One of the most obvious features of the literary response to the Boer War is that all the old narrative modes seem exhausted and redundant, as if they cannot cope with a new, and unprecedented, state of affairs. Romance lends itself well to a story of heroism, but the facts of the Boer War proved too awkward for the simple form of romance. By the same measure, the reality of the Boer War seemed to transgress the acceptable limits of realistic fiction. The consequence is that, wherever we turn, we find, as I show in Chapter 8, narrative forms stumbling in their attempts to respond to the Boer War. In a way, however, this only brings out into the open a tension that has been apparent throughout the century, that the realistic novel cannot cope with the facts of war, and, by the same token, the romance can only cope with war if it ignores those elements that undermine a fairly simple vision of heroism. What we encounter in the Boer War period, however, is some very fine poetry, as if poetry can provide a new perspective on war in a way that the novel and short story could not manage to do at this time. Kipling's Boer War stories are among his weakest works, but a number of his poems inspired by the conflict, poems suffused by a sense of doubt about Britain's imperial mission, are stunning and surprising.

The vastness of the subject matter of this book – something that I had not totally bargained for when I began to research it – should by now be apparent. My nominal subject is responses to and expressions of militarism in literature of the Victorian period, but my real subject has turned out to be a consideration of some aspects of the complex pattern of social, cultural and political change between 1837 and 1901. The eclipse of a military mentality in the first 50 years of the nineteenth century is the easier half of the argument; far more complex is the way in which, and the terms on which, militarism re-established itself in the last twenty years of the century, for this leads one into a whole range of complex questions both about imperialism and about how militarism stands in relation to other strands of feeling and thinking in nineteenth-century Britain.

A book that tackles a vast subject obviously invites criticism on a number of levels. It can, for example, be suggested that I make too many glib claims on the basis of the slight evidence of a few literary texts. I am also aware of the problems involved in attempting to discuss two immense changes in national thinking within the compass of one relatively short book. As a specialist in English Literature, moreover, I am only too aware of gaps in my historical knowledge. Where I feel most vulnerable, however, is on the question of the rationale that has informed my selection of texts for discussion. Why have I focused mainly on novels? Why do I ignore drama? Why do I deal with poetry only when it suits me to do so? And why have I made such a small and selective dip into the largest tranche of relevant material, the innumerable volumes of memoirs from soldiers, war reporters and civilians caught up in conflicts? My choice of texts is, of course, ultimately illogical; I chose to write about the works that most appealed to me. But I was also concerned to select texts that seemed to have some resonance, texts that seemed to have more to say than might be apparent on the surface. I have tended to ignore Victorian war poetry, for example, because so much of it seems little more than a string of patriotic slogans. Rather than focus on transparent works such as these, I have tried to find works that complicate the argument, that enrich (or, indeed, confuse) rather than simplify the picture of what was going on in the Victorian period.

The whole time I was writing this book, however, I was aware of one text that seemed of central importance and which could be described as a Victorian novel, but which at the same time is not actually a part of Victorian literature and, therefore, could not easily be fitted into my scheme of things. Tolstoy's *War and Peace* was published between 1863 and 1869; it is an epic novel of the Napoleonic invasion, dealing with the lives of three aristocratic families. The nature of its achievement perhaps clarifies the issue in this current book: Tolstoy deals magnificently with how domestic life and military life interconnect and overlap. With the exception of Thackeray, none of the novelists discussed in the chapters that follow can deal with both spheres of experience in this way. But Tolstoy is a writer who emerges from a different culture, a culture where war is always at the centre of the national experience. In nineteenth-century Britain the picture is far more muddled: there is simply a gap between the notion of a peaceful, inward-looking, liberal, democratic state and the reality of an aggressive, expansionist, imperialist, military power. The country tries to define and understand itself somewhere in the gap between these two extremes.

It is a pleasure to acknowledge the help I have received in writing this book. My employer, the University of Wales Cardiff, granted me study leave for a semester, during which time I was able to produce a first draft of the whole book. The staff at the University Library in Cardiff have been immensely resourceful in pursuing obscure inter-library-loan demands, which in a number of cases seemed to involve tracking down just about the only surviving copy of some works. I am also very grateful to three of my colleagues, Claire Connolly, Hugh Osborne and David Skilton, who have helped in a variety of ways. My particular thanks, however, go to my collaborator on numerous editing and writing projects, Martin Coyle, who, as always, has been generous with his advice and time, and who has saved me from numerous blunders both in content and expression.

JOHN PECK
University of Wales Cardiff

1

The Army in Victorian Literature and Life

INTRODUCTION

Elizabeth Gaskell's *North and South* (1855) is the story of Margaret Hale who leaves the village of Helstone for the grim industrial city of Milton-Northern. Memorable episodes include Margaret's encounters with the working people, her relationship with a mill-owner, John Thornton, and her confrontation with a mob of strikers. On the opening page of the novel, however, we are introduced to Margaret and her cousin Edith in the genteel setting of London's Harley Street. Edith is about to be married to an army officer, Captain Lennox, and they will then take up residence in Corfu, where his regiment is stationed. This is the kind of detail that we discard in our reading of the text; Edith and Lennox will disappear from the novel, and can apparently be forgotten. But the insignificance of the detail actually tells us a lot about some of Gaskell's informing assumptions in *North and South*. Most strikingly, whereas the reader is told basic facts about life in Milton-Northern, as if it is a foreign country, the fact that the army has a regiment at Corfu – something that is likely to surprise the modern reader – is presented without explanation. Some things, it seems, such as the living conditions of the people of England, require Gaskell's active mediation, while others can be taken for granted.

What the army is doing in Corfu is helping to keep in check any Russian military ambitions to expand into the Ottoman Empire, expansion which would constitute a threat to the Mediterranean and overland routes to India. In a novel published during the Crimean War (1854–6), perhaps this fact did not need explaining to the contemporary reader, but the casual nature of the reference to Captain Lennox remains intriguing. By a stretch of the imagination it could be connected to other army and navy references in the novel; the possibility of calling in soldiers to deal with the strike is

1

mentioned, and, rather surprisingly in a novel about life in an industrial city, Margaret's brother, Frederick, has taken part in a naval mutiny. These details contribute to the debate at the heart of the novel about the use of force as against the path of compromise; Thornton, for example, before his conversion by Margaret, would opt for a show of strength in dealing with the strikers. But the reference to Lennox, as with a couple of references to Edith's father, General Shaw, is never developed sufficiently to become thematically relevant in this way. There is, however, a disturbing dimension to Lennox. Edith is asleep, almost like a baby, for much of the first chapter, and referred to as a 'Poor child' by her mother's friends.[1] There is something alarming about the union between this 'child' and someone as manly as an army officer. While this debate about the roles assigned to men and women will, indeed, prove central in the novel, it is, however, tangential to the information about their posting to Corfu. Gaskell is a radical social critic, and equally radical on questions of gender, but the army and its place in the scheme of things, particularly in relation to defending the empire, can, it seems, go unquestioned.

Gaskell's stance reflects the view of most Victorians for most of the Victorian period. The novel may be the mirror in which the Victorians consider the state of their nation, but the military dimension of their national life merits little comment. Soldiers might appear, but when they do they are often, as in Gaskell, an almost invisible presence. The empire grew, with a succession of colonial wars, but most of the time nobody gave this more than a moment's consideration. Indeed, on only four occasions – in response to the Crimean War, the Indian Mutiny (1857–9), events in the Sudan (1882–98), and the Boer War (1899–1902) – did military matters cause more than a ripple of excitement. A book about literary representations of the army in the Victorian period looks, therefore, in some respects unpromising. But it is, in fact, the paucity of the material that makes the subject interesting, for this is a time when values were changing fast, and, a generation after the era of the Revolutionary and Napoleonic Wars (1793–1815), Britain appears to have re-constituted itself on an almost entirely non-military basis. What makes the story all the more remarkable is that it was the defeat of Napoleon that helped bring into existence this civilian-dominated society.[2] It would be wrong, however, to suggest that a new code entirely eclipsed the old military code; as we shall see, particularly in relation to Tennyson, Kingsley and Thackeray, there were those who were not at ease with the new ways of thinking. And as the century progresses, the limitations of the new liberal, middle-class philosophy will become apparent; after 1870, as a first watershed, it starts to get a little harder to ignore the existence of the army and war. And by the 1890s, soldiering and the empire might be considered to be the most important subjects in literature.

THE NOVELS OF CHARLES LEVER

The story of the relationship between Victorian literature and the army is, therefore, one that involves a number of twists and turns. It is also a story that – because of the oblique nature of many of the military references in Victorian texts – is hard to pin down. What should become apparent, however, is that a consideration of the army in the context of the non-militaristic atmosphere that existed for much of the Victorian period provides a corrective adjustment to some readings of nineteenth-century thinking. Recent work on Victorian masculinity, particularly on Muscular Christianity, stresses the bellicosity of the national temperament.[3] But the moment military questions are put in the context of the nation's widespread indifference to military matters, the emphasis has to change. We can see the difference in attitudes towards Charles Kingsley who is usually seen as an all too typical Victorian imperialist; but when Kingsley is seen as an isolated voice in a period that has abandoned his kind of militarism, he becomes an interesting oppositional figure in a new orthodoxy.[4] I return to Kingsley in Chapters 2 and 6, but at this point, in order to establish the characteristics of the traditional military culture, I want to look at one of the few Victorian writers who is centrally concerned with life as a soldier, Charles Lever.[5] Later in his career Lever changed direction, but in the 1830s and 1840s he was the most successful of a small clutch of military novelists: W.H. Maxwell, G.R. Gleig, and one of the very few writers who ploughed on for years with war stories, James Grant. Even at this stage, however, Lever was an outsider to the military code that they all seemed to share.[6]

As might be expected, the military novels of this period have a great deal in common: they look back to the period of the Napoleonic Wars, nostalgically recreating an era before the age of steam. The novelists themselves had often participated in the events they describe, a fact which probably contributed to the notorious lack of disciplined structure in their works, which often consist of loosely connected tales and adventures. The mixture of elements is apparent in Maxwell's *Stories of Waterloo* (1829); Maxwell served (or possibly did not serve) in the Peninsular War, and as a captain of infantry at Waterloo.[7] Gleig also served in the Peninsula and at Waterloo; he then returned to Oxford, and was ordained in 1820. Following *The Subaltern* in 1826, he produced a string of similar military novels, such as *The Hussar* in 1837 and *The Light Dragoon* in 1844. His history of the Battle of Waterloo was used by Thackeray as a source-book for *Vanity Fair*. In 1844 he was appointed Chaplain-General of the Forces, a post he held for thirty years.[8] James Grant also started with a look back to the Peninsular War – his four-volume *The Romance of War, or The Highlanders in Spain* (1846–7) – but Grant continued producing novels for much of the Victorian period, as late as 1887, the year he died, writing about the hostilities in the Sudan in *Playing With Fire*. John Sutherland refers to him as an opportunist, 'always ready to write a novel on whatever war was going on'.[9] (I discuss his novel about the Indian Mutiny in Chapter 4.) Leaving aside these later works of Grant's, it is possible to extrapolate two central points about early Victorian military novels. For over a hundred years, both on land and sea, Britain and France had been at war (1702–13, 1743–8, 1756–63, 1778–83, 1793–1802, 1803–15); as Linda Colley argues, 'Great Britain was made out of that remarkable succession of wars'.[10] The novels that look back to victory over Napoleon not only confirm a sense of British national identity but also, because of the nature of the revolutionary threat Napoleon represented, reaffirm the importance of traditional, that is to say aristocratic, leadership. But even more importantly, these novels cling on to an aristomilitary code at the very time when Britain is changing its social, political and cultural composition.[11]

The interesting thing about Charles Lever's novels in this mould – most notably, *The Confessions of Harry Lorrequer* (1839), *Charles O'Malley* (1841), *Jack Hinton* (1842) and *Tom Burke of Ours* (1844) – is that, seriously though they seem to assert traditional values, simultaneously they do not take them seriously at all. Unlike the other novelists mentioned so far, Lever did not have a military background; he trained as a doctor, and practised for some years before taking up writing as a full-time occupation. Following the Irish famine of 1845, he alters track as a novelist, emphasising Irish themes far more and abandoning military matters. But it is clear that, as an Irishman, and even though he has always been criticised for producing stage-Irishmen, he always, even in his four famous military novels, remains sceptical of the idea of Britishness that they may seem to assert.[12] There is a consistent pattern in these four novels: in a form of military picaresque, 'a young officer meets with a variety of adventures and intrigues in the garrison or in wider society'.[13] Harry Lorrequer, for example, is a young English officer posted to Ireland with his regiment; his life consists of gambling, steeple-chasing, socialising, falling in love and duelling. He is subsequently posted to France, the novel ending in Munich, where he finally wins the hand of his Irish sweetheart. *Charles O'Malley* features a young man in Galway who is dazzled by Lucy Dashwood. Charles enlists in the dragoons, seeing action in the Peninsular War. At Waterloo he is captured and witnesses the battle at Napoleon's side. He then marries Lucy. Jack Hinton, in the novel of the same name, is a young English officer in Ireland; after a series of adventures, the action moves to Spain, France and Italy. In *Tom Burke of Ours*, Tom, an Irish orphan, as a consequence of his friendship with a French officer, joins the French army. He becomes involved with the Bourbonists, but his release from prison is secured, and he serves at Austerlitz and Jena. He returns to Ireland, goes back to serve Napoleon, who personally promotes him, but with the collapse of the imperial cause returns home, having married Marie, the sister of his French officer friend.

The first point that is apparent in all these novels is that the life of a soldier and the life of a country gentleman are interchangeable: both consist of riding and shooting. It has been suggested that the issue of soldiering is not really very important in Lever's novels, that 'the military background serves only to provide a neutral and unconstraining context',[14] but such a view overlooks the, admittedly light-hearted, way in which a case is being made about soldiering as an extension of a way of life, rather than a middle-class profession that can be acquired. Indeed, there are virtually no middle-class characters in Lever; most of the characters, however shabby their present circumstances, belong to the patrician class, and for all apparent purposes a middle-class world of trade and commerce does not exist. A lot of the time Lever is very similar to Thackeray, and Thackeray's heroes generally belong to the same class as Lever's, but when the two novelists are considered together it is striking how Thackeray's characters are always having to come to terms with a new middle-class world (this includes a middle-class soldier, Dobbin, in *Vanity Fair*). It is possible to read Lever feeling that this is Thackeray without a real story, but this is because English novels so often centre on issues of class, whereas in Lever's world there is no threat from social newcomers. Consider, for example, the Viceroy's dinner in Dublin Castle in *Jack Hinton*, where there is both unreserved admiration for the Ascendancy characters, and an absence of the reservations Thackeray might express about any gathering of representatives of the old order:

> Austere churchmen, erudite chief-justices, profound politicians, privy councillors, military officers of high rank and standing, were here all mixed up together into one strange medley...Play and politics, wine and women, debts and duels, were discussed, not only with an absence of all restraint, but with a deep knowledge of the world and a profound insight into the heart, which often imparted to the careless and random speech the sharpness of the most cutting sarcasm.[15]

This is an elite, immune from middle-class moralising and seriousness. The fact that this might also be a middle-class vision of aristocratic existence is an issue I will return to.

The only real career in this world is that of a soldier. Charles O'Malley begins to train as a lawyer, but abandons his studies to join the army. And even when there is a war on, life goes on in much the same way. In Lisbon, for the Peninsular War:

> Breakfast, dinners, private theatricals, pigeon matches, formed our daily occupation. Lord Wellington's hounds threw off regularly twice a week...The pace may not have equalled Melton, nor the fences have been as stubborn as in Leicestershire, but I'll be sworn there was more laughter, more fun, and more merriment in one day with us than in a whole season with the best organized pack in England.[16]

We are being presented with a picture of how men of a certain class conduct their lives. They are amateurs, untroubled by a life of idleness and privilege, because they can always be relied upon to redeem themselves on the field of battle. Jack Hinton is typical: educated at Eton, where he was 'a smart boy, but incorrigibly idle'

(p. 6), he then proceeded to Sandhurst before life in Ireland, where a typical day might be spent popping down to the 'Curragh, taking a look at the nags for the Spring Meeting' (p. 71). Lever's social assumptions affect the structure of his novels, which lack the pattern of development of most Victorian novels. The plot we might expect to find is that, when war starts, the hero will come to his senses and start to act more responsibly. But such a pattern reflects the assumption that life is a process of education and moral growth, that one must eventually accept responsibility for one's actions. It is, however, just such assumptions that Lever's novels challenge. The heroes sail through their military experiences without any sense of personal crisis. It is because the qualities that matter are seen as being in-born; they are part of the hero's aristocratic inheritance rather than qualities that have to be acquired along the way.[17]

It is in respects such as these that we see the deeply entrenched conservatism of Lever's novels. At heart, such conservatism is a simple code of manly and gentlemanly behaviour. Just occasionally, however, we notice less pleasant aspects of the same picture. In Horse Guards, Jack Hinton encounters

> young officers of the staff, many of them delicate, effeminate-looking figures, herding scrupulously together, and never condescending, by word or look, to acknowledge their brethren about them. In this knot De Vere was conspicuous by the loud tone of his voice and the continued titter of his unmeaning laugh.
>
> (p. 424)

Obviously we are meant to disapprove of such characters, but in touching on their effeminacy Lever acknowledges what seems to have been a feature of the Wellington era: that officers showed their contempt for middle-class standards by exaggerating a non-masculine pose that was the exact opposite of the bravery they would show in battle (it is a point I return to in the discussion of Ouida in Chapter 6).[18] Additionally, there is their arrogance, their sense of themselves as born to lead and therefore above mere politeness. There is a similar display from Captain Hammersly in *Charles O'Malley*, who 'scarcely turned his head, and gave me a half-nod of very unequivocal coldness' (p. 11). This is a man who sneers at all civilians, yet is superb in the hunt, 'the very *beau idéal* of a gentleman rider' (p. 15), and admirable both in his life and his death as a soldier. Lever is always the active mediator, reconciling his middle-class readership and fun-loving heroes, but the picture is complex enough to acknowledge the behavioural gulf between those born to lead and those who have to conform in order to succeed.

A complication in Lever's novels arises, however, from the fact that, although he defends the old aristomilitary code more persuasively than any of his fellow military novelists, it is impossible to avoid the feeling that, simultaneously, he does not take this code very seriously at all. This is partly a matter of Lever knowing his readers. He wrote for the general novel-reading public, appearing in the same contexts as Dickens and Thackeray. There is no reason to believe that Lever's audience would have had any fondness for an aristocratic political dispensation; the likelihood is that they would have regarded the novels as amusing and escapist, and, in so far as any novel-reader bothers to think about the values implicit in a work, would have regarded the values presented as defunct. In addition, there is a level at which the novels pander to their audience, for tales of upper-class licentiousness both appeal to the envious traits of middle-class readers and bolster their self-confidence by confirming their worst suspicions about the class above them. In this respect, Lever's novels owe something to the 'Silver Fork' novels that were in vogue from the mid-1820s to the mid-1840s, novels that portray, with a mixture of excited envy and moral disapproval, the manners of post-Regency society.[19] Lever's world is, however, in just about every respect, an innocent world: there is an almost total absence of real villainy or sexual corruption in his novels. Indeed, it comes as a surprise in *Jack Hinton* when the hero visits a secret gentlemen's club in Dublin where the members dress as monks. This is the kind of scene we might expect in a middle-class novel fantasising about the lives of the aristocracy. But scenes of debauchery do not ensue; this is simply a dining-club, where Jack is dazzled by the wit and intelligence of the members. The episode conveys well the essential innocence of Lever's novels. They recreate a world that has disappeared (although it probably lingered on in Ireland), and, although they might venture towards the issue, do not exploit the tension between an aristocratic order and a middle-class order that is at the heart of many early Victorian novels.

What we find in the place of a class tension is the issue of nationality. As an Irish writer, Lever increasingly seems to realise

that he is an outsider. The novels are marked by a growing awareness that the English aristocracy does not just represent a dominant
class but a dominant race. The result is that, as much as Lever
might present himself as a defender of English aristocratic militarism, he also, if only in details and incidental scenes, identifies with
the victims of English aristocratic militarism. At the start of *Jack
Hinton*, for example, the hero, as he rides alongside the carriage of
the Viceroy, revels in his life as a soldier in Ireland:

> Handkerchiefs were waved from the windows; streamers and
> banners floated from the house-tops; patriotic devices and alle-
> goric representations of Erin sitting at a plentiful board, opposite
> an elderly gentleman with a ducal coronet, met us at every turn
> of the way. The streets were literally crammed with people. The
> band played 'Patrick's Day'; the mob shouted; his grace bowed
> ... On we went, following the line of the quays, threading our
> way through a bare-legged, ragged population, bawling them-
> selves hoarse with energetic desires for prosperity to Ireland
> ... Everything attested a state of poverty, a lack of trade, a
> want of comfort and of cleanliness; but still there was but one
> expression prevalent in the mass – that of unbounded good-
> humour and gaiety. With a philosophy quite his own, poor
> Paddy seemed to feel a reflected pleasure from the supposed
> happiness of those around him – the fine clothes, the gorgeous
> equipages, the prancing chargers, the flowing plumes – all, in
> fact, that forms the appliances of wealth, constituting in his mind
> a kind of paradise on earth. He thought their possessors at least
> ought to be happy, and, like a good-hearted fellow, he was glad
> of it for their sakes.   (p. 38)

It would be easy to dismiss this as an example of the most appalling feature of Lever's work: his readiness to portray the Irish as
both simple and simple-minded. But the glibness – and we should
not forget that this is the voice of young Jack Hinton, rather than
Lever – cannot disguise the fact that there is poverty and political
discontent in Ireland. The force of the passage only really becomes
apparent if we reflect on how little tension there usually is in
Lever's work. French officers, for example, rather than being seen
as members of a revolutionary force, are just like their English
counterparts; they just happen to be on the opposite side. This is a
repeated feature of Lever's novels, that he plays down differences.

The same impulse is evident here – that the poor Irish feel happy for the rich English – but his picture of life in Dublin does acknowledge a gap that is so broad that it strikes a distinctly discordant note.

This tension is sustained in the way that Jack looks at Ireland and misinterprets what he sees; he can only make sense of things in a way that matches his English gentleman's presuppositions. He even acknowledges the naivety of his judgements:

> Deputations there were also from various branches of trade, entreating their graces to wear and to patronize the manufacture of the country, and to conform in many respects to its habits and customs; by all of which, in my then ignorance, I could only understand the vehement desire of the population that the vice-regal court should go about in a state of nature, and limit their diet to poteen and potatoes.   (p. 39)

The political story implicit in *Jack Hinton* is taken further with the murder of a landlord. A priest has to explain to Jack that the Irish peasantry are not content, that 'they look upon your institutions as the sources of their misery and the instruments of your tyranny towards them', and that there is too great a readiness to 'place your faith in your soldiering' (p. 321). Lever slides away from these awkward points as the action of the novel moves on to Spain, France and Italy, but the point has been raised that the Irish are not at peace with their colonial and military masters.

The answer advocated at this stage is compromise: 'When will ye learn that these people may be led, but never driven' (p. 320). But implicit in Lever's position is a far more radical quarrel with English rule, in large measure prompted by his political conservatism. For, essentially, his conservatism makes him an opponent of the course of negotiation and compromise. He is, in particular, at an opposite remove from Elizabeth Gaskell: in *North and South*, as in all Gaskell's novels, the central proposition is that compromises must be made in order to arrive at workable social solutions. But implicit in an aristomilitary code is an absence of any notion of flexibility, or concessions in order to meet specific circumstances; there are simply the rulers and the ruled, the leaders and the led. We can point to the kind of iron discipline that characterised Wellington's army; it was only as the Victorian period progressed that an idea began to emerge that ordinary soldiers might respond to measures other than the lash.[20] In the Ireland of Lever's novels, it would be implausible if soldiers were suddenly to be converted into social workers (this is an issue that is also apparent in a number of novels set in India, in particular W.D. Arnold's *Oakfield*, which I discuss in Chapter 4; that it is impossible to reconstitute military rule on a basis that accepts civilian assumptions). Lever, therefore, writing military novels that feature a military governing caste and an oppressed people, cannot negotiate the kind of fantasy solution that does not seem far-fetched in *North and South*. It is a problem that he continues to consider in his later novels, particularly *Lord Kilgobbin*, where he acknowledges that it takes 'three times as much military force to govern the smaller island'.[21]

In a polarised society, where there is no chance of establishing common ground, all Lever can do is offer us two points of view; he might seem to identify with the rulers in Ireland, but is capable of sympathising with those on the receiving end of English military rule. This is a rare perspective in the Victorian novel. The great bulk of English literature of the nineteenth century simply ignores England's, or Britain's, role as a military power; indeed, the English – who do not have the army present at home as a fact and a force in their lives on a daily basis – always congratulate themselves on the absence of militarism in their national life. But unusually, Lever acknowledges England's military role. It might even be said that nowhere else in Victorian fiction do we find a writer so ready to recognise that England – despite its image of itself as a liberal, peaceful state – is, for the colonised, a military oppressor.

THE VICTORIAN ARMY

It is evident that how the English regarded their army was not the same as others might see it. But how did the army see itself? More specifically, did it make any attempt to respond to social – and technological – changes during the Victorian period? What all the evidence seems to suggest is that the army remained stubbornly committed to ideas that had been defined during the era of the Napoleonic Wars. Indeed, Patricia Morton goes so far as to suggest that 'the army that plunged into World War One was in many respects the same army that Wellington had commanded at Waterloo a century earlier'.[22] This applies both to strategy and to the social composition and attitudes of the army. One of the consequences of Britain's success in the wars against Napoleon had been, as Linda Colley maintains, a patrician renaissance, for 'Waterloo made the world safe for gentlemen again'.[23] Alongside the idea of a service elite, an idea encouraged by Wellington with his distaste for democracy, a new cult of heroism developed.[24] Men began believing in, and playing, a certain role, a fact that was supported by the very impressive military uniforms that began to appear around 1800. An aristocracy of fighting men, or so the myth went, had seen off the forces of revolution.

The army, then, clung on to a certain image of itself, despite the fact that Britain was changing during the course of the 1830s and 1840s. To some extent this is inevitable: an army is always conservative, and will always see itself as embodying a standard of order as the world embraces change. But the fossilisation of the army must also be seen in relation to the forty years of peace that followed the Battle of Waterloo, for in a period of peace the army had no role to play as an instrument of foreign policy.[25] Not that the army was inactive. The Crimean War was the only European conflict involving Britain between 1815 and 1914, but throughout the nineteenth century there were numerous small wars in other parts of the world.[26] The ease with which it was possible to defeat untrained, non-European opponents contributed, however, to the army's reluctance to change. The system that had served Wellington seemed to be working well. But working with considerably fewer men. At the end of the Napoleonic Wars the regular army numbered about 200,000 men; by 1820 the total was down to 80,000, and even in the 1840s was only about 100,000. According to Brian Bond, 'So persistent was the clamour for reductions of the military budget that the Duke of Wellington only managed to preserve a token fighting force at the cost of the non-combatant departments'.[27] The troops were mainly required to garrison the colonies, a commitment that grew as the empire grew, but troops were also needed for Ireland, and at home. In 1819 there were 64,000 soldiers stationed in Britain; by 1825 this had fallen to 44,000, but in the 1840s the number rose somewhat to meet the challenge of Chartism.[28] The only factor that provided some relief was that Britain could rely on its navy as a shield against Continental aggression.

A central point about the Victorian army is that its officers were drawn almost exclusively from the ranks of the aristocracy and gentry, whereas the common soldiers were the lowest of the low.

Charles Lever is accurate, even for this later period, in his representation of officers who see the army as an extension of the country gentleman's life of hunting and shooting. Commissions and promotions (up to the rank of lieutenant-colonel) were obtained by purchase, and most officers regarded the army simply as a temporary occupation. Yet at the same time there was a military caste, men who understood soldiering and with a high level of commitment to military leadership. A caste, however, tends to look inwards rather than outwards; as Peter Burroughs points out, 'restricted recruitment and social homogeneity enabled officers to perpetuate the values and pretensions of the officer gentleman, with accepted standards of behaviour and an acute sense of honour and duty, as well as of regimental *esprit de corps*'.[29] The strangeness of this only really becomes apparent if we compare it with the picture of personal relationships we receive from the vast majority of Victorian novels, where decisions are taken in accordance with the dictates of the individual conscience, and where there is always a fluid relationship between individuals and society. The Victorian novel offers us a world where change is the norm, whereas the Victorian army – at times, it seems, in defiance of the surrounding society – sticks to an established set of rules.

It is in the face of such inflexibility that Victorian society as a whole finds it easy to sideline the army. At times of crisis – the Crimean War, the Indian Mutiny, the death of General Gordon in the Sudan, the Boer War – the army is remembered, but much of the time it seems irrelevant. Soldiers are present to the extent that they are present in *North and South*: part of the picture, but not essential to the plot. And certainly, the vast majority of middle-class and respectable working-class men would never have considered enlisting in the army.[30] The lowly status of common soldiers probably contributed to the infrequency of their appearances in Victorian novels; it renders all the more remarkable those novels – most notably, Dickens's *Bleak House* and Hardy's *The Trumpet-Major* – that feature ordinary soldiers. But the most remarkable development in this area is Kipling's short stories with their entirely fresh, and politically very significant, emphasis on the regular fighting man.[31]

The fossilisation of the army was first exposed during the Crimean War: the fact that its tactics were out of date, that a cumbersome commissariat could not supply and maintain an army in the field, and, most tellingly in terms of public debate, the idea that the army was dominated by aristocratic incompetents. In this last criticism there is, of course, an element of the middle-class public finding the fault it wanted to find. And the fact is that the Crimean War was followed by a range of practical and necessary reforms; the effect of these was that 'between 1855 and 1870...the armed forces ceased to be a mere aggregation of regiments and semi-independent corps, and began to resemble a unified army under a single politically responsible minister'.[32] But significant as these changes were, the fact is that the army 'survived the popular clamour largely unchanged and unscathed'.[33] The explanation is that nobody really cared; the outcry over the Crimean War had 'reflected emotional outrage, not a secure basis for prolonged, constructive pressure'.[34] The Victorians could get back to the important things in life (or possibly the unimportant things in life), and forget the army.

Once again, 'War became a noise far away'.[35] There were occasional invasion scares, but the combination of Britain's industrial strength and maritime power was a good guarantee that the country could feel secure in relation to Europe.[36] Imperial wars, however, were another matter. As Byron Farwell points out, 'There was not a single year in Queen Victoria's long reign in which somewhere in the world her soldiers were not fighting for her and for her empire'.[37] Earlier conflicts tended to be in India and other parts of Asia, although the series of Maori Wars (1843–8, 1860–1, 1863–6, and 1868–70) is not insignificant.[38] The most serious disturbance, however, was the Indian Mutiny or Rebellion of 1857–9. Time and time again events link back to the importance of India: the Second Afghan War (1878–80), for example, was prompted by the need to protect Britain's most profitable colony, on this occasion, as in the Crimean War, the fear being Russian encroachments. Around this time there was also increasing British involvement in the Near East and North Africa, leading to the Egyptian War (1882) and the Sudanese War (1884–5), and the subsequent re-conquest of the Sudan by Kitchener in the campaign of 1896–8, which included the 1898 Battle of Omdurman. There was also fighting in other parts of Africa, for example in the 1873–4 war against the Ashanti threat to British interests in West Africa, but more significantly in the Zulu War of 1879. In all these engagements, traditional military tactics were, by and large, successful. It was only against the Boers – the first time the British fought fellow Europeans in a colonial setting – that the limitations of the British army began to become apparent, first in the Anglo-Boer War of 1880–1, and then in the Second South African, or Boer, War of 1899–1902.

Up until this point, 'The small war mentality of the officer class allowed the British to believe that warfare was something quite remote from business as usual'.[39] This was even true of the Indian Mutiny. The response in Britain to the Mutiny was outrage; partly that troops trained by the British had proved disloyal, but more because of much-exaggerated stories about Indian atrocities against English women. The literary responses to the Indian Mutiny (some of which I examine in Chapter 4) are fascinating: there is a predictable right-wing reaction, but more interesting are the confused thoughts of liberal writers. For the most part Victorian writers were establishing a new standard discourse that conceived of experience in terms far removed from Britain's military inheritance; the Mutiny challenged both the rationality of their liberal convictions and their tolerance. But only briefly. The strength of the new discourse is evident in the fact that, the moment the short-lived anger and bewilderment about the Mutiny had passed, the Victorians seemed to forget all about it and returned to their domestic concerns. The new liberal orthodoxy had been tested, and temporarily derailed, but was soon back on the tracks.

Yet the Indian Mutiny also widened the gap between the army and the general body of the Victorian public. For, in contrast to the Crimean War, the army's handling of the Mutiny was a success; this strengthened the hand of those who, resisting reform, maintained that the army was doing the right things in the right way. The Indian Mutiny did, however, resolve an anomaly, that the East India Company had maintained its own army in India working alongside the British army. In September 1858 the East India Company ceased to exist, the British government assuming responsibility for, and reorganising, the Indian army. From this point on, at least 60,000 British regular troops were stationed in India. It is possible to trace back to the Indian Mutiny the origins of the increased respect for the army that is a feature of the last quarter of the nineteenth century. Peter Burroughs, for example, draws attention to the praise that was lavished on the generals, and suggests that, 'Ordinary soldiers, too, were portrayed as accomplishing feats of heroism, impressions which heightened the popular image and reputation of the army and associated it directly, for the first time, with an Indian empire that had captured the public imagination'.[40] I would not dispute this, yet at the same time Burroughs does seem to be anticipating the works of Kipling, and the reaction to them, by more than thirty years. There might be the first stirrings here of the connections between the army and imperialism that is at the heart of Kipling's stories and poems, but the fact is that the Indian Mutiny found its place in a society that regarded military concerns as both philosophically and physically alien.

One way in which this is apparent is that the army found it increasingly difficult to attract recruits; it is an obvious point to make, but Victorian industry was absorbing vast numbers of men who might previously have enlisted. Edward Cardwell's army reforms, introduced during his period as Secretary of State for War between 1868 and 1874, were primarily intended to tackle the manpower shortage. In a fundamental reorganisation, he recalled battalions from the colonies, abolished purchase, and introduced short service enlistment. The various measures made the army both more professional and humane, although the aim of boosting recruitment was not successful. No amount of political interference, however, could alter the traditional views of the entrenched officer class. Resistance to change was led by the Duke of Cambridge, the Commander-in-Chief of the army, with the support of the Queen. As Brian Bond states, despite Cardwell's reforms, 'Britain's military organisation was so defective that [in the last quarter of the century] out of a regular army of some 200,000 men, nearly half of them stationed at home, it proved difficult to embark an expeditionary force of even 20,000 men'.[41] It was only the Boer War that finally forced serious attention to be paid to these continuing problems of the army.

What we have, then, is a conservative army muddling through, and a general public that is not just indifferent to military matters but speaking a language that has largely eliminated the word 'war' except as a metaphor in contexts such as the fight against poverty or the fight against disease.[42] Such a stance was, of course, myopic. As Lever's novels demonstrate, the belief of the British that they were not a militaristic race was by no means so apparent to those subject to British military power. And the same was true of the series of colonial wars. But British thinking was essentially insular, a view that is borne out by the Stanhope Memorandum of 1891. In response to the request of Garnet Wolseley (who was to succeed Cambridge as Commander-in-Chief in 1895), that the army should be given a definitive statement of the purposes for which it existed, the following list, summarised here by Edward Spiers, was compiled:

> He placed aid to the civil power as his first priority, the garrison-ing of India and the colonies as second and third, home defence as fourth, and the 'improbable' employment of two army corps in a European war as a final task.[43]

The first priority is surprising given that the police now had responsibility for civil order. It is possible to point to specific concerns that prompted Stanhope's response (such as the 'Bloody Sunday' Trafalgar Square riot of 1887), but the impression, none the less, is of insularity; only the first priority anticipates any unfore-seen problems, everything else is business as usual.

The impression as late as 1891, therefore, is still of a low-key attitude towards military affairs. We might link this with the fact that the period between 1871 and 1914, the 43 years between the Franco-Prussian War and the First World War, is an unprecedented period of peace in Europe; the major powers were so busy scram-bling for new colonies that they forgot about fighting each other. But what is also apparent is that some time after 1870 there was a new sense of military tension in Britain, and the first stirrings of a more aggressive imperialism. It is impossible to delineate exactly a change of mood such as this, but it seems to be connected with a growing, if only half-grasped, awareness that Britain's position in the world – as manufacturer, trader, and the country that dictated the terms in international relations – was beginning to be less dominant, that Britain's trade rivals were being revivified as polit-ical rivals. The new mood began to find expression in the arts, but in a way that also acknowledges the strength of the non-militaristic discourse of the Victorians. This is first apparent in the emergence of Jingoism. The term comes from a music-hall song current during the Russo-Turkish War (1877–8), when anti-Russian feeling was running high in Britain and Disraeli ordered the Mediterranean fleet to Constantinople. Subsequently, of course, the phrase sums up everything we find distasteful about English or British national-ism, but one point about Jingoism, as I argue in Chapter 6, is that such belligerent nationalism emerged in a society that had shunned low-key expressions of patriotic fervour. Against the background of the liberal consensus of the time, when aggressive sentiments were expressed they became excessive and unbalanced. This is not to excuse the language of Jingoism, merely an acknowledgement that a cultural shift – the move towards a new militarism in the last quarter of the nineteenth century – has to be seen in the context of the previous cultural shift – the move in the first half of the century from an aristocratic to a middle-class liberal way of thinking.[44]

Jingoism runs to excess; the same is true of a great deal of late Victorian writing in a militaristic vein. This is apparent in the works of Rider Haggard, and in the books for boys that began to appear at the time. But what is surprising is that a similar kind of excess seems to affect life itself. Every age produces its characteristic hero – Wellington as aristocratic leader, Sir Henry Havelock, the hero of the Indian Mutiny, as Christian soldier – but there are few to rival General Gordon, the hero of the Sudan, in terms of oddness. Possibly it is the domestic orientation of Victorian life that makes a military adventurer such as Gordon seem wayward and eccentric, the new normality of Victorian society presuming to define what is abnormal (although, as I endeavour to show in Chapter 6, Gordon is an almost impossible character to pin down). At an opposite remove from Gordon, however, is Herbert Spencer, the supporter of Darwin and believer in scientific progress. In his 1884 book *Man and State* he distinguishes between two opposed types of social organisation, the 'militant' and the 'industrial':

> As a good Liberal, he wanted to see the first of these – which rested on status rather than contractual relationships, and flourished on war rather than peace – superseded by the second . . . his classification illuminates the distaste for violence so deeply rooted in the Liberal mind.[45]

Spenser elaborates a comprehensive theory, but when we realise how many would have instinctively shared his views we see why the newly emerging militarism of the 1880s and 1890s might have sounded extreme, unbalanced, vulgar and disturbing. It is this polarisation of attitudes that I consider in the later chapters of this book, but to complete this opening chapter I want to look again at how the Victorians both related to and began to distance themselves from the elite heroism of the Wellington era.

TENNYSON AND VICTORIAN WAR POETRY

Writing some time around 1918, Arthur Waugh offered a dismissive view of Victorian war poetry: 'The Victorian poets wrote of war as though it were something splendid and ennobling; but as a matter of fact they knew nothing whatever about it'.[46] Ever since Wilfred Owen's 'Dulce et Decorum Est' encouraged us to set the honesty of his own vision against 'The old Lie', this view has become a truism of poetry criticism.[47] And there is plenty of Victorian poetry that supports the impression; the Victorians might have paid little attention to war, but when they wrote poems about it their preference was for a heroic mode. The most famous example is Tennyson's 'The Charge of the Light Brigade':

> When can their glory fade?
> O the wild charge they made!
>   All the world wondered.
> Honour the charge they made!
> Honour the Light Brigade,
>   Noble six hundred! [48]

Bernard Bergonzi, focusing on the literature of the First World War, is patronising about Tennyson's 'large and confident innocence about the state of mind of the unhappy cavalrymen forced to charge the Russian guns'.[49] More positively, M. van Wyk Smith recognises Tennyson's poem as a masterpiece in a battle-piece tradition:

> Like its famous predecessors in the heroic vein, it turns the immediate horror of war into a distant, larger-than-life pageant...Horror and slaughter are redeemed by the necessity for heroic affirmation and patriotic rationalization.[50]

The bulk of Crimean War verse shares Tennyson's heroic and patriotic sentiments, but no other poem begins to rival its impact.[51]

Even if we acknowledge the quality of 'The Charge of the Light Brigade', however, it remains the case that the poetry of the First World War continues to set the standard by which we judge the poetry of the previous century. This assumption is at the heart of van Wyk Smith's otherwise excellent account of the poetry of the Boer War:

One way of tracing out the pattern of war poetry through the ages is to see it as a constant oscillation between two equally ancient views of war as either heroic and ennobling or tragic and brutalizing, with the latter conception of war gradually gaining dominance from the mid-nineteenth century onwards.[52]

This is a false dichotomy in that it implicitly privileges the tragic and brutalising approach. The effect is apparent in van Wyk Smith's book, where he searches for poetry that anticipates the mood of First World War poetry, finding in the American Civil War the first evidence of 'all the conditions as well as the literary sensibility to produce poetry of the kind we normally associate with World War One'.[53] Part of the larger project of his book is to find anticipations of First World War poetry in the poetry of the Boer War. The result is confusing: van Wyk Smith wants to establish the cultural context from which poetry emerges, but fails to pay enough attention to the different contexts of the late nineteenth and early twentieth centuries, and, in relation to Civil War poetry, the different contexts of Britain and America. It is the differences rather than the similarities between periods that tell us most about the poetry of any era. Consequently, in looking at the poetry of the Crimean War, it is unnecessary to look for poems that dwell on the horror of the conflict.[54] It is far more interesting – as it is throughout the Victorian period – to look for the ways in which anything unusual is happening in the handling of received ideas, which in the context of war poetry means the concept of heroism.

Tennyson's *Maud* is the outstanding example of a poem that does something new with heroism, but first I want to look at the end of the century. In the 1890s there are poems where heroism becomes vicious, where there is a lust for blood. In the poems of W.E. Henley, in particular, affirmations about the value of a life of action seem driven and self-punishing rather than positive:

In the fell clutch of circumstance
  I have not winced nor cried aloud.
Under the bludgeonings of chance
  My head is bloody, but unbowed. [55]

As is often the case in Henley's poetry, heroism becomes detached from any tradition or cause, and becomes, even though nationality is stressed, an alienated quest. In the work of Henley, therefore, we are not interested in whether he acknowledges the 'tragic and brutalizing' dimensions of war: what matters is the disturbing direction in which he takes the concept of heroism.

In the Crimean War there is a far more traditional emphasis on heroism. Exceptions can be found. Isobel Armstrong draws attention to the manner in which William Morris in *The Defence of Guenevere* 'takes up the challenge of making a critique of the grotesque through the very form of the grotesque itself'.[56] In poems published the year after the last year of the Crimean War, Morris produces what 'could quite properly be seen as a volume of war poetry, a critique of a society which habitually goes to war'.[57] Rather than setting the tragedy of war against the heroism of war, Morris could be said to venture some way towards seeking political alternatives to war. A case can also be made for Adelaide Anne Procter, that in her Crimean War poems, such as 'The Lesson of War', which views the war from the perspective of home, she starts to articulate a different order: not setting heroism against tragedy, but setting heroism against domestic life, confrontation against negotiation. But her poem, in fact, soon lapses into a routinely expressed idea of a nation united:

> The rulers of the nation,
> > The poor ones at their gate,
> With the same eager wonder
> > The same great news await. [58]

Joseph Bristow, discussing why Crimean War poetry, whether by Cambridge Apostles or Chartist poets, always yields to the same set of patriotic gestures, suggests that, 'The question has, of course, one obvious answer. Poetry was closely associated with the voice of the nation. Poetry – via rhythm and rhyme – could lend urgency as well as dignity to the battle cries leading the British army forward'.[59]

It is in the light of points such as these that – apart from the final chapter – I pay little attention to poetry in this book. The problem is not the poets' stress on the splendid and ennobling qualities of war: the problem is the lack of originality with which they say these things. The need is not for a more 'truthful' poetry about war, just for more interesting poetry. There is, however, one magnificent exception in the Crimean War: Tennyson's *Maud*. Its strength is in part derived from the fact that Tennyson can see a larger conflict

behind the particular military conflict. *Maud* is a dramatic monologue. It tells of the death of the narrator's father, who has been
ruined by his partner in a business speculation, a partner who is
now 'lord of the broad estate and the Hall'.[60] The narrator is in love
with Maud, the lord's daughter. Maud's brother, however, treats
the narrator with contempt. Part II of the poem opens with their
duel and the death of the brother. The narrator flees aboard, laps-
ing into morbid despair. Recovering in Part III, he seeks salvation
through the service of his country in war. It is clear that Tennyson
had the Crimean War in mind:

> Let it go or stay, so I wake to the higher aims
> Of a land that has lost for a little her lust of gold,
> And love of a peace that was full of wrongs and shames,
> Horrible, hateful, monstrous, not to be told;
> And hail once more to the banner of battle unrolled!...
> For the peace, that I deemed no peace, is over and done,
> And now by the side of the Black and Baltic deep,
> And deathful-grinning mouths of the fortress, flames
> The blood-red blossom of war with a heart of fire. [61]

At a simple level the poem seems to set the honour of service in
war against the sordid meanness of a society dominated by the
making of money. In this scheme of things, war is the higher calling.[62]

The issue is complicated, however, by the narrator's mental
disturbance. In order to arrive at a simple reading of *Maud* it is
necessary to ignore both the unbalanced narrator and all the other
disturbing signs in the poem. Maud herself, for example, is
returned to obsessively, but never achieves any separate identity
beyond the narrator's fantasies about her. These appear in fragmented, incantatory lyrics, which, with their echoing of phrases
and small cluster of obsessions, constantly reveal a level of psychic
disturbance:

> There has fallen a splendid tear
>   From the passion-flower at the gate.
> She is coming, my dove, my dear;
>   She is coming, my life, my fate;
> The red rose cries, 'She is near, she is near;'

> And the white rose weeps, 'She is late;'
> The larkspur listens, 'I hear, I hear;'
> And the lily whispers, 'I wait.' [63]

What is so disturbing in a verse like this – and the same is true of the poem as a whole – is that, by repetition and insistence, standard poetic images are stretched and driven to excess. The effect is to create the Gothic underside of Romanticism. In poems such as Wordsworth's, the notion of the isolated individual withdrawing from the world works positively. But when the idea is pushed a little further it produces a sense of a persona with a disturbed relationship to both culture and society. The language and inherited ideas of poetry – including of course the language of heroism – cease to be a sustaining frame and become instead a maze from which the narrator cannot escape. And socially the narrator cannot sustain normal relationships: unable to construct a conventional relationship with a woman, he converts Maud into an alarming projection and representation of his sexual desires and frustration.

In the overall story of *Maud*, the narrator eventually submerges his individuality – along with his desires, which are inextricably sexual and violent – into the collective enterprise of war. The pattern is different from that encountered in many Victorian novels, where time and time again the hero or heroine comes to an accommodation with society; the novel, in other words, offers social integration, whereas Tennyson's poem focuses on social alienation, but with war as a cause that offers the individual a solution. One contradiction in this formula is that war is seen as an alternative to the money-obsessed society of the day, rather than being seen as an extension and expression of the capitalist system. In this connection, we might also notice that the narrator, for all his aloofness to the commercial spirit of the age, is both deeply implicated in this scheme of things – his father killed himself when a business speculation failed – and envious of the wealth of Maud and her family. More importantly, however, at least in the context of a consideration of military issues in Victorian literature, the poem offers us a fresh slant on the idea of military service. In a chivalric code, enlistment is a duty, an obligation to fight for one's country. But in Tennyson's poem, military service becomes an alienated and extreme gesture, the response of a person who cannot come to an accommodation with civil society. It is an idea that is repeated in nineteenth-century literature. In Thackeray's *Barry*

Lyndon, for example, Barry is a vicious bully who is drawn to the cruelty of war; but Thackeray knows he is presenting a despicable hero. In Kingsley's novels, his warlike heroes are as driven and desperate as Tennyson's narrator, but it seems that we are meant to admire these characters. General Gordon (whom I return to in Chapter 6) was a warrior hero every bit as alienated and sexually repressed as the speaker in *Maud*. It seems fair to suggest that, in the new civil order of Victorian society, war was pushed so much into the margins that, even at a time of national emergency, military service was seen as a kind of aberration, a calling for the man who could not cope with civilian society.

The danger in pursuing this line of argument is that it can make Tennyson seem a critic of the military temperament, as if he sits in judgement on his narrator. But the attraction of *Maud* is its ambivalence, the way in which it offers a sense of both the sanity and insanity of an attraction to war. Far from aligning himself with the spirit of rational compromise that is dominant in prose fiction, Tennyson is attracted to a conservative position. This starts with his hostility to the modern world: confronted by the sordid pursuit of money, the narrator, in the words of Chris R. Vanden Bossche, attempts 'to impose a romance plot – containing courtship, rivalry, love scenes in a rose garden, interdiction by the blocking brother, a duel, and heroic death – on his experience'.[64] The poem, seen in this way, can be said to offer two different conceptions of the social universe:

> Both realism and romance imply social values, the values of the classes for which they were created: romance was created for the aristocracy and exists in Tennyson's poem in those elements of the code of chivalry with which he was so concerned; realism arose with the newer genre of the novel, expressing the values of middle-class practicality.[65]

It is clear that Tennyson persists in exploring, and identifying with, the conservative position in the poem. But it is also clear that the complications of tone in *Maud* make the poem ambivalent, Tennyson in the end neither repudiating nor accepting the voice of the narrator.

The tension in *Maud* is the division that dominates this book: on the one hand a traditional culture of war (which found itself renewed and re-energised by victory over Napoleon), and on the other hand a new kind of social thinking. The nature of the new social morality is seen in one of the early responses to *Maud*: Goldwin Smith, writing in *The Saturday Review* in 1855, suggests that rather than 'talking lightly of blood' Tennyson should aim for 'true tenderness, self-control, obedience to the moral law, and fidelity to the end of his mission'.[66] In other words, it would be a better poem if it exhibited the same values we encounter in Victorian novels. But the poem does not embrace these values. *Maud* cannot, however, retrieve the past; it has to consider the new implications of the military temperament in a peaceful society. It is both the mutations of militarism and the limits of liberalism that I consider in this book; in the next chapter, however, I look more closely at the construction of the new civilian vision of the world, in particular how it usurped the old vision even in the midst of war.

2

The Crimean: a Novelists' War

REPORTS AND RESPONSES

The Crimean War is remarkably well established in the popular imagination. Few people could provide more than the sketchiest details about the Napoleonic Wars, but most could summon up some surprisingly detailed knowledge about the later, less significant, conflict. Central, of course, would be the Charge of the Light Brigade and Florence Nightingale, yet, beyond this, many would know the place names, who the allies were, and possibly even about the administrative failings that characterised Britain's conduct of the war. That we are so well informed is due largely to the fact that this was the first war to be reported fully in newspapers of the day; in particular, William Russell's reports for *The Times* created a vivid sense of the war that remains in the public consciousness.[1] In the hands of Russell and then others – Tennyson in his famous poem, the supporters of Florence Nightingale – images were created that passed directly into popular mythology.[2]

What I want to consider, however, is the way in which the impact of another form – the novel – is apparent in Russell's newspaper reports. Russell presents and interprets the war for a novel-reading public, and in order to do this he adopts the characteristics and strategies of a novelist. But he also shares, at a level that is to a profound extent the informing spirit of all his reports, the values and convictions of a Victorian novelist. If this is true of Russell's reporting, it is even more the case in memoirs of the war: narrative coherence is imposed upon the conflict, with the author taking a central role in the same way as a hero or heroine in a novel with a first-person narrator. This is particularly so when the writer is a woman, for, as we shall see in the memoirs of Mary Seacole and Elizabeth Davis, the emphasis is not on military matters but on the narrator's sense of the challenge she has set herself. Indeed, it might be argued that Seacole and Davis reduce the war to a form of domestic fiction. The curious fact is, therefore, that although novels from the period do not deal directly with the Crimean War to any extent, it seems valid to talk about how the war is perceived through a novelist's eye.[3]

Earlier wars had not been written about in this way: contemporary accounts of the Battle of Waterloo, for example, are in an heroic mode.[4] Not everybody, however, wrote about the Crimean War as if it was material for a novel. The tradition of epic, for example, lies behind A.W. Kinglake's eight-volume history, *The Invasion of the Crimea*.[5] Kinglake's account in fact ends with the death of Lord Raglan, commander of the British forces, recalling *The Iliad*, another work that concludes with the death of the hero before the completion of a long siege. Kinglake writes both on an epic scale and in a form that acknowledges an epic model. Charles Kingsley, too, adopts his own approach. *Westward Ho!*, published in 1855, is inspired by the Crimean War even though the subject is at a far remove: it deals with the exploits of an Elizabethan adventurer, Amyas Leigh.[6] It is legitimate, however, to discuss it as a Crimean War novel, indeed the only significant work of fiction that relates to the war. Yet it offers a perspective upon war quite unlike anything encountered in most other novels of the period. There is something of a paradox here: as the last section of this chapter will show, it is the novelist Kingsley who produces the most 'un-novel-like' response to the Crimean War, celebrating, or possibly mourning, values that had fallen out of fashion by the 1850s – or, quite conceivably, touching upon new issues that will prove increasingly important as the century proceeds.

WILLIAM RUSSELL'S CRIMEAN DESPATCHES

The Crimean War was provoked by Russia's claim to the guardianship of the Holy Places and protection of the Greek Christians in the Turkish Empire. The underlying cause, however, was the weakness of the Turkish Empire and an associated fear of Russian expansion into the Balkans and Mediterranean. Turkey declared war on 4 October 1853; the following month its fleet was destroyed at Sinop by the Russians and a Franco-British fleet sailed into the Black Sea hoping to confine the Russians in Sevastopol. France and Britain formally declared war in March 1854. The first allied victory was at Alma in September 1854, which seemed to clear the way to Sevastopol. In November 1854 the British beat back the assaulting Russians at Balaklava (although the battle is best remembered for the disastrous Charge of the Light Brigade) and at Inkerman, but did not feel able to take Sevastopol by storm. Accordingly, the allies settled down to a long winter siege; it was the grim conditions associated with the siege that were at the centre of much of Russell's reporting, and which also established Florence Nightingale's name for her work at Scutari. By the summer of 1855, however, conditions had improved greatly, and in September 1855 the Russians surrendered Sevastopol. In March 1856 the Peace of Paris was signed. As is often the case in war, after the initial success at Alma in September 1854 there was a hope that it would all be over by Christmas. The fact that it was not, the misery of the Crimean winter, and the feeling that those in charge both at home and on the battlefield were to blame, were the concerns at the heart of Russell's reports.[7]

Historians periodically attempt to revise this view of the war, arguing that Russell saw what he wanted to see.[8] The truth, however, is not the issue here. What I am concerned with are the literary resources Russell calls upon to construct his reading of the war, in particular his dependence upon, and his sharing a vision with, the novel of the period. This is apparent from the start of the conflict. Arriving in Gallipoli on 10 April 1854, *en route* for the Crimea, Russell offered his impressions of the town:

> Take dilapidated outhouses of farmer's yards in England – remove rickety old wooden tenements, catch up, wherever you can, any seedy, cracked, shutterless structures of planks and tiles, that have escaped the ravages of time in our cathedral towns – carry off sheds and stalls from Billingsgate, and add to them the huts along the shores of the Thames between London Bridge and Greenwich – bring them all to the European side of the Straits of the Dardanelles and having pitched on the most exposed portion of the coast, on a bare hill, sloping away to the water's edge, with scarcely a tree or shrub, tumble them 'higgldy piggldy' on its declivity, in such a wise that the streets may resemble on a large scale, the devious traces of a bookworm through some old tome – let the roadway be very narrow, of irregular varying breadth, according to the bulgings and projections of the houses, and filled with large round slippery stones, painful and hazardous

to walk upon – here and there borrow a dirty gutter from a back street in Boulogne – let the houses in parts lean across to each other so that the tiles meet, or that a few planks thrown across from over the doorways unite and form a sort of 'passage' or arcade – steal some of our popular monuments, the shafts of various national testimonials, or Irish round towers – surround them with a light gallery about twelve feet from the top, put on a large extinguisher shaped roof, paint them all white, and having thus made them into minarets, clap them down into the maze of buildings – then let fall big stones all over the place – plant little windmills with odd looking sails on the crests of the hill over the town – transport the ruins of a feudal fortress from Northern Italy, and put it in the centre of the town, with a flanking tower extending to the water's edge – erect a few buildings of wood by the waterside to serve as *café*, custom house, and government stores – and when you have done this you have to all appearance imitated the process by which the town of Gallipoli was created.

(pp. 18–19)

This extraordinarily long sentence amounts to far more than just scene setting: what it does is anticipate the narrative (i.e. Russell's reports as a whole) by dictating the central themes of that narrative. As such, it is appropriate to compare it with Dickens's famous opening description of Marseilles in *Little Dorrit*,[9] but with one crucial difference: Dickens is anticipating the themes of his own work of fiction, Russell is anticipating the significance of real events that have yet to take place. The story will develop in directions that cannot be foreseen, but the frame of interpretation has been decided: this is, the need to impose order upon disorder. There is no sense of an alternative culture here in Turkey, for everything is borrowed from England (although other parts of Western Europe are also given a role in providing points of reference); even the minarets are seen as essentially a fraud. This hotchpotch of a place depresses Russell: 'In truth it is a wretched place – picturesque to a degree, but, like all picturesque things or places, horribly uncomfortable' (p. 20). What it lacks is a sense of coherence and identity, although there is perhaps just the faintest awareness that Western Europe has dumped itself here. Overwhelmingly, however, the sense is of a mess; it will be a dirty job, clearing up this shambles, but it is a job that will have to be done.

The reports that follow are not going to contradict this view, apart from the fact that the military disasters and deprivations of the Crimean winter will raise questions about the assumptions of British order and efficiency that are in evidence here. If Gallipoli is a mess, the British will soon contrive an equally extreme mess. But, just as the description of Gallipoli resembles an opening passage in a novel, this overall narrative pattern echoes a familiar structure in Victorian fiction. Characteristically, mid-Victorian novels, while engaged in the forging of national values, can show considerable rigour in simultaneously questioning these values. Dickens's *David Copperfield*, for example, endorses the growth of a middle-class gentleman but also acknowledges everything that is suspect in David's self-development.[10] Russell's narrative follows a familiar trajectory, therefore, in endorsing a British sense of superiority even as it shows British shortcomings.

Is it really necessary, however, to invoke the novel as a model for this? Is it not inherent in war writing to start with a sense of patriotic confidence, to show this confidence being tested, and then to show the eventual triumph of the rightful cause?[11] But what Russell offers is a new sense of where the centre of interest lies. Traditional war writing sees events as an epic struggle, a play, where opposing forces led by exemplary generals engage in dramatic confrontations; at the same time there is, of course, an implicit sense of boys playing games.[12] Russell, however, does not offer us dramatic confrontations and heroic leadership; Lord Raglan is initially seen as such a leader, but this does not extend beyond the Battle of Alma. What Russell offers, by contrast, is a largely static plot, where the fighting is almost incidental; what is of interest is what he sees in the details behind the fighting. And essentially, in the manner of a realistic novelist, what Russell sees is a social problem. Aristocratic ineptitude has produced a disaster, and it is only middle-class resourcefulness that can remedy the situation. By the end of Russell's accounts the war is close to its conclusion, but just as importantly there is a sense of narrative closure, that a social problem has been confronted and dealt with.

The influence of the novelist's way of thinking is equally apparent in the smallest details of Russell's text. We can consider, for example, the act of naming. In the French camp:

The names of the streets, according to a Gallic nomenclature, printed in black on neat deal slips, were fixed to the walls, so that one could find his way from place to place without going through the erratic wanderings which generally mark the stranger's progress through a Turkish town. (p. 25)

The issue goes deeper than imposing order upon this alien environment. A defining feature of the realistic novel is the ability to name the object; if everything can be named, the world becomes a manageable place. Inherent in Russell's approval of a trivial detail like this, therefore, is a whole way of looking at life. Victorian novels return repeatedly to the question of how, if at all, it is possible to regulate an increasingly complex society. Russell is asserting those forms of organisation and control, through naming and defining, that are at the heart of Victorian fiction.

At the same time he can provide an echo of the symbolic confidence of the Victorian novel. In *Bleak House*, Dickens uses disease, specifically smallpox, to exemplify something dangerous, yet hidden, within society that connects the highest with the lowest. It is almost uncanny how the cholera that affected the British forces in the Crimea presents an example of life imitating art. But it is also important to recognise how Russell exploits the symbolic potential of the disease; in a way he deflects attention from the 'real' business of the war, for, rather than the literal enemy, the enemy that must be defeated is the insidious one of a disease that threatens to run out of all control. The disease indicts those charged with responsibility for the health of society. Dickens, in *Bleak House* and elsewhere, draws a distinction between the indifference of those who run society and the practical efforts of those, such as Dr Allan Woodcourt, who take practical steps to alleviate suffering. It was Thomas Chenery, rather than Russell, who reported on the work of Nightingale at Scutari, but we can identify the way in which she is cast in an almost fictional role as a character ministering directly to the sick.[13]

The overlap between life and art is taken a step further when Dickens, responding to the Crimean War in *Little Dorrit*, creates the Circumlocution Office, dedicated to the art of 'HOW NOT TO DO IT'.[14] Dickens – if we ignore the obvious point that he is a comic novelist – is the novelist whom Russell, in fact, resembles most, for both present a panorama of corruption and neglect, and both cling on to such things as cleanliness and middle-class trustworthiness as our best hope in an extreme situation. What can be added to this is a sense of self: if there is going to be a way forward it will be through the individual, almost entrepreneurial, resourcefulness of people with talent. It soon becomes apparent that Raglan, as a representative of the old order, is not capable of inheriting the mantle of Wellington. But there appears to be nobody to take his place, nobody who can point the way forward. To an extent, therefore, Russell's reports ramble and appear diffuse because they do not coalesce around an individual or individuals playing a sustained and positive role. Or, at least, that is the case until we realise that Russell's real hero is himself. He is remarkably to the fore in all his reports; over and over again, we gain the impression that the resourcefulness he demonstrates in acquiring the facts, processing them and reporting home is just the kind of professionalism that is lacking in the conduct of the war. As a journalist he is anything but self-effacing, but what he offers his middle-class readers, in the manner of a mid-Victorian novelist, is both a position with which they can identify and an individual perspective from which the incomprehensible and disturbing can be controlled and given meaning.

What, however, happens to the actual war in Russell's reports, for his main focus seems to be on the state of Britain and the role of the middle-class individual? Although his reports of the battles must have proved exciting reading at the time, to the modern reader they appear exhaustively full, with an excessive fondness for exact times, exact distances, even exact weights:

> At the top of the ridges, between the gullies, the Russians had erected earthwork batteries, mounted with 32lb. and 24lb. brass guns, supported by numerous field pieces and howitzers. (p. 59)

Possibly much of what he writes fails to come to life primarily because he has abandoned a traditional method of writing about war; attention to detail overwhelms any sense of a dramatic confrontation. At a crucial moment in the Battle of Alma, however, Russell returns to an established style:

> And now came the turning point of the battle, in which Lord Raglan, by his sagacity and military skill, probably secured the victory at a smaller sacrifice than would have been otherwise the case.   (p. 61)

The event turns upon the military qualities of the commanding officer. This is the received view: that battles are won by the bravery of those who lead.[15] The isolated nature of such a moment in Russell's reports serves only to highlight, however, the different emphases of so much of what he writes.

Russell invokes these traditional military qualities again as he opens his description of the Charge of the Light Brigade. He writes of

> the most brilliant valour, of the excess of courage, and of a daring which would have reflected lustre on the best days of chivalry.
>
> (p. 103)

This is ironic, however, for he only mentions these qualities in the context of whether they can offer consolation for the disaster that has taken place. It is a masterpiece of tact as a report, for Russell has to be cautious as he questions these soldierly virtues. The men of the Light Cavalry are presented as wishing to give 'an example of courage to the world' (p. 104) to counter the widespread conviction that they have been 'utterly useless in the performance of one of their most important duties – the collection of supplies for the army' (p. 104). Essentially, these 'too fine gentlemen' (p. 104) are criticised for falling back upon a chivalric code in the absence of more practical resources. A report that starts, therefore, with praise for the old way of doing things then takes such values apart, but with due respect for the bravery of those involved.

This is the balance that is struck in the treatment of Captain Nolan, the officer perhaps most to blame for the débâcle. The statement 'A braver soldier than Captain Nolan the army did not possess' (p. 113) is entirely transparent, but when he is referred to as 'A matchless horseman and first-rate swordsman' (p. 113) an impression begins to creep in that he belongs to another world. This is confirmed by Russell's devastating sentence, 'Captain Nolan was killed by the first shot fired, as he rode in advance of the Hussars, cheering them on' (p. 115). We are somewhere between bravery and folly, between heroism and insanity.[16] The aesthetic skill of Russell's epitaph for Nolan reminds us again, however, that Russell's reports are a work of fiction in which the real-life events are being used to create the narrative he wants. Essentially, in a liberal, non-militaristic era, the war is being read by a liberal, non-military minded man. It follows that there are other positions, other dimensions to the war that Russell is missing. But that is inevitable when the imperatives of his account have been dictated by the world view, and even some of the associated techniques, of the novel of the 1850s.

THE MEMOIRS OF MARY SEACOLE AND ELIZABETH DAVIS

Alongside Russell's reports for *The Times*, the other principal accounts of the Crimean War are those of the participants. The two most interesting works of this kind are the biographies of two remarkable women, Mary Seacole and Elizabeth Davis, both of whom worked as nurses in the Crimea. As is the case with Russell's despatches, but to an even greater extent here, we can see the impact of the mid-Victorian novel upon their stories.

In both works, what the reader begins to anticipate most eagerly is the narrator's encounter with Florence Nightingale. Mary Seacole's tone is respectful:

> In half an hour's time I am admitted to Miss Nightingale's presence. A slight figure, in the nurses' dress; with a pale, gentle, and withal firm face, resting lightly in the palm of one white hand, while the other supports the elbow – a position which gives to her countenance a keen inquiring expression, which is rather marked. Standing thus in repose, and yet keenly observant – the greatest sign of impatience at any time a slight, perhaps unwitting motion of the firmly planted right foot – was Florence Nightingale – that Englishwoman whose name shall never die, but sound like music on the lips of British men until the hour of doom.[17]

It is only a passing encounter, but what is apparent is, first, a manner of observation – of extrapolating character from appearance and mannerism – that is particularly reminiscent of Charlotte Brontë. Secondly, and this again seems to echo Brontë, there is an interest in power, in particular how a woman acquires and handles power. In this brief episode, therefore, Seacole has introduced us to several of the central concerns of the mid-Victorian novel: character, gender, social duty, and the idea of being a successful individual.

The inherent contradiction, of course, is that the woman only succeeds by being of service to men, and must continually define her own achievements in deference to the world of men. As we shall see, Seacole's narrative returns repeatedly to how she wishes to be of service. Elizabeth Davis's narrative, by contrast, is less

deferential. Indeed, the impression of the heroine that comes across
– a woman who is repeatedly approached by men who wish to
marry her, but who, for reasons she can never fully understand or
explain, always turns away from committing herself – is of a
narrator who, to a far greater extent than Seacole, echoes the desire
for independence of a Brontë heroine. Davis's lack of deference is
apparent in her encounter with Nightingale. An aside prepares us
for the meeting: when Davis's sister asks her if she intends to be a
soldier, she replies:

> I did not want to be a soldier, but to see what was going on, and
> to take care of the wounded.
>   Then again I read of Miss Nightingale preparing to take out
> nurses. I did not like the name of Nightingale. When I first hear a
> name, I am very apt to know by my feeling whether I shall like
> the person who bears it.[18]

The idea of taking care of the wounded is almost an afterthought,
as if the real motivation is curiosity and a taste for adventure. This
is typical of Davis's narrative: it is always to one side of what we
might expect to encounter in terms of motivation and morality. It is
a perverse streak that is underlined in the odd remark about Nightingale's name.

When Davis meets Nightingale, there is a clash of wills. Davis
speaks first:

> 'I don't like this place, nor anybody in it, nor do I like the system.'
> 'You don't like me, then?' [Nightingale] said.
> 'No, I don't,' I said, 'but I never saw you before.'
> 'Before I go any further,' said Miss Nightingale, 'I want to
> impress one thing particularly on your mind. If you do go to
> the Crimea, you go against my will.'
>   This she repeated over and over again ... She informed me that
> she had made me over to a new superintendent, and I said (my
> Welsh blood being up again),
> 'Do you think I am a dog, or an animal, to make me over? I
> have a will of my own.'   (vol. 2, pp. 115–16)

Davis resents being told what to do: resentment, we might infer, at
being told what to do by an Englishwoman and resentment at
being told what to do by her social superior. It becomes, therefore,

a trial of strength in which, even if Davis has embellished the memory, she pitches her independence against Nightingale's independence. The war is almost irrelevant; this is really a text about Davis's sense of her own identity.

But, even if Davis is more extreme, both women are influenced by the female-penned novel of individual destiny; they are women making their own way in the world in the manner of Jane Eyre or Lucy Snowe. What complicates this picture is an additional fact about Seacole. Davis, as a Welsh dissenter, is a social outsider, but this is even more true of Seacole, who is black. Born in Jamaica, the mixed-race daughter of a Scottish army officer and a boarding-house keeper, she first made her way in the world as a storekeeper in Panama and as a self-supporting widow looking after British officers stationed in Kingston, before arriving in Balaklava in the winter of 1855. She was her own boss, establishing her 'British Hotel', which offered a store, a canteen for enlisted men, a kitchen and mess hall for officers, and a medical dispensary and sick bay.

Her autobiography splits into two parts on the subject of race. Initially it is a central issue, but this is in the setting of Panama, where Americans are repeatedly castigated for their racism. In the British and Crimean settings, however, there is no mention of race. Indeed, what is stressed is Seacole's identification with the British:

> if I could feel happy binding up the wounds of quarrelsome Americans and treacherous Spaniards, what delight should I not experience if I could be useful to my own 'sons', suffering for a cause it was so glorious to fight and bleed for!   (pp. 75–6)

This is the consistent note of the narrative: what Seacole emphasises over and over again is how she wishes to be of service, and the way in which she sees herself as 'doctress, nurse, and "mother"' (p. 124). Her entire object seems to have been to recreate the comfort and security of home:

> their calling me 'mother' was not, I think, altogether unmeaning. I used to fancy that there was something homely in the word; and, reader, you cannot think how dear to them was the smallest thing that reminded them of home.   (p. 127)

A curious contrast between Davis and Seacole is that, whereas Davis is besieged by admirers but never marries, Seacole's husband is introduced and dies within a few lines. Seacole then puts all her energies into her nurse and substitute-mother role, this providing her with a sense of identity. In truth she remains for ever an outsider, but negotiates a position for herself of devoted servant who crosses the line into becoming a proxy member of the family.

The reader's perspective, however, is somewhat different, again reminding us of ideas about identity that we associate with novels of the period. Seacole's eagerness to highlight the role she plays alerts us to the fact that she is merely playing a part, and is never quite the role she adopts. The racism of the first half of the text might have disappeared, but we continue to see the restricted terms on which she is accepted. This is not, however, exclusively an issue of race, for in many places in Victorian fiction – for example, with the character of Peggotty in *David Copperfield*, and with several of Thackeray's women characters, but most clearly with Caroline Gann, a nurse and substitute-mother to the hero of *Philip*[19] – the narrator is only at ease when women are seen in nurturing, non-sexual roles. Seacole stresses that she wishes to be of service, but this extends beyond catering to the physical needs of the soldiers; she is also of service in the way that she slots into the roles that men of the period, including novelists, want women to occupy.[20] At the same time, there is always a level of contradiction in Seacole's text, most obviously in the way that her emphasis on creating the comforts of home clashes with her own nomadic, homeless existence. The text thus endorses central, if somewhat covert, gender assumptions of mid-Victorian England, while at the same time leading the reader to stand back from these assumptions, indeed leaving the reader almost shocked at the eagerness with which Seacole plays the parts that are asked of her.

The main pattern of the text, however, is that, as in numerous Victorian novels, it is the self, and how the self sees and defines itself in relation to society, that is being examined. The Crimean War is symbolically useful, in providing a degree of violence that echoes and reflects the rapid and violent change of the period, but the issues that are worked out in relation to this never turn on the war itself. This is particularly apparent in Elizabeth Davis's narrative, primarily because she simply does not tell us anything unless it concerns herself. In the first volume, for example, before she embarks for the Crimea, she leaves Bala in North Wales and travels the world as a servant, but the feeling that is created at every stage of the journey is that the world is just a side-show put on for her diversion. Every country becomes merely a platform on which she must make her mark. The effect is to create a narrative that is reminiscent of *Moll Flanders*, where, amid a swirl of activity, the narrator is always rather coldly distanced both from events and other people. The general narrative pattern is also similar to *Moll Flanders*: there are sudden reversals of fortune, a sense of being on a journey through life without any clear idea of the direction or purpose of the journey, an occasional religious comment that never quite rings true, odd and unproductive relationships with men, and a curious relationship with the material goods of the society of which she is a member.[21]

Taking up this last point, there is an almost obsessive quality about Davis's references to linen, particularly shirts. Such references start with her arrival in Scutari where, rather than being assigned immediately to nursing work, she is sent to mend old shirts. But what is really odd is that as her account continues she tends to make more references to shirts than to the patients. When she is put in charge of some wards, her success seems distilled in the fact that she 'never found any difficulty in getting proper shirts, both cotton and flannel, for the patients' (vol. 2, p. 157). Even at the end, when her health has failed and she is about to return home, there is a curious interpolation of almost two sides in which she writes about bales of new shirts that have been allowed to rot at Scutari. Indeed, her last confrontation with Nightingale concerns these shirts:

> One day before this, Miss Nightingale had come to the kitchen, and touching the bales with her parasol, asked me what they were.
> I said, 'You should know, I don't. They are not good for anything.'   (vol. 2, p. 198)

There is something unbalanced in these references to material goods, in the same way that Moll Flanders's repeated stealing of watches and rolls of cloth suggests an odd relationship to a time-based, capitalist society. With both women, it is as if in the absence of conventional relationships they can only relate to the goods that society produces.

There is, therefore, a sense of living in a commodity-based, rather than value-based, society. At the same time, however, another set of values is implicit in Davis's need to see clothes kept clean and well-maintained: it represents an upper working-class sense of what is respectable. Davis is anxious to establish a distance between herself and 'the ill-behaviour of two or three of the party [of nurses], who disgraced themselves by drunkenness' (vol. 2, p. 108). In a similar key, in a text that, as Davis travels the world, might have presented endless opportunities for unpleasant remarks about the racial characteristics of the people she encounters, her most extreme comment is a dismissal of West Indians as 'a languid, slothful race, both men and women' (vol. 1, p. 147). The emphasis throughout is on respectability, cleanliness and hard work. It is a simple code in which the most extreme transgression – apart from sexual irregularity – is a lack of respect for property.

But if these are the normative values that Davis holds on to (and they are values at a distinctly lower level in the social scale than those of Seacole, who speaks with the confidence of an employer rather than in the manner of an employee), what really strikes the reader of her autobiography is not her normality but her peculiarity. It is a fact that the original editor of the book draws attention to more than once, for example when she entitles a section of one of the chapters 'Early Indications of Peculiar Character' (vol. 1, p. 36).[22] Davis's refusal to conform first becomes apparent when, as a child, she defies the authority of her father, a Methodist minister, by dancing. He reprimands her, but she replies: ' "I can't help it – when I hear music, something tickles my feet, and I can't keep them quiet" ' (vol. 1, p. 59). It is an apt image for the restlessness she displays throughout the work. The central thread in the story is Davis's rejection of authority. Men propose to her but she always avoids marrying them; the closest she comes to explaining why is when a prospective husband declares, ' "I shall be your master in eight-and-forty hours" ' (vol. 1, p. 122). What makes her encounters with men odd, however, is not their content but the detached manner in which they are presented. In Australia she is accosted by a convict:

> I caught up a broken bough of a tree, knocked him down, beat him severely about his legs and arms, left him on the ground and ran away…The convict, after this occurrence, threatened to waylay and murder me.   (vol. 1, pp. 204–5)

The unvarnished style is, of course, in large measure due to the fact that these are just recollections rather than incidents developed for a work of fiction, but the paradoxical effect is to create the kind of character we might encounter in a novel who is at a remove from ordinary thought and behaviour; this is a heroine fending for herself rather than seeking the role of wife, mother or even nurse.

It is, in fact, in the account of her nursing experiences in the Crimea that the work is at its oddest, for there is no attempt at all to create a picture of the men and their suffering. Nor is there the kind of reference to 'our brave soldiers' that is central in Seacole. Apart from a few cursory references to the 'poor fellows', the entire emphasis is on Davis's own role in relieving suffering. It is always her presence that makes the difference. On one occasion she removes maggots from wounds:

> these men soon got well. I do not believe that maggots ever occur in a case where the wounds are properly cleansed and dressed. I always consider their presence as a proof of neglect. In my experience, I have always found it so.   (vol. 2, p. 129)

This is perhaps simply naive, a narrator who is too unsophisticated to see that she might be striking the wrong note, but the literary effect is less important than Davis's forceful sense of her own value and importance. The impression that comes across is that the war, even the suffering of the soldiers, is less important than Davis's own life story. There is in the work no nationalistic rhetoric, no reference to the justness of the allied cause, no attempt to see the larger picture, indeed nothing other than her account of what she achieves. But what is so powerful about the autobiography is a sense that comes across of a heroine who is as extreme as any heroine in Victorian fiction in terms of being aware of her own isolation and of a strained, if dependent, relationship with society. Working-class dependency is one aspect of this: in a pathetic post-script to the work, there is an appeal for funds to support Davis, who is now destitute. But pulling in the other direction is the feeling that she is an independent woman. It is an idea that is conveyed in a point she makes about her name: the English cannot pronounce her proper name, Elizabeth Cadwaladyr, so she chooses to call herself Elizabeth Davis. In other words, she constructs an identity for herself in English life, but then holds back, retaining a sense of herself as Welsh and an outsider.

CHARLES KINGSLEY'S *WESTWARD HO!*

Given that accounts of the Crimean War have so much in common with novels from the 1850s, it might seem surprising that the war does not feature to any extent in novels from the period. But it is easy to see why. The novel of the 1850s is overwhelmingly social and domestic; war belongs to a quite different category of concerns. By and large, it is no longer a subject for novelists. Indeed, as a culture of war is so remote by this time, Russell, Seacole and Davis can only respond to the war with the assumptions of realistic novelists. This is, however, not universally true. I have already referred to Kinglake's history of the Crimean War, which goes against the grain of everything that I have discussed so far. There is, to begin with, the idea of writing an eight-volume history of the war. This would be comprehensible if Kinglake saw the war as representing some fundamental change, either in the social history of Britain or in the conduct of warfare, but, despite the length of his work, it is never ambitious in this kind of way. Indeed, Kinglake does not even provide a history of the entire conflict, as he concludes with the death of Raglan. This, however, defines the provenance of Kinglake's work: it is a traditional military history, influenced by a heroic tradition. It is not surprising that his style is pompous and dull, for there is no sense of urgency informing his writing,

The only prominent novelist who responds to the war in a novel (if we leave aside Dickens's invention of the Circumlocution Office, and minor references to the war in a few other novels from the period) is Charles Kingsley.[23] *Westward Ho!*, Kingsley's most militaristic novel, is not set in the Crimea, indeed it is the story of a seventeenth-century adventurer, Amyas Leigh, but it was inspired by the war.[24] It reveals Kingsley in his most racist and anti-Catholic guise, but it is too easy to dismiss it as purely symptomatic of distasteful aspects of Victorian thought and feeling. *Westward Ho!* might not be a novel that anyone today would read for pleasure, but it raises questions and confronts issues that Russell, Seacole and Davis do not even start to consider.[25] It looks, for example, at the mentality of fighting: that war involves death and killing, that war calls upon savage instincts, and that, in order to control this fighting, there has to be both strict discipline within an army and a code of conduct that defines what is acceptable in the conduct of war. In addition, to motivate aggression, war has to be placed in a justifying, and encouraging, framework of the national cause. But the text goes further than this in opening up a consideration of the kind of resourceful but displaced individual the nineteenth century seemed to produce: Amyas Leigh might be intended as an old-fashioned hero, but far more is implicit in Kingsley's conception of such a character. It is issues such as these that Russell and others overlook or only hint at, but it is precisely such questions that Kingsley violently barges into.

The first thing that is likely to strike the modern reader of *Westward Ho!*, however, is Kingsley's nationalism, a much-repeated sense of Britain's superiority, which at one level is almost touchingly naive. For example, he claims to be endeavouring to show 'That type of English virtue, at once manful and Godly, practical and enthusiastic'.[26] When this merges with a sense of a militant Protestant cause, however, Kingsley moves towards fanaticism. But what we might also notice in the same material is Kingsley's political sophistication in his recognition that economic and cultural superiority go hand in hand. Russell, by focusing his attention on the failings of the army and the government at home, deflects attention from the deeper political nuances of the Crimean War, converting it into a question of domestic politics. Kingsley, by contrast, and even if only at a fairly rudimentary level, is reaching out to analyse the politics of imperialism. Don Guzman, the Spanish villain of the novel, is clear that the rivalry between Spain and England is primarily commercial, and that the commercial activity both nations are involved in demands territorial expansion:

> Everywhere English commerce, under the genial sunshine of Elizabeth's wise rule, was spreading and taking root; and as Don Guzman talked with his new friends, he soon saw (for he was shrewd enough) that they belonged to a race which must be exterminated if Spain intended to become (as she did intend) the mistress of the world   (p. 231).

The extra twist is that 'cunning policy and texts of scripture' (p. 231) are at the service of Britain's economic activity. This is the surprising honesty of Kingsley's novel: the recognition that if Britain is fighting for a cause, that cause is commercial, and all the rhetoric of religion and nationalism is merely at the service of this higher cause.

This kind of political reading of experience, it has been suggested, disappears with the rise of the Victorian novel, as novelists turn in on the self, reducing a political analysis to a personal analysis.[27] But Kingsley continues to think in terms of politics rather than just personalities. Whereas Seacole and Davis are almost myopically concerned with the self, Kingsley turns out to consider the larger issues implicit in conflicts between countries, and issues that are certainly central in the Crimean War, where religious differences are only the cover for expansion of empire and trade. But the cultural ideal always needs to be in place to serve and support the economic reality. As Walter Raleigh embarks upon a military venture in *Westward Ho!*, he says to himself: 'Shall I not have my Spenser with me, to fill me with all noble thoughts, and raise my soul to his heroic pitch' (p. 241). Spenser obviously inspires Raleigh, but there is also a sense in which he will be used in an almost utilitarian way to underwrite a commercial venture. The other issue implicit here is that, in Spenser's work providing a standard of conduct and behaviour for Raleigh, we are offered an idea of emulating a model rather than being true to oneself. In other words, rather than depending upon individual psychological motivation, as is the pattern in Seacole and Davis, Kingsley works with an outward-looking sense of character. There are, of course, temperamental differences between people (Amyas is warlike: his brother, Frank, is scholarly), but the essential idea is that basic personality types mould themselves in relation to existing models. This is, one might argue, a way of thinking that has never disappeared from military life: that the army imposes ways of thinking upon the individual, rather than the individual's distinctive character mattering all that much.

This sense of the type being more significant than the individual finds its clearest illustration in the institution of the duel; in this text, a meeting between Don Guzman and a Lieutenant Cary. Don Guzman, lacking a second, states: ' "Your nation possesses the soul of honour. He who fights an Englishman needs no second" ' (p. 275). It is the type that counts for everything; there is no possibility that Cary, as a soldier, or his colleagues, will act in an underhand way. Don Guzman does not even need to consider Cary as an individual. But what complicates the scene (apart from the obvious fact that in real life the English gentleman would probably have acted as deviously as the member of any other nationality), is that Kingsley is aware that money overrides all other concerns. The duel is stopped before anyone is hurt, partly because Don Guzman is their guest, but, more importantly, because there is a ransom on his head. This kind of analysis of the economic basis of imperialism is unusual in novels of the period; curiously, it is Kingsley, the most belligerent supporter of the English cause, who is also the greatest cynic.

There is a similar sharpness in his sense of the emptiness that lies behind the militarism he seems to defend so enthusiastically. In *Westward Ho!*, ambitious undertakings usually end in collapse and failure. Thus, Amyas and Sir Humphrey Gilbert embark on a mission with a good deal of rhetoric on the lines of, ' "We are going in God's cause; we go for the honour of God's gospel, for the deliverance of poor captives led captive by the devil" ' (p. 253), but in the very next paragraph we read: 'As early as the second day, the seeds of failure began to sprout above ground' (p. 253). Repeatedly in the novel, rhetoric is undercut by immediate and practical problems. One thing that characterises a great many responses to the Crimean War is disappointment that the allies were unable to follow up their early success at Alma, but Kingsley writes from a different perspective, as if he expects nothing except failure.

What he appears to cling on to is good leadership. As in the case of Francis Drake, this is largely a matter of imposing discipline, for Drake 'knew when to hang a man.' (p. 287).[28] But the ideal is, as always, elusive. Amyas, as hero, displays far more bravery than judgement, and generally in the novel there is more of a feeling of activity for its own sake than a sense of direction and good leadership. It seems a shrewdly aware stance on the whole issue of war, that, for all the talk about the qualities of leadership, what actually matters is hot-headedness. For all the talk about a religious cause and national virtues, fighting in the end is about fighting. Kingsley's racism is pertinent here: it is easy to deplore scenes where the English soldier confronts 'savages',[29] but the fact is that such encounters undermine the notion of war as being bound by the rules of chivalry – the idea that always informs the Englishmen's relations with Don Guzman – for in these battles there are no rules, and Amyas has to rely upon being as savage as his opponents.

In addition, these encounters end in failure. At the end of the most significant battle, Amyas is beaten and defeated, and his brother Frank has been taken prisoner. Kingsley concludes and sums up with the comment, 'so ended that fatal venture of mistaken chivalry' (p. 383). The point that emerges is that *Westward Ho!*

is not the gung-ho text it might initially appear. It is shrewd in its grasp of the economic motives behind war, and equally shrewd in its grasp of the nature of the religious and nationalistic rhetoric that is needed to motivate an army and nation. And, at the same time, it is almost cynical in its understanding of the unbalanced warlike temperament of a character like Amyas.[30] It is easy to imagine that just such a taste for confrontation, for the excitement of fighting, might well have taken over from common sense at the start of the Charge of the Light Brigade. Russell offers a sense of aristocratic folly, but Kingsley, despite appearing to be a novelist who prefers types to individuals, gets inside the mind of the kind of person who might have launched the attack.

The curious thing is that Kingsley, as a novelist, offers what is, for the time, the most uncharacteristic, one might say 'un-novel-like', account of war. This is partly because his contemporaries favour the realistic novel, with its emphasis on the self and society. Kingsley writes in a different tradition, that of romance, with a typical pattern whereby the heroism of romance is tempered with the cold light of experience. It is the fact that he starts with different formal premises that initially permits his different perspective on war. What still comes as a surprise, however, is just how sceptical Kingsley is. Widely regarded as one of the chief proponents of manliness, in *Westward Ho!* he is devastating in his dissection of masculinity. The main thread of the plot is that Rose Saltaire, whom all the men adore, elopes with the Spaniard, Don Guzman. The Englishmen have been so absorbed with their military exploits that they have let Rose slip through their hands; Amyas, in particular, for all his manliness, has not proved man enough to win the girl. At the end of the novel Amyas does have a partner, a native girl Ayacanore, but by now he is totally blind and dependent:

> he stamped on the floor with pettishness, and then checking himself, burst into a violent flood of tears.   (p. 633)

The text ends, therefore, with Amyas weeping, blind and unmanned, having to depend upon a woman from an, assumedly, inferior race. The English hero has been dissected and destroyed.

What makes the text so disconcerting, however, is something that goes beyond this. Kingsley starts with a chivalric code, a chivalric code that is based upon violence, but violence qualified by a sense of being an honourable gentleman and soldier, and acting in the name of one's country and one's religion. His scepticism about the rhetoric of nationhood, religion and honour leaves him, however, with nothing intact except violence. It is this that creates the impression of a sadistic writer. But this is inevitable, for there is nothing that can be relied upon except violence. Kingsley is often criticised for the crudity of his nationalistic rhetoric, but it is important to see why it is so empty and banal; it is because there is no real conviction behind it: the words are just empty words. The fact that Kingsley is left only with violence is most apparent in the closing pages of the novel, where Amyas pursues Don Guzman. His pursuit of Don Guzman's ship is frenzied, irrational and extravagant as he attempts to fulfil the role of his 'brother's avenger' (p. 617). Eventually Don Guzman's vessel is driven on to rocks and sinks with the loss of five hundred men. It is another failure for Amyas, for it is the sea rather than Amyas himself that has destroyed the Spaniard. But Kingsley is almost as frenzied as his hero in these final pages of the novel as he drives Amyas in pursuit of his enemy; the writing itself becomes a pursuit of, and revelling in, violence for its own sake.

Such a stance is problematic: it is easy to make the link between Kingsley and twentieth-century right-wing political violence (particularly where the violence is inspired by a sense of a loss of old ideas and certainties). But it is Kingsley's contemporary role, rather than any ways in which he might anticipate future developments, that is most significant in any attempt to assess his work. And, in this context, what we can see is that, unlike most of his contemporaries in fiction, Kingsley does not approach his work with the kind of liberal premises that had evolved by the 1850s. Kingsley's stance is inevitably more disconcerting than the position of those in the liberal camp, who see a way forward on the basis of social reform and individual integrity. In this respect Kingsley is at an opposite remove from Russell. At the heart of Russell's reports is a call for reform both in the army and in the administration of the army. It is a call that both his newspaper and the country took up. Kingsley is less sanguine: the novel as a genre might have influenced ways of thinking about the Crimean War, turning it into a social problem or a mirror of domestic fiction, but Kingsley shows that war cannot be reduced to such a comprehensible and manageable scale.

What is even more unnerving, however, is Kingsley's sense of his hero. If we think again about the memoirs of Mary Seacole and Elizabeth Davis, we can see that there is a contradiction at the heart of their works that echoes a contradiction in the mid-Victorian realistic novel. The overt stress of a nurse's memoir is inevitably on duty and service, on contributing to the general good of society, but the self-motivated heroines in both texts reveal an excess of energy and independence that makes it impossible for them simply to become dutiful cogs within the social order; Elizabeth Davis, in particular, does not even bother to pay lip-service to the notion of obedience. It is rather different for William Russell, who, as a man, can channel his energy and ambition into his career as a journalist. But in the memoirs of Seacole and Davis – as is the case in a great many Victorian novels – we are aware of the gap between the self and society. One way of characterising this is to focus on the notion of aggression, and a new kind of aggression that seems to have come into existence in the nineteenth century: possibly because war was no longer so commonly available as an outlet, possibly as a by-product of the pace of change of the period.[31] In most mid-Victorian novels there is an attempt to paper over the crack, to play down or condemn or educate the character out of such restless, alienated energy, but Kingsley, despite appearing to favour an old-fashioned sense of character, because of his dissatisfaction with the society of the day, indulges his sense of a displaced and alienated hero. From the evidence of a George Eliot novel we could gain no understanding of why characters such as General Gordon, Cecil Rhodes and Baden-Powell appeared in the Victorian period, but Kingsley's works do provide a sense of the motivation behind such men.[32] His declared intent may be to promote a sense of nation and play down a sense of self, but his novels in fact tell us a great deal about a non-liberal, awkward vision of the self. What is perhaps surprising is that it is in the 1850s, at the very point when a new middle-class peaceful vision of society is superseding the old aristocratic military dispensation, that the limits of the new order become apparent, that attention begins to be paid to facets of the human character that cannot be regulated and contained; indeed, it could be said that it is the new social norms themselves that actually provoke an alienated, frustrated and often furious protest against containment. These are issues that I return to at some length in Chapter 6, in a consideration of the Victorian hero – in particular, why a certain kind of rootless soldier emerges in the last thirty years of the century – but in the next chapter I want to look at how one writer, Thackeray, came to terms with the demise of the aristo-military culture of the Wellington era.

3

Thackeray and the Culture of War

THE CULTURE OF WAR

Thackeray is the one major Victorian novelist who writes extensively about war: the Seven Years War (1756–63) in *Barry Lyndon*, the Battle of Waterloo (1815) in *Vanity Fair*, the War of the Spanish Succession (1701–14) in *Henry Esmond*, and the American War of Independence (1775–83) in *The Virginians*.[1] It is, therefore, somewhat surprising to come across Andrew Rutherford's suggestion that Thackeray's

> sour reflections on traditional poetic treatments of war show his awareness of the novel as a *genre* committed not only to a different subject-matter, but to a different kind of vision and a truer sense of values.[2]

Rutherford's case, in his book *The Literature of War*, overlaps with some of the points I have been developing: that in the Victorian period, especially from the late 1840s, 'there was an increasing tendency for the finest literature to focus on those aspects of experience that fell within the limits of civil life', and that the realistic novel both reflected and helped to determine this trend.[3] It seems odd, however, to associate Thackeray with this new direction in the novel, for what is consistently apparent in Thackeray's works is the difficulty he has in disentangling himself from the military frame of mind.

This is more than a matter of simply including battle scenes and war references in the novels. It involves a sense of experience in which the army is not only the first and natural choice of a career, but also that the disciplines and values of army life provide a framework for controlling and judging civilian life. It is a difficult idea to grasp against the background of the developing liberal democracy of nineteenth-century Britain, but it is extremely easy to understand if we think of warrior societies both past and present, where military conflict is the daily reality of existence. Such societies think along military lines in every aspect of their being.[4] It might seem unrealistic to suggest that such a stance could have survived into Victorian Britain. If we look at the novels of Walter Scott, for example, it is clear that, even in the first twenty years of the nineteenth century, a military code as the whole basis of existence is something that he associates with the past; it is so remote that it can be looked back at with fondness and nostalgia.[5] It would be wrong, however, to draw too many conclusions from a glib summary of Scott's position. It is more relevant to acknowledge, and seek reasons for, the extraordinary degree of growth and change in the Victorian novel from the mid-1840s and in the decade that follows. It is now generally accepted that an unprecedented degree of social redefinition takes place in these years: an urbanised, middle-class society is being established, and the novel not only charts this social change but also defines and interrogates the ideas and values that emerge from this process of social change. A major cultural shift occurs: people's habits of thinking are changing, even how they see themselves as individuals within an increasingly secularised and business-based nation state.[6]

Yet, when we acknowledge the nature of the change in English society and the English novel in the 1840s and 1850s, what we also have to recognise is that old habits of thought would have persisted well into the 1850s.[7] In other words, alongside the emergence of a new cultural order the remnants of an older culture remain. And it is in this context that it seems most appropriate to see Thackeray: for all his professed radicalism, Thackeray is a conservative writer unable to absorb the different social vision that was developing in Victorian Britain.[8] A central aspect of this is Thackeray's instinctive military thinking. For example, when there is a conflict between two men in a Thackeray novel, more often than not the possibility of a duel will be considered. It is true that Thackeray might present the men's actions as farcical, but the important point is that he cannot envisage a dispute between two individuals without turning to the duel, and all that it implies about a masculine honour code.[9] Moreover, in *Vanity Fair* in particular, he not only continues to think in terms of the rituals and conventions of a military code but also seems to endorse the idea of selfless and self-sacrificing heroism that is part of such a code.

For the immediate historical background to Thackeray's position
we need to look back to the period of the Revolutionary and
Napoleonic Wars, where we see the presence of, and strength of,
a traditional military ethos. Indeed, this code acquired fresh energy
from around 1793, when the commencement of hostilities demanded an abrupt and massive enlargement of the army. With
the whole country on a war footing, military values had to be
central. But this was given an extra dimension by the attitudes of
the Duke of Wellington, as described by David Gates:

> Dismissing schemes for the moral welfare and education of
> ordinary soldiers as subversive, he placed his faith in uncompro-
> mising disciplinary codes and the army's reflection of Britain's
> social hierarchy: the rank and file were the tenants of a feudalis-
> tic community; the officers its squires.[10]

It is this sense that the army and society are a mirror image of each
other that constitutes the essence of a military code; the values and
disciplines of army life, including the masculine leadership of an
elite, are the same as the values and disciplines of civilian life. And,
as Wellington's influence confirms – first as a military commander,
but then perhaps even more significantly as a politician, serving
as Prime Minister from 1828 to 1830 and as Foreign Secretary in
1834–5, only retiring from public life in 1846 – the military code
was given fresh life both at the end of the eighteenth century and to
some extent well into the nineteenth century. This is an important
point to bear in mind: a military code might seem timeless, a
constant in a pre-liberal society, simply becoming more visible at
times of war, but the fact is that the military code acquired new
energy and a distinctive new form in the early years of the nineteenth century. The reasons for this include Britain's defeat in the
American War of Independence, the determination with which war
was conducted against the citizens' army of Revolutionary and
Napoleonic France, and the need of the British aristocracy to assert
itself in the face of anticipated, and, as we can now see, inevitable,
social change in Britain. In discussing how mid-Victorian Britain
reconstitutes itself according to a different social philosophy, we
have to recognise that the mid-Victorians were reacting against a
military code that, in its particular form, had been constructed little
more than a generation earlier, in response to specific conditions,
and to some extent as a defensive bulwark against the social code

that was to succeed it; in other words, the old code was put together precisely because there was a fear of the coming order within society.[11]

An aristocratic sense of being someone born to lead both on the battlefield and in politics is conveyed well in the impression that has come down to us of Uxbridge, later the Marquess of Anglesey, Wellington's second-in-command at Waterloo. He believed that a cavalry general should 'inspire his men as early as possible with the most perfect confidence in his personal gallantry. Let him but lead, they are sure to follow, and I believe hardly anything will stop them.'[12] But just as significant as Anglesey's own words are the anecdotes he inspired – and the same is true of Wellington – for these apocryphal stories fostered and sustained the values of the military code in the imagination of the public at the time. The most famous story about Anglesey concerns the wound he received at the close of the Battle of Waterloo:

> Uxbridge exclaims 'By God, sir, I've lost my leg!' Wellington momentarily removes the telescope from his eye, considers the mangled limb, says 'By God, sir, so you have!' and resumes his scrutiny of the victorious field.[13]

The story conveys everything that needs to be conveyed about how an English aristocrat conducts himself in war.

This was a war, moreover, against the French, who were fighting in the name of a political radicalism that threatened 'Order, hierarchy, and sexual propriety'.[14] This added a harder edge to British militarism, something that is most apparent in a new view of the military opponent that developed at this time. It is part of a traditional military code that enemies who are equally honourable – that is, sharing both tactics and values – confront each other. They have a shared view of the rules of the engagement. Part of Napoleon's success as a general, however, was that he rewrote the rules of strategy,[15] but more significant in English representations of the behaviour of the French was the conviction that they had abandoned gentlemanly standards:

> The frank unassumingness and contentedness of the British officers and troops, were the themes of eulogium in every mouth, and were by every one contrasted with the ferocity, greediness, and insolence of the French.[16]

This is a comment by John Scott, who, like so many other Britons, travelled to Belgium in 1815 to see the battlefield at Waterloo. His view might be dismissed as a naive case of patriotism, but it does offer us a sense of the view of an ordinary member of the educated English public, and is also interesting in terms of the identification it sees between military and social virtues.

What is even more interesting about Scott's views, however, is that he sees a vibrant and progressive society flourishing in England within the secure structure that the old order provides. Before embarking for the continent he passes through Margate and Ramsgate, where

> business supplied pleasure, and pleasure gave circulation and vigour to business. It is only in England, and but lately there, that the intermingling of the different orders of society, and the intermeddling of one class of people with the proper habits of others, which constitute the life of a watering place, could occur. A very long and highly prosperous settlement of national institutions, and personal pursuits, is necessary, before any great number of individuals can have the power so to quit for a time their natural track, and respite their routine tasks: and an active, stout and independent turn of thinking can alone account for the inclination to do so.[17]

This is a rebuke to the French, who have promoted change through revolution rather than trusting to evolution, but there is little danger of the English following the French route, as they value their independence rather than acting as a mob. It is not a democratic society that has arrived in England, simply a society where there is sufficient money and leisure for the usual boundaries to be crossed occasionally in the setting of a holiday resort.[18] In Scott's book as a whole it is the army that provides the framework of security in which this freedom can flourish; it serves as one of the vital 'national institutions'. In a peaceful era the early Victorians had less cause to think about the role of the army in their national life, but in a quiet way they continued to place their faith in the army as guaranteeing this level of domestic security. Indeed, what was so shocking about the Crimean War was that the army, which had remained untested in Europe since 1815, proved not to be the dependable element in the national equation that people had assumed it to be.[19] The shock brought home to people the real change that had occurred since Waterloo: that the army and society were no longer a mirror image of each other. Society had changed, but the army had failed to change. At that point, the redundancy of a military code becomes transparently obvious. This is the context in which we have to consider Thackeray's continuing instinctive allegiance to aristocratic and militaristic habits of thinking. In the year of Waterloo it is not surprising that John Scott sees the military code as relevant in every area of life, but by the 1840s the very fact that he writes novels based around military campaigns identifies Thackeray as an outsider in the novel of his time.

BARRY LYNDON AND VANITY FAIR

Moving from the rhetoric inspired by the Battle of Waterloo to Thackeray's *Barry Lyndon*, we move from the giddiest heights to the lowest depths. It is the story of an Irish adventurer who enlists as a soldier during the Seven Years War but eventually deserts the English army to serve as an infantryman for the Prussians. He then deserts again in order to pursue the life of a professional gambler. He mistreats his stepson, Viscount Bullingdon, but his cruelty to his wife, Lady Honoria, is so extreme that Bullingdon publicly horsewhips Barry. His luck having finally run out, Barry dies of *delirium tremens* in the Fleet Prison.[20] On the face of it, *Barry Lyndon* strips away every scrap of heroic idealism in the military code: this is the soldier as mercenary, coward and absolute rogue.

Yet, *Barry Lyndon* is, in various respects, a conventional military narrative, for the debunking it offers complements rather than subverts a traditional view. Inherent in the very concept of an ideal is the awareness that there are those who cannot live up to the ideal; the aristocracy are born to lead, but beneath them is an unruly mob displaying all the worst traits of human nature. Looked at in this light, everything in *Barry Lyndon* can be seen as an exact inversion of what we might expect to find in a heroic military narrative: the emphasis is on the common soldier rather than officers, these soldiers show no respect for women or property, when Barry fights he fights as a mercenary rather than for his country, and, for Barry, saving his skin is always more important than dying a heroic death. This alternative perspective serves to endorse traditional values. The tactic can be compared with the conservative stance of the eighteenth-century rogue narrative and later Newgate novel. In Fielding's *Jonathan Wild*, for example, an infamous criminal becomes the chief of a gang of thieves and victimises a former schoolfellow. Wild's actions are in part a satirical comment on the life of the Whig politician Sir Robert Walpole, a fact that indicates the provenance of Fielding's work: the Tory Fielding demonises a new and unruly force within society.[21] The Newgate novel expresses a similar fear of the social outsider.[22] *Barry Lyndon* operates in the same way. In particular, it bears out Wellington's view that the great mass of soldiers are the scum of the earth:

> People talk of their enlisting from their fine military spirit – all stuff – no such thing. Some of our men enlist from having got bastard children – some for minor offences – many more for drink.[23]

A similar patrician arrogance informs *Barry Lyndon*: the potential for indiscipline of the common recruit confirms the case for discipline and a military elite.

At the same time, however, we do need to acknowledge that there are original and disturbing qualities in *Barry Lyndon*. Primarily this is a matter of the degree of violence in the novel, particularly in the latter stages when Barry has left the army; his treatment of his wife and stepson is essentially psychopathic. He is an extreme figure, literally an Irish fugitive, but also outside any community of values and beliefs. He assumes identities (he is never an officer, but passes himself off as one), changes his name, and, in the most extreme example in the novel, refers to the

> strange frightful custom of *child-murder*. The men used to say that life was unbearable, that suicide was a crime, in order to avert which, and to finish with the intolerable misery of their position, the best plan was to kill a young child, which was innocent, and therefore secure of heaven, and then to deliver themselves as guilty of murder.   (p. 101)

This is a line of thinking that is bizarrely outside conventional morality, but so many of the incidents in the novel are extreme that it might seem hard to determine exactly what kind of impression Thackeray is creating. We can make some progress, however, if we compare Barry with Bill Sykes in Dickens's *Oliver Twist*.[24]

Both *Oliver Twist* and *Barry Lyndon* emerge from a context of social unrest (their respective dates are 1837 and 1844), more precisely a fear of violence from the lower reaches of society. Barry and Bill Sykes are similar in the unbounded nature of their villainy; both represent a terrifying, in some ways less than human, threat from below.[25] Far from being a politically radical text – which is how *Barry Lyndon* would appear if it was seriously questioning military culture – the novel is motivated by these conservative fears about social change and social disruption. It is a conservative stance that becomes far more pronounced in *Vanity Fair*.

Thackeray offers a seemingly plain statement of his position in *Vanity Fair*. As the protagonists prepare for the Battle of Waterloo, the narrator writes:

> We do not claim to rank among the military novelists. Our place is with the non-combatants. When the decks are cleared for action we go below and wait meekly.[26]

His main focus, consequently, is on social life in Brussels, from the 'business of life and living, and the pursuits of pleasure especially' (p. 340) before the battle, through to the camp followers fleeing when a French victory looks imminent. The military campaign seems simply an opportunity for outrageous displays of self-interest. Indeed, even war itself can be seen as an extension of Vanity Fair. In a novel which is centrally concerned with buying and selling, and in which stockmarket imagery is always prominent, it is not surprising to see the same imagery used in a military context:

> The august jobbers assembled at Vienna, and carving out the kingdoms of Europe according to their wisdom, had such cause of quarrel among themselves as might have set the armies which had overcome Napoleon to fight against each other, but for the return of the object of unanimous hatred and fear. This monarch had an army in full force because he had jobbed to himself Poland, and was determined to keep it: another had robbed half Saxony, and was bent upon maintaining his acquisition: Italy was the object of a third's solicitude.   (p. 340)

Thackeray's facts are correct – at the Congress of Vienna between September 1814 and March 1815, the allies squabbled over the pickings of the war, only to be reunited again with the news of Napoleon's return – but his choice of imagery recasts the issue according to the controlling terms of his own novel.[27]

Another real-life event provided Thackeray with his most stunning illustration of the frivolity of Vanity Fair: the Duchess of Richmond's ball on the eve of the Battle of Waterloo.[28] But Thackeray again manipulates the facts to present his own vision of a world where values have become confused:

> All Brussels had been in a state of excitement about it, and I have heard from ladies who were in that town at that period, that the talk and interest of persons of their own sex regarding the ball was much greater even than in respect to the enemy in their front.   (p. 355)

Repeatedly there is an inversion of values as the language of war is applied to social life (Becky battles with Miss Pinkerton and conducts a campaign to advance in society), and the language of social life turns war into a business:

> It was a blessing for a commerce-loving country to be over-run by such an army of customers: and to have such creditable warriors to feed.   (p. 336)

When 'warriors' are seen as 'customers', any sense of what is trustworthy in the world becomes elusive. Theatre imagery is common in relation to war, but in *Vanity Fair* it is taken to an extreme as news of their departure for the Continent provides the characters – especially Jos Sedley, who grows a soldier's moustache even though he is only a camp follower – the ideal opportunity for dressing up and playing a part.[29] Sourer notes do intrude, but for the most part it is a giddy social round that continues after the battle as the characters move on to Paris.

At the same time, important points are being made. The 'Corsican upstart' (p. 211) challenges the received social order. Just as Napoleon represents a new and dangerous force, a lot of the questionable behaviour we see in *Vanity Fair* is not a matter of timeless human failings, but the expression of new, aggressive energies. Becky Sharp, who is repeatedly compared to Napoleon, is the embodiment of these anarchic impulses.[30] As is the case with Barry Lyndon, Becky constitutes a destructive threat from below, but she appears in a novel that offers a much more comprehensive sense of a whole society in flux. Against such a background, the self-contained and self-regulating men's world of the army seems simple and straightforward: George Osborne, for example, is 'famous at field-sports, famous at a song, famous on parade' (p. 143), an excellent drinker, an excellent boxer, and 'the best batter and bowler, out and out, of the regimental club' (p. 143).[31] But the picture is less straightforward than it appears, as class rivalries conflict with the simple ideal of the military code. Rawdon Crawley, as an officer in the Guards, belongs to a socially more desirable regiment than George and Dobbin, and George aspires 'to exchange into some better regiment soon' (p. 338). Meanwhile, Rawdon pays 'scarcely any attention to Dobbin, looking upon him as a good-natured nincompoop, and under-bred City man' (p. 294). Significantly, after the Battle of Waterloo, whereas Dobbin moves up one rank from Captain to Major, Rawdon moves up two steps, to Lieutenant-Colonel.

The overall effect of details such as these in *Vanity Fair* is to create a sense of a society in a process of change; Becky Sharp might represent the most extreme threat, but the emerging middle class constitutes an equal challenge to the old military pattern of hierarchy and deference. A process of social change is taking place, and Thackeray delineates the nature of that change. If we put it that way, however, it might suggest that Thackeray reports these matters dispassionately, whereas *Vanity Fair* is anything but a detached account of events that have taken place thirty years earlier. On the contrary, Thackeray is still entangled in the divisions at the heart of the novel. The way in which this is most apparent is that Thackeray, in a work that claims to have no hero, clings on to the one virtue of heroism. George and Rawdon are both wasters, yet when called upon to do their duty rise to the challenge. Neither man flinches for a moment when he hears that he will have to fight at Waterloo. It does not have to be this way. If Thackeray had continued with the logic of *Barry Lyndon*, the principal characters in *Vanity Fair* could be as devious in battle as they are in all other areas of life, but this is not the case. There are those who run away, but this is only people like the Belgian hussar, Regulus (p. 392). No officer deserts his post, no officer is found wanting in any way. By some miracle, men who are weak in all other respects suddenly become exemplary. In real life, the army at Waterloo did prove itself to be the backbone of the nation, but it is surprising to find the

English officer class presented unironically as the backbone of Thackeray's novel.[32]

The idea of duty surfaces repeatedly in *Vanity Fair*. In particular, a mocking passage will frequently culminate in a statement such as each officer 'was bent upon doing his duty, and gaining his share of honour and distinction' (p. 220). Mrs O'Dowd is a comic figure in the novel, but her husband is presented almost reverentially as a man who has 'paid for every step in his profession by some more than equivalent act of daring and gallantry' (p. 327).[33] Rawdon Crawley, normally 'a selfish heavy dragoon' (p. 225), is grave as he prepares for war, dresses in his shabbiest uniform, and goes off to war quietly and thoughtfully. And even George Osborne, who plays the part of a repentant sinner as he departs, proves his courage in battle. This is all summed up in one sentence from Thackeray: 'All our friends took their share and fought like men in the great field' (p. 405). In a novel where most of the enduring images are of falseness and deception, the one area where things are true is in battle. It might be argued that even a satirist is going to worry about offending his audience, and that Thackeray knows better than to ridicule the British victory at Waterloo, but the position is not as simple as this. For, rather than just celebrating a British victory, what he celebrates are the traditional military virtues as exhibited by a military elite. In returning to a traditional military code, Thackeray clings on to known values as his only safeguard against the general instability – including the stirrings of class upheaval – that he detects in contemporary society; fearing much of what he documents, he retreats to the security of a chivalric code. But more is involved than just a retreat to the past, for Thackeray's intuitive allegiance to a military code is by no means incompatible with a serious interest in Britain's military inheritance.

HENRY ESMOND

The sequence of Thackeray's major novels is revealing. After *Vanity Fair*, he writes a domestic novel in *Pendennis*, but then returns to military matters in *Henry Esmond*. The domestic *The Newcomes* is then followed by *The Virginians*, which is based around the American War of Independence. Thackeray cannot break free from war; he ventures into civilian life, but repeatedly comes back to a military perspective. It is only at the end of *The Virginians* that he manages to establish a new position, looking at war with a social vision rather than looking at society with a military vision. In *Henry Esmond* he is still thoroughly caught up in the culture of war. Most of the army passages in *Henry Esmond* relate to the War of the Spanish Succession, which attempted to curb the power of Louis XIV in Europe. Britain, Austria, Prussia, Denmark, Holland, Portugal and Savoy – the Grand Alliance – confronted France, Bavaria and Spain. The Duke of Marlborough's victories at Blenheim (1704), Ramillies (1706), Oudenaarde (1708), and Malplaquet (1709) all feature in the novel, along with a number of lesser campaigns and battles. But war has affected the lives of all the characters well before this, for the recent past of the novel is the Civil War and subsequent upheavals, including the Battle of the Boyne (1690) where James II landed in Ireland with a French army to try to regain his throne.[34]

As the novel opens, therefore, both the lives and the homes of the characters are scarred by war. The description of the damage inflicted upon Castlewood Hall, in particular, sets up a frame of reference for the narrative. There has been extensive damage, but there is also a garden-terrace where

> the flowers grew again, which the boots of the Roundheads had trodden in their assault, and which was restored without much cost, and only a little care, by both ladies who succeeded the second viscount in the government of this mansion.[35]

The novel will deal with male aggression, but it will also deal, as this passage suggests, with gentler, nurturing impulses which, as we might expect, are going to be associated with women. More ambitiously, this account of the domestic damage inflicted in war suggests that the novel will examine the relationship between public life and private life, between the sphere of war and the sphere of the home. This is a more complex topic than in *Vanity Fair* where war is seen primarily as a simple arena in which men can do their duty and show their sterling qualities. In *Henry Esmond* war and domestic life overlap in a troubling way. It is apparent in the control that is exercised over the Castlewood family as potential rebels. A soldier informs Castlewood that 'he was not under arrest, but under surveillance' (p. 55). This is a sinister aspect of military power, the intrusive control of people's lives. The modern reader is, of course, fully aware of the limitations on personal freedom in any country where the military assumes control, but the issue is a new one in Thackeray's novels; he seems to be reaching out to ask ambitious questions about control and freedom, the state and the individual, questions pertinent in the 1850s as Britain moved slowly towards a new kind of liberal democracy.

The focus of Thackeray's interest might also point us towards a fact that is hard to grasp today: that Thackeray took himself seriously as a historian, and was taken seriously by the public as a historian, albeit that he worked in the medium of the novel. The temptation for the modern reader is to think that Thackeray chooses to escape to the past as a way of avoiding the present, but inherent in his concern with large-scale European conflicts is a desire to understand the deeper historical forces – specifically the military legacy – that have led to and shaped the pattern of nineteenth-century life, and shaped the national identity of the English, both as a nation and as individuals. When we are reading works such as *Jane Eyre* or *David Copperfield* there is a sense in which we are reading the history of one life; in Thackeray there is nearly always a larger sense of historical process. Similarly, many Victorian novels seem to establish a path from the present to the future, as the characters, by the end of the text, define their working relationship with society. In Thackeray, by contrast, and again indicating the genuine historical dimension to his novels, there is always a far greater sense of how the nation's past has led to the present. Reporting on the history of a country which, by the 1850s, had achieved a dominant position in the world largely as a consequence of its victories on land and sea, Thackeray inevitably must adopt the role not just of historian but more specifically of military historian. The three major European conflicts he deals with could be said to be the wars that determined the nineteenth-century balance of power, not just in Europe but throughout the world. At a more difficult to define level, they are also the wars that shaped nineteenth-century Britain. The War of the Spanish Succession (1701–14) thwarted the territorial ambitions of Louis XIV, the Seven Years War (1756–63), the most successful war Britain has ever fought, established British global supremacy particularly at the expense of the French, and the Revolutionary and Napoleonic Wars (1793–1815) finally consolidated the sense of national self-confidence. In focusing on these three areas Thackeray explores how the eighteenth century led to the nineteenth century.

(The one setback Britain experienced in the eighteenth century was the American War of Independence (1775–81). As I will argue in the last section of this chapter, Thackeray needed to disentangle himself from his attachment to a military code before, as a historian, he could really find a way of incorporating defeat into his view of the past.)

As ambitious as Thackeray's novels are, however, much of the time in *Henry Esmond* he presents a very simple impression of war and army life. At the most basic level, the army offers a chance to escape from domestic responsibilities. Henry Esmond enlists when his relationship with his family comes under strain; he enjoys his first campaign, which 'if not very glorious, was very pleasant' (p. 199), providing 'that excitement of action and change of scene, which shook off a great deal of his previous melancholy' (p. 202). And there is much to admire in the 'splendid...gallantry' (p. 281) of commanders such as Marlborough and Webb. But there is also a darker side behind the splendour. Lord Mohun, the villain of the novel, for example, is 'a person of a handsome presence, with the *bel air*, and a bright daring warlike aspect' (p. 126), with entertaining 'stories of his campaigns and his life at Vienna, Venice, Paris, and the famous cities of Europe which he had visited in both peace and war' (p. 131). But, unlike *Vanity Fair*, where the rogue always distinguishes himself in battle, Mohun's conduct is all of a piece, for his life of dissipation includes duelling, resulting in the death of Castlewood. The aggression that has served him in war taints his private life. The same might be said of Marlborough, as he is presented in the novel, a great commander who is finally tripped up by his vanity and greed.[36] By way of contrast with these aggressively masculine figures – Castlewood himself could be added to the list – who bring the less acceptable aspects of army life into the home, Henry Esmond, for all his military involvement, is a gentler, more feminised, character, making a distinction between public and private conduct.

This is the awareness that emerges in the post-Waterloo era, that society and soldiering are not synonymous, that a different network of values is established in a society where war is marginal rather than the daily reality of existence. *Henry Esmond* takes a long-term look at the evolution of this contrary impulse in western society. But what is apparent in *Henry Esmond*, as in all Thackeray's novels, is that he cannot fully take on this new domestic vision of experience; he cannot make the break with militarism. The way in

which this is most apparent in *Henry Esmond* is in Thackeray's
reliance upon duelling, both to advance the action and to resolve
the plot. He cannot see a way of resolving a conflict between two
people that does not involve the idea of a duel; even when an
alternative solution is found, the very fact that he has introduced
the concept of the duel indicates the essentially militaristic way in
which his mind works. The last serious duel in Britain was fought
in 1852, which is, coincidentally, the year *Henry Esmond* was published. There are a number of later incidents, but the encounter
between George Smythe and Colonel Romilly at Weybridge is
generally regarded as 'the last duel'.[37] The informing principle of
the duel is that a man defends his honour (or the honour of a lady).
Aligned to this is the fact that the duel is part of an aristocratic code
of behaviour: the participants must be social equals, and of sufficient standing to have a reputation to defend. One reason why
duelling disappeared in the Victorian period is that those with a
grievance turned increasingly to the courts. But in *Henry Esmond*
duelling is still a central feature of life.

Of the three significant duels in the novel, the first, between
Mohun and Castlewood, may be regarded as a classic, text-book
duel: it is prompted by a dispute over the honour of Castlewood's
wife. What a duel tells us about attitudes towards women and
notions of masculinity is so obvious that it does not need stating.
But what is also involved in a duel is a ritualised and institutionalised containment of violence; underlying any duel is brute
savagery – something that is particularly evident in the second
duel of the novel, where Mohun kills the Duke of Hamilton and
is then killed himself – but the violence is controlled by a set of
rules, a code of honour. Honour is, indeed, more important than
life itself; the duellist always sets his reputation above self-interest
or self-preservation. This reflects the issue at the heart of *Henry
Esmond*: war might be brutal, but inherent in the military code is a
sense of selfless honour that must be set against the new kind of
self-centred, self-justifying individualism that Henry represents,
and which is precisely the kind of sense of being an individual
that comes to dominate the nineteenth century (we need only
think of *David Copperfield*, published in 1850, to find an example
of the new kind of Victorian hero, who is self-serving, hardening
himself only to cope with the demands of family life and a
career rather than the extra sacrifice that might be involved in
military service).

Thackeray's inability to disentangle himself from the merits of the old military ethos is apparent again in the token duel between Henry and the Pretender with which *Henry Esmond* concludes. Their duel amounts to nothing more than crossing swords:

> The swords were no sooner met, than Castlewood knocked up Esmond's with the blade of his own, which he had broke off short at the shell; and the colonel falling back a step dropped his point with another very low bow, and declared himself perfectly satisfied.
>
> 'Eh bien, vicomte,' says the young prince, who was a boy, and a French boy, 'il ne nous reste qu'une chose à faire:' he placed his sword upon the table, and the fingers of his two hands upon his breast: – 'We have one more thing to do,' says he; 'you do not divine it?' He stretched out his arms: – 'Embrassons nous!'
>
> (pp. 458–9)

Robin Gilmour argues that 'With this token duel, following on Esmond's bitter denunciation of the Stuart cause and the symbolic breaking of his sword, the old code of honour is renounced. The history of Colonel Esmond is a farewell to arms'.[38] This, however, seems a rather too neat and tidy reading of the scene. If the end of the novel really represented a 'farewell to arms' there would be no need for even a token duel: Esmond could demonstrate the irrelevance of the old ways – and his maturity – by refusing to rise to even the token challenge. But the duel does have its attractions: primarily, the institution formalises conduct, enabling these two men to resolve their differences in a clear-cut, visible manner. The circumstances behind the duel have been grubby: the dispute has been provoked by the Pretender's sexual misconduct, by his advances upon Beatrix. The novel could, therefore, end with undignified brawling or festering resentment, but the duel – even if it is only a token duel – restores some dignity to the relations between the two men. And the token duel does seem necessary to maintain honour, for Esmond cannot just walk away from this situation. It would seem a failure to defend his family's reputation; self-respect demands some sort of confrontation. A handshake, as a gesture of reconciliation, would not be enough. A lot of nineteenth-century duels echo this one: meetings in which neither man has any intention of wounding the other, but in which honour can be satisfied merely by enacting the ritual. The note on which *Henry*

Esmond ends is, therefore, an ambivalent one: Thackeray offers a shrewd sense of the tawdry reality behind duelling, but at the same time is drawn by the clear-cut values inherent in a military code. As one might expect, the duel enjoyed a particular revival both in Britain and elsewhere in the Napoleonic era, but the survival of duelling well into the nineteenth century – for example, the Duke of Wellington and the Earl of Winchilsea went through the ritual of a duel in 1829 (both men deliberately firing wide) – suggests that many others found it just as difficult as Thackeray to discard such a valued and valuable code of conduct.[39]

THE VIRGINIANS

The Virginians is Thackeray's American War of Independence novel; we have to wait a long time, however, for Thackeray to reach the war, which only begins to feature in the last hundred pages of a thousand-page novel. Before that we have to endure, as many would see it, a slow-paced, interminable narrative. George and Harry are brothers, the American grandsons of Henry Esmond. George serves with the army in Canada and is thought to have been killed. Harry goes to England, where he becomes involved with the degenerate main branch of the Castlewood family. He has lost all his money and is in a debtors' prison when George reappears; he clears his brother's debts and settles down to live the life of a man of letters in London. While George marries, Harry goes off to fight with Wolfe against the French. Then, in the American War of Independence, George fights on the side of the British, and Harry with Washington. There have been many critical comments about Thackeray's failing powers in *The Virginians*, and the novel is often long-winded, yet it could be that Thackeray is writing at length on a subject that is important to him but which fails to register with the modern reader.[40]

This suggestion stems from the impression that, while other Victorian novelists seem to be looking forward, Thackeray is a novelist who looks back. What we also need to consider, however, is that *The Virginians* is a novel prompted very directly by events in the 1850s. Published in monthly parts between November 1857 and October 1859, this is Thackeray's first post-Crimean War novel. As with all his contemporaries, Thackeray was deeply affected by the war, particularly by the setbacks and all too obvious shortcomings of those in command both in the Crimea and at home.[41] For someone like Thackeray, who, as we have seen, was still deeply imbued with a military way of looking at the world, the time might have come to reconsider his views. Indeed, what seems evident is that, although he cannot move directly to the kind of thinking that characterises his contemporaries in the novel, Thackeray does in *The Virginians* at last manage to disconnect himself from an old set of values as he moves away from a culture of war.

What the novel starts with, however, is an American society that is fundamentally and comprehensively warlike in character. It is a new society, a society that is still expanding, and involved in the conquest and annexation of additional territory as well as the taming of its existing territory. Engagements with the French and with Native Americans are the daily reality of the Americans' lives. The facts of their present existence inevitably determine how they view the past. For example, young Harry Warrington studies a map of England, piecing together a historical picture that is predominantly military in character:

> London...its grim tower, where the brave and loyal had shed their blood, from Wallace down to Balmerino and Kilmarnock, pitied by gentle hearts; – before the awful windows of Whitehall, whence the martyr Charles had issued to kneel once more, and then ascend to Heaven; before Playhouses, Parks and Palaces... before Shakespeare's resting-place... before Derby, and Falkirk, and Culloden, where the cause of honour and loyalty had fallen, it might be to rise no more.[42]

There is, as the passage acknowledges, another dimension to Britain – its cultural history – but in this American view war dominates and surrounds everything else. The idea is extended in various ways in the novel. For example, Rachel, the daughter of Henry and Rachel Esmond, and the mother of Harry and George, visits Europe to search for her ancestors: she constructs an elaborate lineage in which she sees the family descending from Charlemagne and Queen Boudicca (p. 29). Not surprisingly, therefore, when Washington plans to raise a regiment to fight the French, Rachel is keen for her sons to volunteer. Her son George, who is a bookish, scholarly young man and by no means a natural fighter (unlike his brother Harry), accepts that it is 'the law of Honour...I must go' (p. 72). Similarly, when they suspect Washington has made romantic overtures to their mother, Harry and George expect that one of them will inevitably fight a duel with him, demanding 'the reparation that is due to gentlemen' (p. 105).

The cumulative effect of an extraordinary number of references of this kind in the opening chapters of *The Virginians* is to create a sense of a society that has adopted fully a military code, viewing aggression and masculine honour as vital, indeed as the key to survival. Oddly, this can combine with a gentleness that has all but disappeared in European life. When the brothers' disagreement with Washington is resolved, Washington, demonstrating 'a custom in those days which has disappeared from our manners now ... took [Harry] fairly to his arms, and held him to his heart' (p. 116). This detail – which echoes the embrace from the Pretender at the end of *Henry Esmond* – tells us more about masculinity in a military code than all the aggressive and brutal examples of militarism in the text: in a male culture of war, male affection is not open to misinterpretation. Emotions, whether hostile or friendly, are openly displayed. There is none of the concealment, none of the secrecy, none of the self-containment which could be said to be a repeated aspect of nineteenth-century characters in fiction. Scores are settled and resolved, rather than resentments being allowed to fester.[43] There is, therefore, in *The Virginians* a comprehensive impression of a set of values that are engrained in American life – or at least, in American life as Thackeray chooses to present it in the novel – that echo the values to which he has shown a consistent commitment in his fiction, even if, throughout his career, there is a simultaneous awareness that these values are no longer relevant in the modern world. This contradiction – that he both believes in yet can see the shortcomings of a military code – is particularly apparent in his presentation of the potential duel with Washington. Given a disagreement between two men – particularly if a woman is the subject of the dispute – Thackeray's automatic response is to construct a scene where a duel will resolve the conflict, but as is the case in this disagreement with Washington, and as is nearly always the case in his novels, the men have been misinformed, or there is some grubby aspect to the potential duel, or the actual duel collapses into farce. The facts, that is to say, undermine all the male posturing involved in the situation. Yet, up until the latter stages of *The Virginians*, Thackeray cannot move forward, he cannot find a narrative convention for handling a disagreement that moves beyond the traditional real-life and narrative convention of the duel.

None the less, there are numerous indications throughout *The Virginians* that Thackeray is at least trying to change direction. If we consider the England that Harry travels to in the novel, it is to a large extent a country that has distanced itself from a culture of war. There are circumstances in which people have to fight, but even the career soldiers in England make a distinction between their professional role and the standard that applies in their everyday lives. There are a number of scenes where the impetuous Harry, desperate to fight, finds his dreams of military glory being checked by the temperate thoughts of Colonel Lambert and Colonel Wolfe. Wolfe in particular dismisses 'glory and honour' (p. 248) as an illusion, claiming:

'True love is better than glory; and a tranquil fireside, with the woman of your heart seated by it, the greatest good the gods can send to us.'   (pp. 248–9)

What is most interesting about these scenes advocating the primacy of a domestic vision of happiness is the fact that it is the leading English military figures in the novel who make this distinction between their professional calling and the standards that apply in their private lives. This difference between English and American thinking in the novel is underlined when Harry, exasperated that Lambert and Wolfe are 'for ever preaching morality to me' (p. 451), says to Lambert: ' "Such a slight may mean nothing here, sir, but in our country it means war, sir!" ' (p. 451). But Lambert and Wolfe, living in a country that has reorganised its scale of values, refuse to rise to his taunt. What adds weight to the English stance is the fact that Harry's aggressive masculinity is, as must be apparent even in these brief examples, always more than a little ridiculous. This is compounded by the point that Harry, for all his posturing and warlike talk, is not a serving soldier: 'He led a sulky useless life, that is the fact. He dangled about the military coffee-houses' (p. 637). And even when he does manage to enlist, his first campaign on the continent is such a mundane, even if successful, affair that he is home again 'Exactly four weeks after his departure from England' (p. 678).

Thackeray's stance in *The Virginians* does, therefore, seem new, as if he is at last trying to distance himself, in a way that he has not been able to do before, from the culture of war. This is something that becomes most clear in his consideration of the concept of 'honour', which is one of the most used words in the novel. Honour, as we have seen, is the idea at the heart of the duel: a man's reputation, a man's honour matters more than anything else, indeed more than life itself, and it is only by means of a duel that honour can be satisfied. In *The Virginians*, however, something has started to change, for there are, with the minor exception of a passing reference to a duel George fought in Canada as a young man, no duels, only potential duels. This is, in fact, one of only two novels by Thackeray – the other is *Pendennis* – in which a duel never takes place. Even in *The Newcomes*, which is by no means a military novel, duelling is central to the plot.[44] In the England of *The Virginians*, however, people have learned to shrug off or ignore a suspected insult, or, as is the case with Harry and George's cousin Will Castlewood, would rather appear cowardly than accept a challenge. A traditional sense of honour is increasingly irrelevant in the England of the novel. What Thackeray begins to suggest is that being at ease with one's conscience is more important than any defence of a public sense of honour; the battle is an internal battle with oneself rather than an external battle with another person. *The Virginians*, consequently, begins to move towards a redefinition of the meaning of honour, shifting from a public to a private meaning of the word. If we look at a potential duel between George and Will, the dispute is trivial, nothing is said that could not be ignored, and George should be able to rise above the insult. None the less, they arrange to meet, but, probably tipped off by Will, the police arrive and stop the duel (p. 747). George appears ridiculous, anxious to defend his honour in a world that no longer takes the idea seriously.

But how can Thackeray dismiss honour, and, by implication, the associated military code, as easily as this? Just a couple of years earlier, in *The Newcomes*, a sense of honour, however flawed and futile, seems worth clinging on to as better than the selfish, business-motivated standards associated with the character of Barnes Newcome. *The Virginians* spends a lot of time discussing precisely this question; indeed, one of the reasons why it is such a long novel is precisely because it agonises at length on the concept of honour. The most important sections, however, centre on George's relationship with Theo Lambert. George has been forbidden by General Lambert to see his daughter Theo. George explains to her sister, Hetty, that he gave his word of honour that he would not attempt to see Theo. Hetty turns on him:

'Honour! And you are the men who pretend to be our superiors; and it is we who are to respect and admire you!...to desert an angel...an angel who used to love me till she saw you...is what you call honour?' (p. 802)

Hetty tears into the male notion of honour, insisting that the word has a private meaning which is far more important than its public sense of reputation. The point is reinforced and extended when George meets General Lambert. Lambert feels that George has acted dishonourably:

'You break your word given to me!' cries Mr Lambert.
'I recall a hasty promise made on a sudden at a moment of extreme excitement and perturbation. No man can be for ever bound by words uttered at such a time; and what is more, no man of honour or humanity, Mr Lambert, would try to bind him.' (p. 816)

There is a shift in the meaning of the word 'honour' when it is coupled with 'humanity'. Honour has ceased to be a matter of public reputation and has become an issue of private conscience. This is confirmed within a few pages when Lambert accepts that he was wrong in demanding his daughter's 'utter submission' (p. 822): he realises the shortcomings of the kind of traditional paternal authority he has imposed upon Theo. This shift towards acknowledging the woman's view contributes to the undermining of the male sense of honour. George, and now Lambert, have moved on to a new sense of how to relate to other people and the world at large.

It could be argued that it has taken Thackeray a long time to arrive at a conventional piece of wisdom, but it has been far from easy for him to move from old values to the new values emerging in the Victorian period. Throughout his career, he is ambivalent about military-based values, but it has taken him until *The Virginians* to see how social relations can be constructed upon a different basis. The difficulty he has experienced is that the personal code he has now arrived at did not exist as a definable entity before the writing of his novels; he is participating in a redefinition of the self, moving away from the sense of a man playing a role towards a private sense of the self that is characteristic of the mid-Victorian period. A significant way in which this shift is indicated in the novel is that in the closing stages, covering the actual war, George becomes the narrator. We move from an external view of the events, which inevitably tries to see the whole picture, to the perception of one of the participants.

It would be wrong, however, to suggest that *The Virginians* arrives at a point of resolution and stability. Certainly the novel ends cheerfully, with the two brothers reconciled, but when they are on opposite sides in the war the word honour is again prominent:

> Never did I say my prayers more heartily and gratefully than on that night, devoutly thanking Heaven that my dearest brother was spared, and making a vow at the same time to withdraw out of the fratricidal contest, into which I had entered because Honour and Duty seemed imperatively to call me.
>
> I own I felt an inexpressible relief when I had come to the resolution to retire and betake myself to the peaceful shade of my own vines and fig-trees at home.   (p. 977)

George rejects 'Honour and Duty' for the lower-case 'honour and humanity', but there is something suspect about his escape to a rural retreat. It is an escape that manages to side-step the complications inherent in the novel's new sense of the word 'honour'. In the past, honour was a public concept; now, when a man defines his own sense of his honour, relationships become more, rather than less, complicated. Indeed, as we see in the conflict between the two brothers, there now emerges a form of internal strife, for when brother is set against brother the scenes convey the idea of a split individual battling to reconcile warring impulses in his personality. The duel both formalised and externalised conflict; conflict now becomes internalised, and, as such, more complicated. It has taken Thackeray a long time to exorcise a military code from his novels; now that he has done so, he is casting his characters onto stormier rather than more peaceful waters. When the Duke of Wellington and the Earl of Winchilsea decided to settle their differences with a duel, perhaps they knew what they were doing in keeping the issue relatively simple.

4

The Army Abroad: Fictions of India and the Indian Mutiny

THE INDIAN MUTINY

On 10 May 1857, the Bengal units of the East India Company's army in India mutinied, massacring British officers, officials and traders, along with their families.[1] The immediate cause of the so-called Indian Mutiny was the introduction of new cartridges for the Enfield rifle; the word soon spread that the grease for these cartridges was made from cow and pig fat, a fact that caused consternation among both Hindus and Muslims. At Meerut, the sepoys (Indian soldiers in service with the British army) refused to touch the new cartridges, and 85 of them were given long prison sentences; the following day the Meerut sepoys mutinied. Behind the immediate explanation, however, is a more complex web of political, economic and religious grievances that had developed as the British, with increasing insensitivity, imposed an alien culture upon a subject people.[2] The Mutiny spread rapidly through Bengal, Oudh and the North-West Provinces, and, with Indian troops outnumbering the British by a ratio of more than six to one, for a time it seemed as if the British might lose control of the whole of India.[3] The Punjabi, Sikh and Gurkha troops remained loyal, however, and the rebellion failed to spread beyond the north of the country. There was, none the less, a bitter struggle with atrocities on both sides – including a massacre of British prisoners at Cawnpore that deeply affected thinking in Britain – before Delhi was recaptured by the British in September 1857 and before Lucknow was finally secured in March 1858.[4] It was the end of 1858 before the Oudh rebels were finally subdued.

The Indian Mutiny is both typical and untypical of the kind of military action the British army was involved in during the Victorian period. The Crimean War was the only European conflict

Britain was engaged in between 1815 and 1914; all other military campaigns were in colonial possessions or countries, such as China and the Sudan, where Britain was defending its overseas interests. With the exception of the final Boer War, all of these military engagements were relatively small-scale affairs. They were also very one-sided; the army could uphold the reputation won for it by Wellington at Waterloo by fighting enemies far worse equipped than itself. The Indian Mutiny, however, was distinctive in a number of ways. It would be possible to discuss specific points, such as the fact that the enemy in this case was not a totally alien force but regular troops trained by the British, but what I want to consider is something more nebulous in the area of the ways in which the mutiny contributed to a new Victorian image of the army and to a changing sense of national identity. The proximity of the Crimean War and the Indian Mutiny is significant here; just as success in the Napoleonic Wars compensated for the blow to national self-confidence created by the loss of the American colonies in the American War of Independence, the Indian Mutiny offered the public an impression of the army that moved on from the sense of aristocratic incompetence that was so damaging in the Crimea. In the Crimean War, men from the Wellington era still set the tone; in the Indian Mutiny, a new image of the army and the country started to develop.

It could be argued, however, that the Mutiny on its own did not change anything, that it merely confirmed changes that were already taking place, while some things did not change at all. But, if one accepts Linda Colley's claim that Britain has 'a culture that is used to fighting and has largely defined itself through fighting', we should be able to see that Britain's sense of national identity was given a fresh emphasis by this conflict.[5] It helped that the dispute was easy to visualise: the defence of a beleaguered town offered the Victorian public a clear picture of both a community and a community of values under attack. In addition, Christians were being threatened by non-Christians; the resources that enabled the British to win were, inevitably, seen as uniquely Christian. Indeed, what one sees in responses to the Mutiny – or, at least, in some responses – is the putting together of a particular mixture of religion, politics and patriotism that comes to be seen as distinctively Victorian. The clearest form this takes is 'Christian militarism', a concept that assumes increasing importance as the period continues, and which in this conflict is embodied in the person of

Sir Henry Havelock.[6] In Christian militarism, the military code of the Wellington era has been refashioned into a moral and religious cause. The picture becomes more complicated, however, when we consider the inherent instability in a mixture of religion, politics and patriotism. It is a combination that can boil over into a blood-thirsty desire for revenge, something that is apparent in the early responses to the news from Cawnpore.

But what we also have to consider is that, as important as Christian militarism is as a new factor in mid-Victorian thinking, it co-exists with a widespread indifference to military matters. The point is often made that, after their immediate anger, the British forgot about the Mutiny (or at least, did so until the end of the century, when military matters assumed a new centrality).[7] In literature, in the thirty years immediately following the Mutiny, we have to turn to a handful of largely forgotten texts to find considerations of the event.[8] The majority of novelists, in particular, continued to find military issues both philosophically and physically alien, preferring to dwell on domestic matters. But those novelists who did turn their attentions to India un-avoidably touched upon important matters; most interestingly, they exposed a form of myopia in British social fiction. As against English-based novels, novels set in India reveal, if only by default, the gap between the ideal of Victorian domesticity and the brutal reality of colonial power. This is true of the noisy fantasies of revenge and the old-fashioned military romances that continued to appear, which, by and large, do not bother with the new uniform of Christian militarism, but the gap is most evident in the very small number of novels that resist the idea of an extreme military solution to colonial problems. It is the most celebrated of these novels, *Seeta* by Philip Meadows Taylor, that I consider in the last section of this chapter, but at this point I want to look at W.D. Arnold's extraordinary, if bewildered, novel, *Oakfield*, published four years before the Mutiny in 1853.

W.D. ARNOLD'S *OAKFIELD*

At first sight, *Oakfield* seems to anticipate the Christian militarism that was to become established at the time of, and in the wake of, the Indian Mutiny.[9] It is Olive Anderson who has done most to define the nature of Christian militarism: she identifies a change between 1854 and 1864, prompted by both the Crimean War and the Indian Mutiny, in which the compatibility of Christian and military virtues began to be stressed.[10] There is plenty of evidence of a new religious spirit among many soldiers, particularly commanding officers, but Anderson also points to an 'official policy of creating an almost ostentatiously Christian army', through such measures as the introduction of chaplains.[11] This change of emphasis in the army was a way of matching changing military needs with changing political and social circumstances, something that included the new moral attitudes of the period; in line with the demands of British society at large, a different moral framework was imposed on the activity – although it might now be more appropriate to say 'duty' – of soldiering. There was a reciprocal response within society, as religious organisations, specifically the Salvation Army, the Church Army and Boys' Brigades, began to borrow the 'military discipline, titles, uniforms and accoutrements' of the army.[12]

This final development, however, belongs more to the 1880s, by which time Christian militarism – particularly as associated with General Charles Gordon – was developing in a more extreme direction. The essential quality of Christian militarism in the mid-Victorian period is that it seems to offer a way of coming to terms with war for a society that wants to be seen to be working in line with clear standards of ethical responsibility. The army, rather than being seen as an instrument of the state, is reconceived as an expression of the moral character of the state.[13] The majority of mid-Victorians might have been routinely indifferent to military matters, but, when required, Christian militarism provided, for those who needed such moral justification, a convenient and coherent acceptable position on the subject of war. *Oakfield* seems to be participating in just such an attempt to define a post-Wellington style for the army that the middle-class public could feel at ease with. It also seems appropriate that a member of the Arnold family – W.D. Arnold was the son of Thomas Arnold and the brother of Matthew – should be engaged in the kind of moulding of public opinion that his family had such an aptitude for.[14] The flaw in this thesis is that *Oakfield* is a wretchedly confused novel that signally fails to provide any clear lead for its audience. But what we will see here is a pattern that repeats itself within the entire Victorian period, that the subject of

India always exposes the contradictions of British social and political thinking.

The hero of the novel, Edward Oakfield, arrives in India as an officer in the East India Company's army, and is shocked at the behaviour of his fellow officers. Offended by their language and morals, he boycotts the mess, withdrawing to eat alone in his own quarters. The mess bully, Stafford, sees an opportunity to provoke a duel, but Edward refuses to rise to the challenge. As a result he incurs the displeasure of his commanding officer and is court-martialled on a charge of cowardice. He is exonerated, but even the decent men in the Company's service are puzzled by his code of ethics and repudiation of the traditional honour code. The court martial concludes the first volume of *Oakfield*. In the second volume, Edward regains the respect of his fellow officers by his heroism in the Sikh Wars of 1846. He is rewarded with a civil appointment as District Commissioner at Lahore. He dies after six years' exhausting work raising the moral tone of the colony. It is easy to identify the moral stance in this. Edward's ethical sensibility puts him at a remove from the old order that prevails in India, something that is confirmed by his inability to accept the honour code of his fellow British officers. His principled stand represents a move away from a traditional gentlemanly idea of soldiering, an idea with very little substance, something that is confirmed by the fact that Edward's challenger, Stafford, is simply a bully looking for a fight. Edward moves to a position where his actions are determined by his own moral convictions; essentially, he sets his own rules rather than following the army's rules.

There could be a problem here, with Edward, as an individual, setting himself above military discipline, but the issue is overtaken by the fact that he distinguishes himself in battle. In addition, far from Edward's individualism being a problem, there is the implication that his principled behaviour makes him a better soldier. This is a central element in a mid-Victorian reorientation of ideas about duty, the idea that one serves – in this case, as an officer – because of one's convictions, rather than the army (or the law or the church) being simply an automatic choice of career, as it would traditionally have been for members of the aristocracy and gentry.[15] The pattern of *Oakfield* does, therefore, seem to resemble the pattern of Christian militarism that developed in the late 1850s, but with a particular emphasis that is specific to the novel as a genre. Victorian novels time and time again examine the individual in a complex and changing society. The apparent success of *Oakfield* is that, rather than seeing a sense of the self as problematic, it seems to reconcile the integrity of the self with a cause that passes beyond self. It appears to offer a neat integration of what might be conceived of as contrary impulses in Victorian Britain. In Elizabeth Davis's Crimean War memoir, for example, she finds it impossible to reconcile her wish to be true to herself with a self-effacing idea of service.[16] In *Oakfield*, however, the solution seems to have been achieved. The two major events in the novel – the duel and the battle – are the two elements that are central in the plot of all military novels, but here they are tweaked to give the work a new kind of moral emphasis. The novel seems to anticipate what Olive Anderson describes as 'peculiarly the accomplishment in an indirect way of the Indian Mutiny', the view 'that Christians make the best soldiers'.[17]

Oakfield is, however, not as simple as this. For a start, it is only hesitantly a religious novel; indeed, it is the hero's religious reservations that lead him to decide against a career in the church. As an alternative, he opts for the army. At an early stage he makes it clear that he has little sympathy with 'the party bitterness and ignorant self-satisfied narrow-mindedness' (vol. 1, p. 28) of the Evangelicals, and it is also clear that in refusing to fight a duel he has not chosen to 'come the religious dodge' (vol. 1, p. 271). Francis Hutchins takes up the point that there is form rather than substance to the Christianity of *Oakfield*, but then proceeds to argue that Arnold's Christianity, becoming 'what distinguished Englishmen from Indians', is

> transmuted from a faith into a code of ethical self-discipline, which made it easier for Christians to reprove rather than to convert those who differed from them. Indians had become characters in a Christian morality play, the villains in a religious drama in which Englishmen played the central role.[18]

This view, however, is too simplistic in its superiority to the text, identifying *Oakfield* as revealing the hypocrisy at the heart of Christian militarism, in which religion and nationalism swagger together in contempt of an inferior opponent; how much easier than in those years when the enemy was the Catholic French, when the English might have been dogged by both a fear of national inferiority and a sense of the opportunism of their religious convictions. Viewed from Hutchins's perspective, *Oak-field*, for all its reservations about military coarseness, can be seen to belong firmly within the camp that advocates an imposed milit-ary solution to every colonial problem; the novel might appear to ask questions, but moves rapidly towards enforcing convictions.

What undermines the neatness of this approach to *Oakfield* is the hero's romantic malaise. He is subject to the kind of intro-spective examination of his conscience that we associate with the novel of domestic realism rather than the military novel. It is not uncommon in military novels for people at a loose end to join the army, but, as in a Charles Lever novel, this instantly solves their problems, for they are given a larger issue to think about rather than focusing on themselves. In *Oakfield*, however, joining the army exacerbates the uncertainties the hero has been experiencing. What comes across is a split between national identity and private identity. Christian militarism in a colonial setting helps the Victorians define themselves and their role in the world, but the exploration of private identity can, as we see in a great many Victorian novels, lead towards a questioning of these shared convictions.[19] In Charlotte Brontë's novels, for ex-ample, there is a sense of the world existing around the individual, rather than the individual fitting easily into the general scheme of things. In the domestic novel, however, the problem can be solved by manipulating the hero or heroine into a marriage that is both personally fulfilling and socially productive. In India, by contrast, there is nothing but a sense of a huge gulf between personal feelings and the alien environment, with any sensitive individual ill-at-ease with the codes of conduct that have developed in this foreign land.

Where this gulf is revealed most clearly in *Oakfield* is in the hero's reservations about manliness as he encounters it in colonial military life. When Oakfield's friend Vernon attempts to talk glibly about borrowing money, Edward distinguishes between 'sham manliness' and 'a genuine manly shame' (vol. 1, p. 52). Edward despises the sham that considers it 'unmanly – griffish I suppose your friend Cade would call it – to appear to care for home' (vol. 1, p. 63), and even expresses his regret that the mess is not 'the abode of luxurious refinement, even it might be to effeminacy' (vol. 1, p. 40). There is a characteristic development in the plot of mid-Victor-ian novels, most notably in *David Copperfield*, where the hero moves beyond feminine softness and becomes as hardened as any other man by the end. In *Oakfield* it is different, for what the hero expects the military world to do is to adjust to his definition of masculinity.

What this contempt for traditional manliness has to be set against in *Oakfield*, however, is the fact that Edward distinguishes himself by a display of the traditional manly virtues in battle; or, to put it another way, after one volume in which an old idea of honour is rejected, it is, paradoxically, honour that matters in volume two. This level of confusion is characteristic of the work. It is a novel in which the various elements will not unite into a coherent whole, something that is evident again in the displacement of the love interest. A Miss Middleton is introduced, Arnold writing:

> And now doubtless the reader supposes that we have at last come to the heroine, and that Oakfield is forthwith to fall in love. Alas! we fear not.   (vol. 1, p. 235)

Love, it seems, would only prove another source of agonised self-questioning for Edward. But the cancelling-out of love means that *Oakfield* cannot move towards an ending based upon marriage, an ending which would allow the hero to find success in both his private life and public life while remaining true to his principles. The impression in the novel is, in fact, just the opposite: Edward cannot reconcile his private feelings with any sense of a public role.

This gap is again evident in what might appear to be the dream solution, when Edward is appointed to the post of District Commissioner. But Edward continues to view India as a place of torment, and, as he approaches his death, continues to be beset with 'doubts and perplexities' (vol. 2, p. 286). The absence of answers in *Oakfield* seems to indicate a fundamental doubt about the whole imperial enterprise, as if the man with a liberal conscience is bound to find himself at odds with the military reality of colonialism. Intriguingly, the Victorians' new sense of the self and individual integrity develops simultaneously with the expansion of the empire, creating situations where the ethical and humane standards that were increasingly taken for granted at home could all too easily be forgotten when one was far from home. Christian militarism is about to emerge as a way of bridging the gap between high moral standards and questionable military behaviour in the empire, but Arnold has already identified the inherent contradiction. It is illuminating to compare Edward with St. John Rivers in *Jane Eyre*, another character drawn to India because of his inability to settle in England.[20] Rivers is disturbed and disturbing, with a manic level of energy that, in the fevered atmosphere of *Jane Eyre*, suggests a level of sexual disturbance. But the suggestion at the end of *Jane Eyre* is that he has managed to channel his storming energies into his missionary work in India. Edward Oakfield is altogether more languid and cautious, but, most of all, unlike Rivers, he is unable to reconcile the contradictions in his temperament and life: he is pulled between a sense of his religious and ethical duty, a sense of the importance of proving himself in battle, and a sense of the importance of being true to himself, but it is impossible for him to reconcile God, the world and the self – and especially in India, where the glaring contradictions become all too apparent. *Oakfield* is, therefore, a novel that contributes towards the emergence of Christian militarism, but it is also a novel that undermines the basic premises of this distinctive blend of religion, politics and patriotism even as it is in the process of taking shape.

FROM ANGER TO CHRISTIAN MILITARISM

As one might imagine, Arnold's agonised soul-searching is not typical of the period. For most mid-Victorians there was no problem: questions of colonialism and Britain's role in India never crossed their minds. And when the Mutiny occurred, the atmosphere at home was hardly conducive to reasoned reflection on its significance; in 1857 and 1858, the most humane people could, quite inconsistently, express their loathing of the Indians.[21] Even in the case of W.D. Arnold, there is a distinct difference between the doubts revealed in *Oakfield* and the views he expressed in a series of articles on the Mutiny in *Fraser's Magazine* between December 1857 and December 1858. These articles, published anonymously, focus mainly on the causes of the Mutiny, but combine an awareness of the justified sense of grievance of the Indian population with a call to take the native army firmly in hand, ensuring that Europeans are established in position of control.[22] This, it could be said, is the official voice of mid-Victorian colonialism: there is a job to be done, which must be done responsibly, but with the use of force if necessary. There is no sense in Arnold's magazine articles of a debauched British soldiery, specifically at command level, which is one of the most striking aspects of *Oakfield*.

Arnold's magazine articles are, none the less, reasoned and reasonable; a lot of other responses to the Mutiny are far less measured. In particular, when the news from Cawnpore reached Britain
there was a widespread feeling of revulsion, often combined with
calls for revenge.[23] It is, of course, one thing to express such feelings in the heat of the moment, but quite another to carry over such
feelings into a literary text, and then to allow that text to be
published. When, as in the case of the short story 'The Perils of
Certain English Prisoners', the author is Charles Dickens (or, one of
the authors, as Wilkie Collins wrote the middle section of a three-
part story), the work in question becomes particularly interesting.
The Indian Mutiny touched a raw nerve in Dickens. As Patrick
Brantlinger has suggested – taking up an earlier suggestion by
William Odie – *A Tale of Two Cities*, published in 1859, can be seen
as a response to the events in India: 'His Carlylean view of the
Revolution as irrational, frenzied and bloodthirsty is close to his
view of the Mutiny'.[24] Brantlinger draws attention to the way in
which Dickens likens his French characters to tigers, and, more
generally, there is the question that runs through so many of
Dickens's novels of how, if at all, society can contain and control
dangerous forces. The Mutiny seems both to renew Dickens's sense
of the criminally destructive elements in existence and to reinforce
his commitment to the need for regulation and control. But there is
more to it than this, for, whereas *A Tale of Two Cities* is an achieved
work of art, a form of racist hysteria seems to overwhelm Dickens
in 'The Perils of Certain English Prisoners'. As Brantlinger points
out, the story more or less 'suggests genocide as a solution to the
Mutiny'.[25]

Brantlinger is not only illuminating on Dickens's response to the
Mutiny, but also provides the best account of the overall literary
response, how 'Innumerable essays, sermons, novels, poems and
plays expressed a general racist and political hysteria about
the Mutiny'.[26] The texts he considers include eye-witness accounts
of the Mutiny, such as Mrs J.A. Harris's *Lady's Diary of the Siege of
Lucknow* (1858), Robert Gibney's *My Escape From the Mutineers in
Oudh* (1858), and Mowbray Thompson's *Story of Cawnpore* (1859).
There are also historical works, such as Charles Ball's *History of the
Indian Mutiny* (1858), Sir John William Kaye's *Sepoy War In India*
(1864–80), and Sir George Trevelyan's *Cawnpore* (1865); poetry,
including poems in *Punch*, and Tennyson's 'Havelock' (1857) and
'The Defence of Lucknow' (1880); and drama, including *Nana Sahib*

(1857), *The Fall of Delhi* (1857), *The Indian Revolt; or, The Relief of Lucknow* (1860), and Dion Boucicault's highly successful *Jessie Brown; or, The Relief of Lucknow* (1858).[27] Brantlinger focuses on how these works reduce matters to simple oppositions between good and evil, victims and villains. This is particularly true of the melodramas, which were staged within weeks, sometimes days, of the events in question, and which capture the mood of a moment rather than revealing a process of evaluation and reflection. The pattern of racist thinking in these works is, however, also in evidence in the memoirs and histories of the Mutiny, even if the rough edge of anger has been subdued. Indeed, with a few exceptions, the same assumptions are in evidence in all nineteenth-century responses to the Mutiny. Against such a background, 'The Perils of Certain English Prisoners' falls into place, therefore, as an immediate, angry and overtly racist response to the news from India.

To an extent, however, all of this is obvious. What is more interesting to note is that sometimes, even in the most hysterical works, there is a realisation that the events in India have consequences for, and perhaps demand a reconsideration of, domestic attitudes in Britain. This is the only saving grace of Dickens's 'The Perils of Certain English Prisoners': the story is mainly characterised by its anger, but it does reveal Dickens fumbling towards a new, or modified, sense of national identity. Brantlinger rightly condemns it as Dickens's 'least compassionate' Christmas story, but he does not consider how it might fit into a different Victorian debate in which anger begins to yield to a new social vision.[28]

The narrator of 'The Perils of Certain English Prisoners', Gill Davis, a former private of the Royal Marines, tells how the small English community on Silver-Store Island held out against pirate attack. The settlers are captured, led off into the jungle, but eventually escape. Even though the story was prompted by the Mutiny, as Peter Ackroyd points out, a story of 'struggle, heroism, endurance, self-sacrifice and, running beneath all of these, a thin strain of unrequited and unfulfilled love' was a much-repeated pattern in Dickens's work at this time.[29] It is, however, the desire for revenge that we are most likely to notice initially. Captain Carton, the principal character in the story, speaks:

I presume you know that these villains under their black flag have despoiled our countrymen of their property, burnt their homes, barbarously murdered them and their little children, and worse than murdered their wives and daughters?...Believing that I hold my commission by the allowance of God...I shall certainly use it, with all avoidance of unnecessary suffering and with all merciful swiftness of execution, to exterminate these people from the face of the earth.[30]

Outside the story, Dickens was even more intemperate: he told Miss Burdett-Coutts that he would have liked to have been the Commander-in-Chief in India, in order 'to exterminate the Race upon whom the stain of the late cruelties rested...to blot it out of mankind and raze it off the face of the earth'.[31]

What Dickens was responding to was reports of the atrocities at Cawnpore, the destruction of a domestic order – property, homes, wives, children – that represented the essence of a Briton's existence. Napoleon as a revolutionary force had represented a threat to the political structure of British life, but the events in India struck a symbolic blow to an idea of the order of home life, albeit cloned in a foreign setting. Of course, it could be argued that the situation in India was so extreme as to justify a response of righteous anger, but it seems that the reports were being fictionally embroidered before they reached England; the truth, which, significantly, did not involve the rape of English women, was overlaid with vivid stories of the abduction of white women by natives.[32] The sexual threat is obliquely treated in Dickens's story, but is perhaps more disturbing for this very reason. Miss Maryon, the heroine, who will eventually marry Carton, asks Gill to make her a promise: '"That if we are defeated, and you are absolutely sure of my being taken, you will kill me"' (p. 219). The threat comes from 'swarms of devils – they were, really and truly, more devils than men' (p. 225). It is a dangerous force that is represented as both sexual and demonic; Carton sees it as his Christian duty to use force against force.

In some respects, what we encounter in the story is the timeless pattern of romance: the hero battles with the forces of darkness. As we will see in the next section, the majority of novels dealing with the Mutiny employ the same romance format. But if we emphasise romance we are likely to lose sight of the interesting ways in which Dickens's tale contributes to changes that were taking place in the mid-Victorian era. We can see some of these changes if we consider paintings dealing with the Indian Mutiny. Battle paintings are uncommon, but there are a number of paintings dealing with the personal suffering of the British in India. Also characteristic is Henry Nelson O'Neal's 'Eastward Ho!', which depicts families saying good-bye to their menfolk as they embark for India.[33] It is clear that the family is assuming a new significance in both the pictures and narratives of war, but it is also the case that, whereas the heroes of Waterloo were aristocrats, the private soldier now begins to find a place in art.

This is a notable aspect of Dickens's story, that the narrator is a private in the marines. Initially there is some resentment on his part at the lives of both the civilians and officers in Silver-Store, but he realises he has been misguided as the officers begin to show their true spirit: 'I was heart and soul ashamed of my thoughts ... The spirit in those two gentlemen beat down their illness (and very ill I knew them to be) like Saint George beating down the dragon' (p. 210). Not only does Gill respect his officers, but increasingly he comes to feel that he shares their values. That might seem an obvious point to make, but the idea of the common soldier being morally motivated is a significant change from the Wellington era. This change is underlined in the way that Gill becomes a convert to the idea of caring about England during the course of the tale. Initially he claims that 'England is nothing to me' (p. 234), but Maryon encourages him to be proud to be an Englishman, suggesting that his reward for his service to his country will be 'to make some good English girl very happy and proud, by marrying her' (p. 234). The fact that he does not marry, that wounded and destitute he becomes dependent upon the Cartons, provides an unexpected sting in the socially cohesive picture. But up until this point Dickens has been contributing to a new vision of militarism: united against a non-Christian enemy, the different classes in British life see it as their duty to work together to protect a domestic order that is built around the family.

Even in the anger of 'The Perils of Certain English Prisoners' Dickens can, therefore, be seen to be expressing a new sense of national identity and a new attitude towards war. What he, like Arnold, is moving towards, if only in a tentative way, is Christian militarism. Indeed, his story adds to our understanding of what is involved in the term. There are two issues here: one is that, in Christian militarism, the world of the domestic novel meets the subject of war, and an accommodation is established between the two – war becomes a means of defending family life, and so finds its justification in this. The obvious elements in Christian militarism are patriotism, politics and religion, but it also has this domestic dimension. The other element in Christian militarism that Dickens's story alerts us to is the overwhelming importance of the empire in determining the new face of Victorian militarism. No longer did the British army define its function and character in relation to the French; it was now the empire that determined both the nature of the army and its mission, and, in addition, the public perception of the army. This is evident if we consider why the Indian Mutiny is historically more significant than the Crimean War. It can be argued that the Crimean War (which has to be considered in relation to Britain's possession of India), was only a symptom of a bigger issue in the nineteenth century, the issue of colonialism. With the Indian Mutiny we move from the symptom to the thing itself. What we also move on to is the fact that, even at the time, colonialism required an explanation and a justification. This could start with the sense of a religious mission (a modern-day crusade), but had to extend to include a defence of what might be represented as the exploitative and unfair nature of the colonial relationship. [34] Christian militarism provided a coherent explanation of why the British were exercising military power in such a range of remote places. Whereas Napoleon had been challenged by gentlemen supporting the status quo, the Indians were fought by the British as a nation convinced of the rightness of their religious, moral and family mission.

These might seem large claims to build upon the flimsy evidence of Dickens's story, but it is very clear that a new attitude was being established at this time. This is brought home to us in the career – and, even more, in the accounts of the career – of Sir Henry Havelock, the hero of the Indian Mutiny.[35] Havelock was the essence of a Christian soldier. He entered the army a month after Waterloo, and went out to India in 1823. He became interested in religion on the voyage out, and in 1829 became a Baptist, marrying the daughter of a missionary, Joshua Marshman. He served in the Afghan and Sikh Wars, before playing a central role in the relief of Cawnpore. Crossing the Ganges, he then fought eight victorious battles before having to rest due to illness. In September 1857, however, he led the force that relieved Lucknow, although he then found himself trapped at Lucknow until November when Sir Colin Campbell forced his way to the rescue of the town. A week after the town was relieved Havelock died of dysentery. In various ways this is a traditional tale of leadership: a somewhat undervalued commander who distinguishes himself when the confrontation comes, revealing both his tactical skills and his bravery. Then, as is traditional in such a story, he dies at the height of his glory. But what makes Havelock's story different is his social class and his religious persuasion.

A middle-class hero, he was motivated by a sense of his Christian duty. This, at any rate, is the message of the accounts of his life that appeared in the wake of the Mutiny, in particular in the work of Havelock's brother-in-law, John Clark Marshman. His *Memoirs of Major-General Sir Henry Havelock, KCB* was published in 1860.[36] As Richard Dawson points out, Marshman produces 'the narration of a Havelock whom the reader is invited to value in particular ways'.[37] The vision is of a middle-class, Christian soldier, but there is a contradiction at the heart of the book. Marshman 'presents, as of public interest, the spiritual, intellectual and emotional life of the "private" man in his domestic as well as public relationships'.[38] This is again characteristic of how Christian militarism seeks a link between the private domain of the home and the public stage, using each to justify the other; it constitutes a kind of 'novelization' of experience, in which even the business of war is read in the light of the routine concerns of domestic fiction. But, even though this adds complexity and depth to the public image of Havelock, it also draws attention to the contradictions between the private and public spheres in Victorian thinking, and how the subject of India always exposes these contradictions.

What we see in the case of Havelock is essentially the same problem that is apparent in *Oakfield*, that being true to one's principles does not combine easily with the reality of military conduct in the empire. Christian militarism endeavours to paper over the crack, but the phrase 'Christian militarism' is essentially an oxymoron, attempting to reconcile contrary impulses. In practice the idea works well, but in literary texts, either by design or default, it is the contradiction that becomes most apparent, that the domestic and liberal frame of mind is at odds with the mentality required for military involvement. Marshman's biography actually draws attention to this contradiction in the very act of trying to deny it. Richard Dawson makes an interesting point when he states that the new versions of Havelock's life that appeared in the more militaristic period at the end of the century stressed a cruder version of 'exemplary imperial masculinity', foregrounding 'Havelock's military adventures at the expense of other aspects of his life'.[39] In other words, there was no longer a perceived need to connect Havelock's private life with his public life. In the mid-Victorian period, however, Christian militarism sought to reconcile the values that we find in the domestic novel with the business of war, even if the enterprise was fundamentally flawed.

INDIAN MUTINY NOVELS

Christian militarism is an important strand in nineteenth-century thinking, yet it is arguable that in the years following the Indian Mutiny Christian militarism becomes a side-issue. On the one hand, there is a widespread indifference to military matters; there are hundreds of novels which seem to include representatives of every profession except that of soldier. On the other, old-fashioned military novelists continued to write war novels, even about the Indian Mutiny, as if nothing had changed. It is useful to bear these facts in mind in considering the treatment of the Mutiny in fiction. The figure is sometimes given that more than 30 novels about the Mutiny were published during the Victorian period, thus creating the impression that this was a major subject in Victorian fiction. The figure, however, requires a gloss. Basing my analysis on the list compiled by Shailendra Dhari Singh, it appears that *The Wife and the Ward, or A Life's Error* by Edward Money, published in 1859, was the first Mutiny novel.[40] There were then six more novels about the Mutiny in the next ten years, including works by James Grant, G.A. Lawrence and Henry Kingsley. After this there was a mere trickle of novels over the next twenty years.

At the end of the century, however, the Mutiny really came into its own as a subject, with 16 novels about the Mutiny appearing in the 1890s. The obvious conclusion is that the 1890s was the decade of the Indian Mutiny novel, the topic reflecting the period's new enthusiasm for militarism and tales of colonial adventures. In the ten years following the Mutiny, by contrast, it was a minor theme, appealing mainly to established military novelists who, by and large, were content to fantasise on revenge without thinking the issues through. They produced military romances in a traditional vein, even if they had a nastier edge than usual, a fact prompted by the issue of race. In James Grant's *First Love, Last Love* (1868), for example, we are presented with a story about the Weston sisters,

Kate, Lena and Polly, who are the talk of Delhi.[41] As the Mutiny starts, Lena makes a dash and manages to escape, but Kate and Polly are abducted. Polly, rejecting the advances of Prince Abubeker, is sent into the streets where she is raped and tortured before she dies. The other sisters, however, eventually find happiness with two British officers, Rowley and Jack, who have behaved heroically throughout the Mutiny. The new element in Grant's novel is the extent to which the enemy is associated with cruelty and sexual lawlessness, a point that has been examined in detail by Brantlinger and also Nancy L. Paxton, but the two heroes, Rowley and Jack, are as straightforward as the heroes in a Charles Lever romance.[42] In other words, Grant focuses in a distorted way on the nature of the enemy, but pays no attention to the fact that a change of enemy together with a change of locale might have consequences for, and alter the nature of, British militarism and the conception of the British soldier.

The pattern in Henry Kingsley's *Stretton* (1869) is rather similar.[43] On the one hand are the atrocities at Cawnpore, and on the other three straightforward young officers, Roland, Eddy and Jim. The formula is that of chivalric romance: whereas in a realistic novel the main characters might be expected to change, develop and mature as a result of their experiences, in works such as this the heroes arrive in the novel with the qualities that enable them to cope with any problem, and possess exactly the same qualities at the end of the novel when they emerge triumphant. It could be argued, therefore, that, rather than engaging directly with the Indian Mutiny, these novels respond to what they perceive as an alarming new threat by retreating to old convictions about heroism. There are some works, though, where the conception of the hero does change. Most interestingly, G.A. Lawrence's *Maurice Dering* (1864) seems to sidestep, and move beyond, Christian militarism.[44] Maurice's fiancée is murdered in India while he is away in England. As in Grant and Kingsley, a lot of the emphasis is on the cruelty of the enemy and the need for vengeance, but Lawrence's hero is vicious and extreme. A parson tries to persuade Maurice to be merciful, but in rejecting the parson's advice it is as if he shrugs off the need for a religious sanction for his actions. In Lawrence's muscular hero we get perhaps the first anticipation of the cruder nationalistic militarism that will become central in the last twenty years of the century.

The general pattern in the other Mutiny romances, however, is a change in the conception of the enemy rather than in the conception of the hero or militarism; the novelists seize their subject, but do not bother to think through the implications of the subject. By contrast, one novel from this period, *Seeta*, by Philip Meadows Taylor, published in 1872, considers in an entirely different way the nature of the relationship between the Indians and the British.[45] Taylor went out to India at the age of fifteen and spent his entire working life there, initially in business, then in the army, and finally in a series of important administrative posts. He published six novels, all of them set in India, but it is *Seeta* that stands out as a quite exceptional work. Praise from modern critics includes Brantlinger's comment that *Seeta*, as the 'only pre-1890s novel about [the Mutiny] which does not focus reductively on Nana Sahib and the massacres at Cawnpore', is 'the only complexly imagined intersection between British and Indian characters in Mutiny novels before 1914'.[46] Nancy Paxton is even more enthusiastic, seeing *Seeta* as 'open to the heteroglossia of colonial life and...perceptive about the conflicts generated by the racist and sexist ideologies at work in the "contact zone" of British India'.[47] What I want to suggest, however, is that a more insidious, and as such more dangerous, form of racism is at work in *Seeta* than in the general run of Cawnpore-revenge fantasies.

At the heart of *Seeta* is the subject of inter-racial marriage. Seeta is the wife of Huree Das, a banker. Their house is attacked by Azráel Pandé, at the instigation of Ram Das, the brother of Huree Das. Huree Das is killed, and Seeta and her son move to her grandfather's house. A year later, Azráel and his gang are on trial in Deputy Commissioner Cyril Brandon's court. Brandon is struck by the beauty and dignity of Seeta, who begins to recognise her own love for Brandon. Azráel, sentenced to death, escapes. In a subsequent attack on the home of Seeta's grandfather, Azráel wounds Brandon, and Seeta nurses him. When her son dies her thoughts turn increasingly to Brandon, and eventually they are married in a Hindu ceremony. With a few exceptions, the British deplore the match. The Mutiny now enters the plot, with Azráel as one of the leaders; he leads an attack in which Seeta is killed while saving Brandon. Azráel himself is killed by a Captain Hobson. Brandon fulfils Seeta's wish of opening a school in her village. He then leaves India and marries Grace Mostyn (one of the few English people who had tolerated Seeta), and on the death of his brother becomes a peer.

A summary can distort a novel, in this case making *Seeta* seem like a romantic farrago, but, in fact, there is much to admire in the novel which is far more rooted in a real India and real attitudes than other Indian Mutiny texts. It is particularly astute on the causes of the Mutiny, for example the lack of recognition of cultural differences, something that is expressed in an arrogance that the novel captures marvellously. The Nawab Sahib, an Indian colonel, speaking to an English brigadier, is felt to have overstepped the mark:

> 'Silence!' cried the Brigadier, interrupting him, 'you are forgetting whom you are speaking to: this is beyond the limit of respect, and you had better go, sir, before I forget who you are, and turn you out of my house. You have permission to depart,' he continued, rising, 'and begone!'
>
> Dil Khan rose, and glared savagely at the two officers. 'When there are no English!' he muttered between his teeth, 'when there are no English! this insult will be avenged.'   (pp. 138–9)

This is the tone in which a mill-owner might speak to a worker in a British industrial novel, except that the relationship here is clearly master and slave rather than employer and employee. Taylor places himself at a contemptuous remove from those who regard the Indians as ' "niggers" and "black fellows", as if they were negro savages' (p. 70). This last comment, however, indicates a fundamental problem in the novel. Taylor is only prepared to tolerate 'otherness' on his own terms: the Indians are acceptable because they have more in common with the English than 'negro savages'.

What is in evidence here is a difficulty that besets liberal novels throughout the Victorian period: the authors want to promote social reconciliation, but on the basis of the notion of a community of values in which everyone endorses the same code. But *Seeta*, as is the case with any novel set in India that puts forward a liberal view, is flawed simply because the reality of colonialism is the triumph of force over negotiation. It is easy to condemn those Victorians who indulge in fantasies of revenge in the wake of the Mutiny, but *Seeta* expresses rather similar views in a covert way. At the heart of Taylor's text is the assumption that if the British rule well then the Indians will be happy to accept, and indeed see the benefits of, British rule. Brandon provides the model:

> as he became better known, year by year, the fine qualities of his character had become more and more appreciated... Many a

rude village poet had written ballads, and the minstrels had sung
them to his praise, at village festivals.   (p. 69)

The assumption, at heart, is that the Indians are like children who
need to be led.

A consequence of this is an undercurrent of contempt in Taylor's
narration, an impatience with signs of cultural difference. The
existence of the system of caste provides the biggest difficulty.
Taylor finds it impossible to mention caste without sneering, yet
this is a novel that concludes with the hero taking up his position
in the British aristocracy. A note of contempt is also evident when
Taylor writes about the mutineers' motives. He runs through a
cross-section of Indian society, from princes and barons, through
landowners and bankers, down to the criminal classes, arguing that
they are all motivated by a consideration of how they can exploit
the crisis to their own advantage:

> Thieves, Dacoits, and the lawless swash-buckler soldiery, who
> had ill-succeeded in turning their swords into ploughshares, rose
> in thousands, plundering the peaceful and industrious.   (p. 315)

At one level the novel acknowledges the sense of grievance that has
provoked the rebellion, but there is an even stronger impression
that the motives of the participants are personal rather than political. The contradiction is most apparent in the treatment of Azráel:
a respected native leader, he is also seen as a villainous bandit,
with the added complication of a sexual motive in his worst
excesses.

The manner in which Azráel is presented, in fact leads one to the
realisation that *Seeta* is just as much a violent and erotic fantasy as
any other Indian Mutiny novel. The overt tone of the narration is
liberal, but the incidents in the narrative are the fundamental
materials of romance, with a succession of violent episodes. It is,
however, the erotic dimension of the text that is most disconcerting: there is a very unclear line between love and a lust for possession. This is most evident in the questionable terms in which
Brandon's feelings for, and physical contact with, Seeta are
described. One can see what Taylor is trying to achieve when he
tells us that Brandon 'took both her hands and put them into
Mrs Mostyn's and Grace's' (p. 212), but it is hard to resist the
impression that she is being seen, and handled, as an object, an

embodiment of the idea of dark and unfamiliar indulgence. Patterns repeat themselves in fiction: David Copperfield moves beyond the sexually enticing Dora when she dies, and marries the highly suitable Agnes, but there is something more disconcerting in the way that Brandon moves on from Seeta to Grace. He has been distracted by the east, with its aura of violence and eroticism, but now needs to put this behind him, rejoining his own race.

This might seem a less than generous account of *Seeta*, which is a remarkable text for its time, repeatedly challenging received prejudices. But it cannot avoid the difficulties that appear in any liberal text about colonialism: there is just too wide a gap between the values cultivated at home and the reality of colonial life.[48] The problem appears again in Taylor's treatment of the actual Mutiny. The action of the novel takes place on the fringes of the Mutiny, as if it is a distraction, something that does not quite relate to the main stream of life in India. And then Taylor undermines his own reading of the political significance of the Mutiny, by turning it into a family affair in which the unbalanced Azráel seeks to wreak revenge upon his relatives. As in *Oakfield*, we are confronted with the gap between liberal ideals and reality, but whereas Arnold is overwhelmed by a sense of confusion, Taylor is committed to seeking an answer. In the end, however, he only demonstrates the deep division between the liberal position and the military position.

This tension is, as *Seeta* suggests, one that is, for the most part, stumbled across rather than explored in Victorian fiction. There is, however, one novelist who does seem sharply aware of the contradictions; this is Wilkie Collins. *The Moonstone* starts with the storming of Seringapatam in 1799, an event that left the British as the masters of Southern India.[49] After a siege lasting a month, Seringapatam was plundered and destroyed. It is the looting of the Sultan's palace that provides the foundation of Collins's novel. John Herncastle steals the Moonstone during the course of the siege, murdering at least one of the three Brahmins guarding the diamond. Back in England, the diamond is again stolen. It could be argued that the Indian episode is simply an enabling mechanism for the detective novel that follows, but with *The Moonstone* appearing in 1868 it seems just as plausible to suggest that this is, indirectly, another Indian Mutiny novel. Consider, for example, the theft of the diamond. One aspect of the British response to the Mutiny was to stress the Indians' lawlessness, but in Collins's novel it is the British soldier who is the criminal, and, moreover, behaving 'like a madman' (p. 5) as he steals the diamond. In one episode, Collins has reduced the imperial mission to frenzied plunder.

The subsequent theft of the diamond in England is investigated, but the original crime, a crime fraught with symbolic and religious significance, is left uninvestigated. Indeed, it is only in retrospect that we realise that two crimes have been committed in *The Moonstone*. Concerned with the righting of a wrong in England, we only focus on criminality in the domestic context. The novel, as it proceeds, pays a great deal of attention to the issue of the ways in which the characters support or challenge the legal and domestic order of life in Britain. There are servants, such as Rosanna Spearman and Ezra Jennings, who, to judge by their physical appearance, would seem to be outside the social compact, but who demonstrate their loyalty. As against these characters, Godfrey Ablewhite, who is eventually exposed as the thief, is a hypocrite as well as a villain. This is part of a pattern in the novel, that dishonesty is shown to combine with dependence upon others, ranging from dependence upon servants to dependence upon the benefits of plunder from India.

There seems to be a comprehensive reversal in *The Moonstone*, therefore, of some core assumptions of the English novel of the mid-Victorian period. The British presence in India is seen as exploitative and rapacious rather than beneficial. This is particularly the case because Britain, seeped as it is in criminality, does not in reality possess a set of values that can be set above the values of the east. Indeed, to get at the truth about the Moonstone, one of the characters, Franklin Blake, has to use opium; he has to rely upon the so-called irrationality of the east, together with a morally suspect product of the east, to sort out a mystery in the west. At one point in *The Moonstone*, a solicitor who is narrating says to Murthwaite, a traveller in the east:

> 'The Indian plot is a mystery to me.'
> 'The Indian plot, Mr Bruff, can only be a mystery to you, because you have never seriously examined it.'   (p. 314)

As long as the 'Indian plot' remains a distant complication, to be judged and evaluated by the standards of those at home in Britain, it will remain a mystery. But if, as happens in Collins's novel, the focus becomes the extent of criminality and transgression in

Britain, as against the integrity of the Indians (as reflected in the conduct of the Brahmins in *The Moonstone*), the position that is evident in many novels begins to fall apart. It is no longer a question of how a liberal, moral state reconciles itself to the activity of colonialism, more an illustration that Britain's behaviour abroad is simply consistent with and a product of questionable standards at home.

Collins's novel is a very rare example of a novel that is aware of the relationship between Britain's global role and its domestic standards. In other Mutiny novels, events in India might inadvertently raise doubts about the conduct and convictions of the British, but in Collins there seems a calculated subversion of the self-image of the British. In comparison with Collins, Taylor in *Seeta*, for example, seems almost smug about the superiority of the British. At the heart of Indian Mutiny novels, however, is the overwhelming fact of Britain's occupation of the country, a fact that a novelist such as Taylor is always slightly uneasy about. It is in the non-liberal reality of the physical domination and subjection of India that we get our first clue as to why Britain moved again in the direction of militarism in the last twenty years of the century. This is the theme that I take up in the final chapters of this book, but in the next chapter I want to consider the role of the army in Britain itself.

5

The Army at Home: from Disraeli to Hardy

MILITARY DUTIES IN THE UNITED KINGDOM

Alongside defending and advancing Britain's interests in and against other countries, the army has always had a complementary role to play in maintaining civil order at home. It is in the nineteenth century that this assumes the form we are most familiar with: the army is called in, as at Peterloo, to suppress political unrest.[1] Scenes of this kind, although less extreme, feature in a number of Victorian novels, or, to be more precise, early to mid-Victorian novels, for, as the century progressed, the police increasingly took over such work.[2] In the second section of this chapter I discuss four novels that present military intervention in a domestic context; the interesting thing about these novels, by Gaskell, Eliot, Disraeli and Charlotte Brontë, is that, in a period when most people all but ignore the army, these works actively consider its role. What we might expect to encounter is a straightforward idea that the army must maintain social order, but the nuances of the authors' attitudes create a far more complicated impression.

First, however, we need to establish a context. In Gaskell's *North and South*, faced by a group of striking workers, one of the characters asks, 'When can the soldiers be here?', as if, like the modern police force, the army is an emergency service that can be summoned at a moment's notice.[3] But was this the case? Public riot and disorder were certainly not uncommon in the first half of the century; those involved included industrial workers, farm labourers and miners. Things were at their worst between 1811 and 1817, as Luddite disturbances convulsed the Midlands. By contrast, the Chartist demonstrations of the 1830s and 1840s were a problem mainly because of the large numbers involved. Most incidents, however, were small in scale. Those obliged to respond were local magistrates, who were expected to muster a force and lead it to the scene of disorder. Before the advent of police forces in the 1840s, however, the magistrates had no civil force to call upon. They turned, therefore, to the regular army, the militia or volunteer forces. Most commonly the regular army was called in, but the yeomanry is also of interest. This was a volunteer force, officered by the aristocracy and landed gentry, with tenant farmers and small landowners as the rank and file. The total force in 1838 was getting on for 15,000. They were under local control, but could be ordered into neighbouring counties to counter unrest on the direction of the Home Office.[4] There were, though, areas of the country, such as South Wales, that did not possess a single troop of yeomanry.

For various reasons, the authorities preferred to call upon the regular army at times of disturbance; the yeomanry could appear to be interested parties, and as natural Tories they were less than popular with Whig governments. It was, therefore, the army that interfered most frequently in the civil strife of the 1830s and 1840s. There was a further development in 1859 when, in the wake of a French-invasion scare, a Rifle Volunteer Force was established; this is recognised as the first middle-class auxiliary force. By 1859, however, the social picture is fairly stable, whereas in the first fifty years of the century things were often unsettled. Yet, as Ian Beckett points out, despite the number of instances of disorder, 'few troops were required to disperse those few disturbances which did seem to have more than rudimentary purpose or organisation'.[5] What we are considering for the most part, therefore, are small disturbances in which approaches were made to local magistrates for a token show of army power. At times the sanction of the Home Secretary was required, but he could not always be consulted as this might lead to disastrous delays. If trouble was predicted, as was often the case in South Wales for example, soldiers might be garrisoned in a town. The civil authorities, however, were only expected to call in the army as a last resort. The call had to come from the magistracy, rather than the army itself taking the initiative. When the army was deployed, the force was required to arrive in regular order; only the commanding officer could give the order to fire, and the soldiers then had to exercise a 'humane discretion' regarding the line of fire.[6] It is, of course, arguable that such caution was expedient rather than humanitarian, yet there is plenty of evidence that there was a genuine concern for people's rights in such confrontations.[7]

Despite the caution with which civil unrest was tackled, there were casualties; for example, as many as 25 demonstrators were killed at Merthyr Tydfil in 1831.[8] Loss of life on this scale was, however, rare. Indeed, calling in the troops at all was seen as a drastic measure. And by the 1850s the police had an increasing role to play. Yet the changes of the 1850s are only partly a matter of new mechanisms of social control; they have more to do with the transition to a different kind of orderly society, a society which could, for the most part, function without the visible presence of the army.

'WHEN CAN THE SOLDIERS BE HERE?': ELIZABETH GASKELL, GEORGE ELIOT, BENJAMIN DISRAELI AND CHARLOTTE BRONTË

Of the four novels discussed here, it is *North and South* that seems to offer the most uncomplicated view of military intervention in an industrial dispute. As we will see, Gaskell's stance is more complex than it initially appears, but on the face of it *North and South* presents a solidly middle-class view of the army as a service at the disposal of employers. During the course of a strike at Thornton's Mill, a mob arrives, enraged by Thornton's importation of unskilled labourers from Ireland. At this point Thornton's mother asks, ' "When can the soldiers be here?" ... in a low but not unsteady voice' (p. 207). No comment is offered on the idea of calling in the army, suggesting that Gaskell shares Mrs Thornton's view that this is a reasonable response to an unreasonable development. Indeed, the narrator shares Thornton's view of the workers as 'wild beasts' (p. 209):

> As soon as they saw Mr Thornton, they set up a yell, – to call it not human is nothing, – it was the demonic desire of some terrible wild beast for the food that is withheld from his ravening.   (p. 209)

As we might expect, there is always this kind of lurch to an extreme even in the most liberal nineteenth-century writers when they engage with the mob. In *North and South* as a whole, Margaret Hale, the heroine, questions the assumptions of the mill-owner Thornton, but at a moment of crisis they are as one, with a common enemy.

Margaret does criticise Thornton, but the essence of her criticism is that he does not display enough of the quality that distinguishes him from the 'wild beasts'. She urges him to negotiate a compromise:

> 'Go down and face them like a man... Speak to your workmen as if they were human beings. Speak to them kindly. Don't let the soldiers come and cut down poor creatures who are driven mad.'
> (p. 209)

The conviction that reason will prevail is rather undercut by the view that the 'creatures' have to be approached 'as if they were human beings'. A liberal stance seems to fall apart in the very process of being put together. There is a similar failure of reason as the mob disperses:

> the retrograde movement towards the gate had begun – as unreasoningly, perhaps as blindly, as the simultaneous anger. Or, perhaps, the idea of the approach of the soldiers, and the sight of that pale, upturned face, with closed eyes, still and sad as marble, though the tears welled out of the long entanglement of eyelashes, and dropped down; and heavier, slower plash than even tears, came the drip of blood from her wound.   (p. 213)

The narrator is trying to decide why the mob has dispersed: perhaps there is no logical explanation, or perhaps it was the fear of the approaching soldiers, or perhaps the sight of the injured Margaret. But the odd thing is that the sentence loses direction, becoming illogical and confused. It is as if a power to think disintegrates; there is only the visual image of the mob and its victim.

Gaskell's faltering illustrates how violence tests the limits of the social vision of a realistic novelist; words fail her in trying to comprehend the encounter. But such hesitancy is, of course, totally compatible with a commitment to 'the power of authority and order' (p. 214), although underwriting the authority of factory owners is a curiously utilitarian, and unglamorous, expression of military power. Yet the industrialist is recognised by Gaskell as the inheritor of the traditional qualities of military leadership:

> The sound of [Thornton's] well-known and commanding voice seemed to have been like the taste of blood to the infuriated multitude outside.   (p. 206)

Thornton is, indeed, frequently described in terms appropriate to a military commander: 'his eyes gleamed, as in answer to the trumpet-call of danger' (p. 206). This excites Margaret:

> She liked the exultation in the sense of power which these Milton men had. It might be rather rampant in its display, and savour of boasting; but still they seemed to defy the old limits of possibility
> (p. 193)

We can, therefore, see contradictory strands in *North and South*: the liberal novelist, eager for negotiation, and a novelist who, confronted by a difficult situation, thinks in terms of military power, a concept that surreptitiously always excites her.

Gaskell's most characteristic position, however, is one that involves a fundamental challenge to the old military model of confrontation. This is primarily achieved by setting a female discourse against an inherited male discourse. Margaret's liberal plea for discussion may falter in the strike scene, but it has considerable force in the novel as a whole. There is, in addition, the physical intercession of Margaret at a key stage:

> She only thought how she could save [Thornton]. She threw her arms around him; she made her body a shield from the fierce people beyond... Then she turned and spoke... 'For God's sake! do not damage your cause by this violence.'   (pp. 211–2)

It could be argued that Thornton is unmanned in accepting a woman as a shield in this way, but this is not the impression the scene creates. What matters is Margaret's intervention, attempting to forestall a clash. It is the clearest example in the novel of Gaskell's view of how a confrontational model of human relations can be replaced by a gentler approach.

We can set it against Thornton's silent confrontation with his employees:

> He stood with his arms folded; still as a statue; his face pale with repressed excitement. They were trying to intimidate him – to make him flinch.   (p. 210)

It is a masculine confrontation; for both sides, their masculinity is on trial. Margaret, by contrast, speaks to the crowd. The effect is that, although at one level the scene seems to reject the possibility of negotiation, the case for a dialogue is, none the less, asserted throughout. There is one moment of violence, but in the broader context the actions of Margaret have proved effective, for the mob disperses before the army arrives. It might seem to be stretching a point to extrapolate a general truth about Victorian attitudes from this one scene, but its implications are substantial. Inherent in the scene is the idea that problems can be resolved in a new way; the military model might have worked in the past, but it is divisive. Gaskell expresses a different feeling about the government of civil society, a feeling that moves beyond the assumptions of the Peterloo era. We have seen Thackeray trying to grasp a new non-militaristic basis on which social relations can be established, but in Gaskell's novel such thinking seems instinctive, and to become the whole basis of her social philosophy. Her preference is for social negotiation which will, in the end, and if only in an ideal world, eliminate the need for confrontation, even the need for war.

This stance is taken further in the novels of George Eliot, something that is most apparent in *Felix Holt*. Published in 1866, *Felix Holt* is set at the time of the 1832 Reform Act. The unrest in the novel takes place on election day:

> The Tories began to feel that their jokes were returned by others of a heavier sort, and that the main strength of the crowd was not on the side of sound opinion, but might come to be on the side of sound cudgelling and kicking. The navvies and pitmen in dishabille seemed to be multiplying, and to be clearly not belonging to the party of Order.[9]

Eliot's tone is jocular, superior to the confrontation that is being anticipated. This might be a matter of historical distance, that Eliot can be ironic about the events of 1832, but it seems to have more to do with an attitude of mind that disdains violence. Whereas Gaskell shares her characters' anxieties about the mob, Eliot invests her characters with her own sense of proportion. Urged to send for the army, 'the Rector felt that this was not the part of a moderate and wise magistrate, unless the signs of riot recurred' (p. 257). As against the direct summons for the army in *North and South*, Eliot suggests that the army is only turned to as a last resort by people who are reluctant to think in terms of military solutions to social problems.

It transpires in *Felix Holt*, however, that conciliatory measures do not work, and, when a riot breaks out, the army has to intervene. Furthermore, the consequences of the riot are serious: whereas Margaret, in *North and South*, is merely injured by a pebble, Felix Holt is shot through the shoulder by the soldiers, two men are killed, and Felix is charged with assault, manslaughter and leading a riotous onslaught. Curiously, none of this makes much of an impression. The riot concludes the second book, but there are no further references to disturbances in the novel. In *North and South* there is a sense of angry people with a real grievance, but in *Felix Holt* the election day events seem self-contained, with no roots in any social malaise. This might be a reflection of Eliot's Tory leanings, but it also reflects a change of focus in the society of her day. In book three of *Felix Holt*, Eliot takes her eye off the political issue and concentrates on the fate of Felix; what matters is his integrity as an individual. In this new dispensation, military matters belong to the past. There is, in fact, a sub-plot within *Felix Holt* that is full of military references. A servant, Christian, left the country in 1808 as a soldier, eventually swapping identities with another soldier, but the idea of swapping identity in this way belongs to the romantic past. It is at odds with Felix's desire to be true to his own identity.

This emphasis on self-realisation involves Felix rejecting his inheritance from his father, a quack apothecary. More generally, a male code of inheritance, aggression, defence of property, and confrontation is set aside in favour of individual integrity, negotiation and social conciliation. And, as in *North and South*, the principal female character plays a central role in this. In court, it is Esther Lyon, the heroine, who, at her own prompting, speaks up for Felix; a case is being made both about the importance of speaking and the female voice. Felix's trial follows his involvement in the riot, but here again we should see that his intended role was conciliatory, that he assumed control of the rioters in an attempt to limit their actions. A riot did ensue, but the fundamental stance of the novel is that trouble can be controlled and contained. The aim, as in *North and South*, is to rationalise out of existence the need for military confrontation. By 1866, the year of *Felix Holt*, we can see just how deeply engrained a non-militaristic philosophy is in British social thinking.

Such confidence in the redundancy of militarism would prove short-lived, but in the 1850s and 1860s there is clear evidence of a shift in the dominant discourse of society. This becomes even more apparent if we turn back 20 years, to 1845, the year of Disraeli's

Sybil, where we can see how some writers in the 1840s were still committed to a different code. *Sybil* offers militarism in a traditional mould, Disraeli seeming to revel in the idea of violence. The disturbances in the novel relate to Chartist activity in the town of Mowbray. Charles Egremont, the hero of the novel, is drawn into politics by a desire to change the lives of the working people. His position, however, is that the people themselves are not strong enough to achieve the changes they seek; they need the assistance of a new generation of aristocrats like himself with awakened consciences. Consequently, when the Chartists present their petition, Egremont argues that the aims of the charter can be achieved by the ruling class taking the initiative. As against this, the Chartists are preaching open insurrection. The editor of a radical newspaper, Stephen Morley, is alarmed by the increasing association of Walter Gerard with extremists. Gerard is arrested but, thanks to the intervention of Egremont, receives a comparatively light prison sentence. Coinciding with his release, a sequence of events is initiated that culminates in rioters attacking Mowbray Castle. A detachment of yeomanry led by Egremont arrives. Morley draws his pistol and is shot dead by one of the troopers. The castle goes up in flames. Meanwhile, Egremont's brother, Lord Marney, leader of a larger troop of yeomanry, encounters Gerard and his followers. Marney attacks them, shooting Gerard, and, as Gerard's men fight back, Marney is killed too. With Egremont succeeding his brother and marrying Gerard's daughter, Sybil, a new and more hopeful era begins.

A summary gives an impression of Disraeli's form of enlightened conservatism, but it might also suggest that he is exasperated by the violence that seems so central in society. Sybil, who intervenes as a peace-maker, trying to speak to the mob storming the castle, obviously fits into this reading. But Sybil's actions amount to little more than a gesture in the novel. Indeed, talk and negotiation are largely irrelevant in *Sybil*, for the central premise of the work is that those who have always held power know best and will do the best for the country; people like Egremont are born to command. This connects with the military thinking in *Sybil*, specifically the fact that it is the yeomanry, led by men of rank and standing, who take a leading role. Egremont is in his rightful place in this traditional military structure.

But there is more to the issue than this. It might, on the basis of a summary, seem that the riot is a tragic waste of life, but the

impression that comes across in the work as a whole is that Disraeli
revels in confrontation:

> The Riot Act was read with the rapidity with which grace is
> sometimes said at the head of a public table – a ceremony of
> which none but the performer and his immediate friends are
> conscious. The people were fired on and sabred. The indignant
> spirit of Gerard resisted; he struck down a trooper to the earth,
> and incited those about him not to yield. The father of Sybil was
> picked out – the real friend and champion of the People – and
> shot dead. Instantly arose a groan which almost quelled the spirit
> of Lord Marney, though armed and at the head of armed men.
> The people who before this were in general scared and disper-
> sing, ready indeed to fly in all directions, no sooner saw their
> beloved leader fall than a feeling of frenzy came over them. They
> defied the troopers, though themselves armed only with stones
> and bludgeons; they rushed at the horsemen and tore them from
> their saddles, while a shower of stones rattled on the helmet of
> Lord Marney and seemed never to cease. In vain the men around
> him charged the infuriated throng; the people returned to their
> prey, nor did they rest until Lord Marney fell lifeless on Mow-
> bray Moor, literally stoned to death.[10]

Disraeli, as a novelist, naturally wants to make the confrontation
exciting, but the energy of the scene seems to have more to do with
the fact that it suits his purpose to visualise a clear clash between
different interest groups. It is a vision of society that owes something to Shakespeare's history plays, where we see violent strug-
gles between different factions, and in which the only answer is the
emergence of a winner who is stronger and wiser than his rivals. At
a fundamental level, therefore, there is not only a hierarchical
vision of social relations in *Sybil*, but also a vision of society constructed on a military basis.

What *Sybil* offers amounts to the kind of social vision that all but
disappears in the 1850s and 1860s. As such, Disraeli's vision might
seem old-fashioned, but it can also be argued that he acknowledges
an aggressive streak in human nature that writers such as Gaskell
and Eliot fail to do justice to.[11] Charlotte Brontë is equally ready to
confront disturbing and violent impulses in human behaviour, as
we can see in *Shirley*. This novel is set at the time of the Luddite
protests of 1811 and 1812, a period when the Napoleonic Wars

have had a depressive effect on trade leading to industrial unrest. Robert Moore, the mill-owner at the centre of *Shirley*, has, along with other employers, provoked trouble by installing new machines. The events of the novel centre on an attack on his property. Moore approaches Colonel Ryde, seeking military support. This will, however, be on a small scale: no more than half-a-dozen men. We are also told that Moore has already been in contact with the Home Secretary, who is prepared to offer active support for strong action against troublesome employees.

The impression in *Shirley* is that Brontë seems to lack the kind of social concern that is in evidence in a number of other Victorian industrial novels. Her focus is almost entirely on the middle-class characters, with very little concern for the poor.[12] Moore, in particular, belongs to a middle-class elite, displaying, like Thornton in *North and South*, what might be regarded as traditional military virtues as he defends his property:

> He had fortified and garrisoned his mill, which in itself was a strong building: he was a cool, brave man: he stood to the defence with unflinching firmness; those who were with him caught his spirit, and copied his demeanour. The rioters had never been so met before. At other mills they had attacked, they had found no resistance; an organized, resolute defence was what they never dreamed of encountering.[13]

The implication is that this is a new kind of man, but with roots to the past. This is most evident in the way that he conducts himself like a soldier, the troops he has requested merely supplementing his own martial qualities.

Generally, then, Brontë seems appreciative of the military virtues, even if Helstone, an arms-bearing clergyman, strikes a ridiculous figure as a soldier *manqué*. He fits, however, into a network of military images that is deeply infused into the novel. For example, the Anglicans in *Shirley* have a semi-comic Whitsuntide battle with the Dissenters, and, at another level, Caroline, the heroine, and Moore read *Coriolanus* together. Set against a background of the Napoleonic Wars, the military references sustain an idea of life as a clash of wills and beliefs. The fact is underlined by having just one character, Mr Yorke, who takes a contrary line, arguing, in the manner of the conciliators in Gaskell and Eliot, for flexibility and negotiation:

'If Moore had behaved to his men from the beginning as a master ought to behave, they never would have entertained their present feelings towards him.'   (p. 356)

It is not a view for which Brontë has much sympathy. There are critics who have sought to place her in the liberal camp, but instinctively, and as a novelist with her roots in the 1840s, she imagines social relations in adversarial terms.[14]

At the same time, she does subvert the traditional order, but does so in a way that maintains the case for aggression and confrontation. For what Brontë maintains is that the women in the novel, rather than playing a passive or emollient role, long to be involved in confrontations and danger. In Gaskell and Eliot the female characters are the articulate proponents of a post-militaristic code of conducting social relations, but Brontë speaks for women who want to be at the heart of the action. The women in *Shirley* long to be agitators rather than healers. Caroline Helstone and Shirley Keeldar live in a world that routinely belittles women. Helstone the clergyman, for example:

> could not abide sense in women: he liked to see them as silly, as light-headed, as vain, as open to ridicule as possible; because they were then in reality what he held them to be, and wished them to be, – inferior: toys to play with, to amuse a vacant hour and be thrown away.   (p. 138)

Moore is less openly dismissive, but laughs, even if 'very quietly, though' (p. 350) at Shirley's eagerness to help in the feeding of the men who have been defending the mill.

But these are not submissive women. Both Caroline and Shirley are confident handling weapons, and keen to handle them. On the question of using a carving-knife as a weapon, Caroline feels she could not nerve her arm to strike home with it, whereas Shirley feels that she 'could do it, if goaded' (p. 327). But when the attack takes place, it is Caroline who has to be restrained by Shirley. The significant point is that neither has any intention of intervening in the conciliatory way that is the woman's usual role in Victorian fiction. Just the opposite: they are as excited as the men at the prospect of a violent confrontation. Shirley, who calls herself Captain Keeldar and Mr Keeldar, is as warlike as the men, only more so:

'I feel like Robert, only more fierily. Let them meddle with Robert, or Robert's interests, and I shall hate them.'   (p. 268)

And Caroline is never far behind: ' "I would stand by him as you mean to stand by him – till death" ' (p. 268).

The relevance of *Shirley* to the overall subject of this book is that it can be seen to undermine one of the central propositions upon which mid-Victorian realistic fiction is built. Gaskell and Eliot propose a female discourse of negotiation as an alternative to the male discourse of confrontation. But *Shirley* mocks the idea that there is this kind of female role.[15] It could even be argued that *Shirley* undermines, before it becomes fully established, the pattern at the heart of so much mid-Victorian fiction in which negotiation takes over from the social model of confrontation. The idea at the heart of *North and South,* for example, which emphasises Margaret's role as peace-maker, can be seen as the formulation of a social philosophy relevant to a specific era rather than a fundamental change in social relations. Far from moving beyond a militaristic model of confrontation, society has merely rationalised it out of existence for a brief, mid-Victorian moment. Militarism is in recession, but will re-emerge by the end of the century. But what we must also recognise is just how fundamental the rejection of military habits of thinking was in the mid-Victorian years, a fact that is strikingly apparent in Dickens's novels.

CHARLES DICKENS'S *BLEAK HOUSE* AND *GREAT EXPECTATIONS*

There is, of course, no obligation upon writers to deal with military matters, but, on the face of it, the total absence of soldiers in most of Dickens's novels is surprising. At a basic level, he presents such a broad panorama of the characters of his day that we might expect a fair sprinkling of army types. More significantly, however, the recurrent themes and anxieties of Dickens's novels might also lead us to expect that they will feature soldiers. Nobody can compete with Dickens in conveying a sense of a society that is running out of control, where an explosion of new social energies and old human desires creates a state of chaos. The complement of Dickens's awareness of the closeness of anarchy is his interest in ways of regulating the world he creates. It is in this context that the army, particularly in its domestic role, and perhaps especially in Dickens's industrial novel *Hard Times* (1854), might seem to have a role to play. The extent to which Dickens ignores the army, however, suggests that we have to see his novels as reflecting a reorientation of thinking in the mid-Victorian period. The distinctive form this takes is Dickens's presentation of the new mechanisms of social control, in particular the police force, which were taking over from the army on the domestic stage.

A consideration of the rare appearances by soldiers in Dickens's works will, none the less, help us forward in understanding changes in Victorian attitudes. There are very few soldiers in Dickens: Colonel Bulder, commanding officer of the Rochester Garrison, and Captain Dowler, a bombastic ex-army officer in *The Pickwick Papers*; Captain Adams, who acts as a second in a duel in *Nicholas Nickleby*; a passing reference to Colonel Granger, the first husband of Edith Dombey in *Dombey and Son*; and Captain Bailey, David Copperfield's rival at the Larkinses' ball. These military characters are not only few in number but also totally insignificant. A slightly more substantial figure is Major Joseph Bagstock, in *Dombey and Son*, a retired soldier who worms his way into Dombey's friendship. There are, however, rather more references to soldiers in *Bleak House* and *Great Expectations*, which I discuss below. But even with these exceptions, the overall impression remains that soldiers are peripheral in Dickens's vision of society, that his novels reflect a new sense of how society operates.

A possible complication in this proposition is the large number of naval references in Dickens. These, however, have a distinct function. As can be seen in the character of Captain Cuttle, in *Dombey and Son*, there is an honesty about naval men that contrasts with the corruption endemic in society. The idea is taken further in the portrayal of Allan Woodcourt, a ship's doctor in *Bleak House*, who can be contrasted with the selfish Harold Skimpole, in the same novel, who has trained as a doctor but does not practise his profession. The figure of the sailor is, then, significant in Dickens as a symbol of honesty, but the merchant navy serves his purpose just as well as the royal navy. This is an appropriate point at which also to acknowledge the importance of the police in Dickens's novels, who indicate the direction in which society has developed: a new kind of regulation of civilian society has taken over from the overt display of force that one associates with the army. If Gaskell and Eliot look towards a sense of social order rooted in negotiation rather than confrontation, Dickens offers us a sense of how such a society polices itself. In addition to policemen and detectives, there are numerous lawyers in Dickens's novels, again adding to the sense of a new contractual rather than confrontational model of how society increasingly conducts its affairs.

Against this background, one of the more unusual features of *Bleak House* is that, alongside policemen and lawyers, it features a number of retired and serving soldiers. There is Captain Hawdon, a retired officer who, under the name Nemo, lives in poverty as a law writer; George Rouncewell, also known as Trooper George, who ran away from home to join the army, and then, on leaving the army, opened a shooting-range; Matthew Bagnet, an ex-artillery man and friend of George's, who now plays the bassoon in a theatre and keeps a musical instrument shop; and Richard Carstone, one of the novel's Chancery wards, who makes false starts in a number of professions, including the army. Trooper George and Matthew Bagnet are uncomplicated characters in a world of labyrinthine perversity. Bagnet, married with three children, is, in a novel where family life is in disarray, a member of the only united and stable family in *Bleak House*. Indeed, when we look at this 'most respectable man with a wife and family', we see that there is an admirable order about army life that reproduces itself in the life of this family.[16] This might seem trivial, but something significant is in evidence here about changing attitudes towards the common soldier. The traditional image of the ordinary recruit is of a social misfit. In the course of the 1850s, however, the image of the soldier began to change; he began to be thought of as an honest man doing his duty.[17] Bagnet is a minor character, but it would be hard to find an earlier example in fiction of the ordinary soldier being so directly connected with ideas of home, family and marriage.

Rather than focusing on an elite, Dickens presents the common soldier as a model for society. George makes just as positive an impression as Bagnet. He is loyal to his former commanding officer, Hawdon, refusing to betray him, and has an active sense of duty, as can be seen in his readiness to provide shelter for Jo. What is also of interest is that both Bagnet and George are now small businessmen, one owning a shop and the other a shooting-gallery. Traditionally, the world of the soldier and the world of commerce would be seen as having nothing in common, but Dickens associates the soldier with a range of virtues – efficiency, attention to detail, orderliness – that are entirely compatible with running a business.[18] It is, in addition, a good populist stance on the part of Dickens to represent these values as typical of ordinary recruits rather than well-born officers.

Richard Carstone, for example, is a gentleman waster, a super-fluous figure in society who flirts with a variety of careers. This is characteristic of the representation of the aristocracy and gentry throughout Dickens's works; he engages in an exercise of self-definition for himself and his middle-class readers by stressing the ways in which they are superior to the class above them. Similarly, the class below, represented by George and Bagnet, might differ from the middle class in some respects, but are pres-ented as endorsing middle-class values as they share the same commitment to home and family, together with an awareness of the importance of duty and application. Richard Carstone and Captain Hawdon have no awareness of these values. Richard enters the army because it might impose a framework of discipline upon his life:

> His name was entered at the Horse Guards, as an applicant for an Ensign's commission; the purchase money was deposited at an Agent's; and Richard, in his usual characteristic way, plunged into a violent course of military study, and got up at five o'clock every morning to practise the broadsword exercise.   (pp. 391–2)

The sentence pulls in two directions: the description of the frame-work of order that Richard adopts is also a description of an absence of moderation and balance.

But Richard is more than just a typical young man of his class; he is someone who has been psychologically damaged by the endless Chancery case. He is always close to madness:

> He was only half-dressed – in plain clothes, I observed, not in uniform – and his hair was unbrushed, and he looked as wild as his room.   (p. 675)

The army at this point offers a refuge for someone who lacks a sense of his social identity; it can, however, offer no real security. In the case of Hawdon, the army provided a rank, as captain, but leaving the army he becomes Nemo, ending his life as a drug addict. A similar sense of things dark and frightening is even associated with George; the army is still the place people can run to when they want to escape from their families, and this is the case with George, who 'ran wild, and went for a soldier, and never came back' (p. 134). In his separation from his mother, he becomes one of the many characters in Dickens's novels who lose their identity. In the army, 'Trooper George' has a role, but his life story is a familiar one in Dickens's novels of separation from family, social dislocation and psychological disturbance. At one level, therefore, Dickens associates the army with discipline and order, but he also links it with a sense of psychic and social disorder, and, more precisely, with an awareness of the potential for violence that is for ever simmering in life.

This issue is focused in the image of the shooting-gallery, which provides, or is meant to provide, a means of channelling dangerous impulses. Even George himself is aware that his shooting-gallery provides 'a safety-valve' (p. 398), but it can barely assimilate the 'Mad people out of number, of course' (p. 397). When we put these various army references in *Bleak House* together, it becomes clear just how far Dickens has moved to a new pattern of thinking. The army is not associated with warfare or even deeds of bravery. Such positive qualities as the army has are entirely associated with the family-oriented common soldier. Primarily, however, the army is associated with disturbed and violent psychological states. The traditional image of the army has, consequently, been reversed; it does not provide a guarantee of security for civilian society, but symbolically represents those forces that threaten the security of civilian society.

It is not, of course, the real army that Dickens is writing about; as is clear at the time of the Crimean War and the Indian Mutiny, Dickens endorsed the army when necessary.[19] What he is writing about is a range of anxieties about violence, punishment and guilt for which the army is purely an appropriate symbol. Rather than looking out, in the sense of considering the army and its place in modern life, Dickens is looking in, identifying a state of combat in the mind; the military images prove effective for bringing such an idea to life. The approach is taken a step further in *Great Expectations*, the only other novel by Dickens with a significant number of military references. At the beginning of the novel, a party of soldiers arrives at the blacksmith's cottage, where Pip, the hero, lives, with a set of handcuffs that need unlocking.[20] The soldiers are primarily a means of expressing the psychological anxieties of Pip; they serve as an apt expression of his feelings of guilt, his feeling that he lives in the shadow of constant and unnerving surveillance. There is a similar psychological dimension to a brief scene featuring a character called the 'Colonel', who is in prison for 'coining'. He is, in fact, an impostor, someone who has passed himself off as a colonel, forging himself just as he has forged money. But this act of imposture, of wearing a false uniform, echoes the behaviour of Pip, who, with an alarming sense of his own dishonesty, has been passing himself off as a gentleman.

Dickens has moved on a long way from traditional representations of soldiers when military images are used in this manner. He offers no sense of, and has no interest in, the army as an institution in society; it is, on the contrary, a symbol, expressing other ideas relating to states of mind. But in choosing this direction Dickens starts to suggest a new, and altogether more disturbing, vision of society, for what he starts to present in *Great Expectations* is the kind of nightmare regime in which security forces arrive unannounced, and where there is always the possibility of unexpected, perhaps undeserved, arrest and punishment. In his portrayal of George and Bagnet, Dickens expresses a new respect for the common soldier, but beyond this he moves towards a sense of an insidious punishment squad called into operation by the guilt feelings of his protagonists.

THOMAS HARDY'S *FAR FROM THE MADDING CROWD* AND *THE TRUMPET-MAJOR*

Dickens's novels shift as far away as possible from traditional military thinking. Reading *Bleak House* or *Great Expectations*, it is easy to see why the army in the 1850s and 1860s saw itself as under threat, increasingly conceiving of itself as an embattled citadel. It was all too clear that society was changing and that the army was being sidelined.[21] In the 1870s, however, militarism re-enters the picture. The re-emergence of militarism, and how literature both responded to and contributed to this development, is the subject matter of the remaining chapters of this book. The first foretaste of a change of mood was provided by the Franco-Prussian War of 1870–1. A French force of nearly 250,000 men faced nearly half a million Germans. Napoleon III ordered an advance on Berlin, but the Prussians advanced too, and, after several major battles, began to march on Paris, the city eventually surrendering after a lengthy siege.[22] The scale and ferocity of the war can be said to have undermined a liberal vision of the sane and civilised conduct of social, and even international, relations. Dickens, we might add, had always offered a disturbing vision of violent impulses in life, but as we move towards the end of the century there is an increasing emphasis on the myopic limitations of the liberal vision of the world. We can begin to see this in Hardy's surprising rehabilitation of the soldier as a significant character in fiction.

Sergeant Troy, in *Far From the Madding Crowd* (1874), is the most striking soldier in the whole of Victorian fiction. Behind the glamour, and nastiness, of his character, however, there is a complex set of issues. We can start with the simple fact that it is surprising to see a soldier as a central character in a mainstream Victorian novel. While the absence of soldiers suggests that they embodied ideas most Victorians had little interest in, Hardy's reintroduction of a soldier indicates his concern with these neglected ideas. It is an impression that is confirmed by all the details about Troy. He is a wayward, outlaw-like figure, pursuing, marrying, then abandoning the heroine, Bathsheba. After Troy's death, Bathsheba marries Gabriel Oak, who is as solid and virtuous as his name. Troy, by contrast, represents excitement and danger. Hardy, and perhaps the Victorians in general, are becoming curious again about the riskier aspects of experience. With Troy, we witness the reintroduction of a character who is so traditional that his reappearance has to be seen as revolutionary.

At the same time, there is a lot about Troy that is new. Significantly, Hardy takes considerable care over defining the social class – or, perhaps, the indeterminate social class – of his soldier. Troy is, at least in name, the son of a doctor who was married to a French governess, but it is generally accepted that his father was Lord Severn. Troy started out in life as a clerk in a lawyer's office, and 'might have worked himself into a dignified position of some sort had he not indulged in the wild freak of enlisting'.[23] He is now a sergeant in the army. The point would seem to be that Troy was at first connected with the middle-class professions of medicine and law, but breaks free. The secret of his birth, however, suggests that there is a degree of aristocratic arrogance in his personality that attracts him to a life outside middle-class routine. When we reflect on the domestic novel of the 1850s and 1860s, it is as if it has been so busy defining the rules for middle-class existence that it forgets about excitement; in *Far From the Madding Crowd*, Hardy appears to rediscover the riskiness that the realistic novel had outlawed.

Even the most trivial details confirm this impression. For example, on Troy's first appearance we are told that marriage was 'looked upon with disfavour in the army' (p. 120). The cluster of ideas informing so much of Victorian fiction – a cluster of ideas linking the family, marriage and domestic life – is suddenly seen from a different angle. Dickens's Matthew Bagnet is, in equal measure, both soldier and married man, but Hardy's casual aside exposes the picture of Bagnet as an unlikely mid-Victorian construction. A similar but more extended sense of the way in which Hardy distances himself from familiar patterns of thinking is evident in a remarkable description of Troy's character, the emphasis falling upon how he lives only for the moment:

> He was a man to whom memories were an incumbrance and anticipations a superfluity. Simply feeling, considering, and caring for what was before his eyes, he was vulnerable only in the present. His outlook upon time was as a transient flash of the eye now and then: that projection of consciousness into days gone by and to come, which makes the past a synonym for the pathetic and the future a word for circumspection, was foreign to Troy. With him the past was yesterday; the future, tomorrow; never, the day after.   (p. 197)

The effectiveness of this analysis is that it incorporates a critique of both the temper of middle-class life and the assumptions inherent in realistic fiction. In both, the individual and the novelist are repeatedly having to take stock in preparation for the future; there is always a privileging of thought over feeling. But with Troy a mentality that is based upon action rather than long-term calculation finds its way back into the Victorian novel.

Part of the attraction of such a life is that it is dangerous. It is this that Bathsheba finds so seductive. In one of the novel's most celebrated scenes, Troy demonstrates the art of sword-play, the blade coming perilously close to Bathsheba:

> In an instant the atmosphere was transformed to Bathsheba's eyes. Beams of light caught from the low sun's rays, above, around, in front of her, well-nigh shut out earth and heaven – all emitted in the marvellous evolutions of Troy's reflecting

blade, which seemed everywhere at once, and yet nowhere specially.   (p. 216)

Bathsheba seems to pass into another dimension, but Hardy himself is also passing beyond the domestic limits of Victorian fiction. Troy's behaviour towards women throughout *Far From the Madding Crowd* clearly puts him beyond the pale of middle-class respectability, but he also appears to be able to transcend the usual limits on identity. He fakes his death, reappearing in disguise as Dick Turpin. It is as if he has the power to reinvent himself. This is, however, a routine feature of the military novel, that the soldier on enlisting can make a clean break with his past and assume a new identity. This continuity with an older fictional model is important in *Far From the Madding Crowd*, for in the character of Troy an old pattern of masculine behaviour, based upon the primacy of action over thought, reasserts itself in a culture that has for over a quarter of a century committed itself to marriage and moderation. In Gaskell and Eliot the army is seen as a force at the disposal of the community, but in *Far From the Madding Crowd* the soldier threatens the stability of civilian life.

It could be argued that it is misleading to make too much of one example, that Troy might be simply an anomaly rather than a symptom of a change of direction in Victorian fiction. As the next chapter will suggest, however, *Far From the Madding Crowd* is just one early sign of a widespread reorientation of ideas in the last quarter of the nineteenth century. Hardy's particular interest in military matters is taken further in *The Trumpet-Major* (1880). This might, at first sight, seem little more than a rural idyll, but it explores the implications of issues raised in *Far From the Madding Crowd*. What is noteworthy about *The Trumpet-Major* is that it is in many respects a domestic novel, but one that happens to be set at a time of preparation for war. It is set in the Napoleonic era, more specifically at a time when England is making preparations for a possible invasion. The trumpet-major, John Loveday, the son of a miller, is a suitor for the hand of Anne Garland, but John's sailor brother, Bob, also loves Anne, and, after winning glory at Trafalgar, is the one who gains her hand in marriage. John goes off to fight, and die, in the Peninsular War.

The Trumpet-Major engages in a significant rewriting of history. The common soldiers in the novel (John in particular) are presented as thoroughly decent young men from respectable families. Their families may be disappointed at the vocation they have chosen to follow, but remain close and committed to their sons. Historical evidence provides a very different impression of the common soldiery at the start of the nineteenth century; the rank and file were social misfits, the unemployed, and those who by mere chance had fallen into soldiering. There is no precedent for Hardy's portrayal of John, the son of a mill-owner, making a career choice of the army. But John is just one of many peaceful men in the novel, men 'of a quiet shop-keeping disposition', who have enlisted.[24] Hardy repeatedly emphasises the quiet respectability and good manners of his soldiers; far from being, as we might expect, a lawless rabble, these are young men of some education and with a considerable degree of delicacy of feeling.[25]

It is clear, then, that Hardy is rewriting the past, making the ordinary soldiers representatives of, or, at least, extensions of lower middle-class society. Troy is an outlaw, but in *The Trumpet-Major* the soldiers are at one with civilian society. Hardy's rewriting of the Napoleonic era is part of a wider pattern; in the late-Victorian period there is an immense revival of interest in the Napoleonic period, and also a reinterpretation of the events to make them a part of bourgeois experience. It is an interesting development: militarism is re-emerging, but the resurgent militarism of the late-Victorian period has to be reconcilable with the views of the mid-dle-class majority. Hardy's class stance is underlined in his presentation of Festus Derrinan, the one gentry character in the novel and the leader of the local yeomanry. Festus's actions reveal the shortcomings of his class. Unlike the common soldiers, Festus is offensive in his behaviour. This is evident in such a trivial matter as his misjudgement in singing a coarse verse of a song at Miller Loveday's party. Sergeant Stanner, who started singing the song, has the innate tact to skip the verse in question in deference to the female guests.

Where Festus proves really offensive, however, is in his consistently threatening attitude to the heroine, Anne Garland. In a gentle novel, this is kept within limits, but there is an unmistakable sense of a man presuming to exploit his privileged social position in order to take sexual advantage of a woman. And at one point his behaviour becomes genuinely alarming. Locked in a deserted house, Anne is threatened by an enraged Festus. The scene, with its images of violation and entry, inevitably implies an intended rape, the violent connotations of which relate to the military theme of the novel, that is to say the threat that Napoleon might penetrate the English defences. Compared to Festus, the Loveday brothers are natural gentlemen, whereas Festus is only a gentleman by birth. John Loveday's delicacy and sensitivity, in particular, make him almost feminine in feeling rather than the traditional rough soldier. John is often tongue-tied and tentative:

> But the gallant musician's soul was so much disturbed by tender vibrations and by the sense of his own presumption that he could not begin   (p. 112)

But John is so hesitant that the picture becomes disturbing. As Roger Ebbatson suggests, he 'functions through repression and self-abnegation to such a degree that the heroism upon which the narrator insists begins to feel psychotic'.[26]

This is just one aspect of a surprising sense of uneasiness that is generated by *The Trumpet-Major*. Throughout the novel there is a sense of a threat to the quiet, routine lives of the characters, a threat posed by the likelihood of invasion and war. In the quiet landscape of Wessex, there are repeated troop movements, indeed a general sense of movement and upheaval. As Hardy combines a sense of the small scale and the large scale, we receive an impression of passive characters being acted upon by large forces that are outside their control. But perhaps even more unnerving is the suggestion of an incompatibility between the usual domestic routine of this community and the force of the impact of military life. John and Bob Loveday are kind and sympathetic characters, but both are committed to conquering the resistance of Anne Loveday. There is also something uncomfortable about the manner in which they seem almost to bargain over Anne as an object to dispose of as they wish. Implicit in their behaviour, as in their professions, are aggressive assumptions which are at odds with the domestic, peaceful values that the novel seems to want to endorse.

In *The Trumpet-Major*, superficially an idyll, we see some difficult questions being confronted. The dominant spirit of the mid-Victorian novel is insular. After 1870, however, doubts begin to emerge about the long-term sustainability of such an ordered, but blinkered, existence. Hardy, in reintroducing military figures into the mainstream of Victorian fiction, both anticipates and begins to explore the implications of these changes. On the one hand, there is the domestic world of the Victorian novel, endorsing the idea of individual choice and the concept of relationships founded upon trust. But, on the other hand, such liberal sentiments conflict with the idea of aggression that is at the heart of all military thinking. Hardy, in both *Far From the Madding Crowd* and *The Trumpet-Major*, starts to examine the inadequacy of the old liberal perspective in a society that is starting to become more belligerent. Yet, at the same time we have to recognise that both novels are pleasant rural diversions. Moreover, in *The Trumpet-Major* in particular, Hardy has imported lower-middle-class morals and manners into a society where they can only have existed in embryonic form. There is, consequently, a contradiction at the heart of both novels: that, as much as they undermine a liberal view of society, they also embody liberal convictions, in their choice of characters, selection of detail, narrative stance, and, more generally, in their quiet confidence as novels. It is just such a mixture of a new military emphasis together with a resilient liberalism that is in evidence in British literature right through to the end of the century.

6

Heroes

OUIDA'S *UNDER TWO FLAGS*

In the preface to his 1851 book *The Fifteen Decisive Battles of the World*, Sir Edward Creasy apologises for his subject matter:

> It is an honourable characteristic of the Spirit of this Age, that projects of violence and warfare are regarded among civilised states with gradually increasing aversion...For a writer, therefore, of the present day to choose battles for his favourite topic, merely because they were battles; merely because so many myriads of troops were arrayed in them, and so many hundreds or thousands of human beings stabbed, hewed, or shot each other to death during them, would argue strange weakness or depravity of mind.[1]

This is more than a gesture: for over 600 pages Creasy makes it plain that it is possible to combine an interest in military history with the essentially liberal values that we encounter in novels from the period. Creasy's book is not a celebration of a military elite; indeed, one of the first points he makes is that the military virtues of courage, honour and, significantly, 'human intellect' are 'found in the basest as well as in the noblest of mankind'.[2] Nor is it the kind of nationalistic book about war that began to appear in the last twenty years of the nineteenth century. Creasy's principal concern is to show how his chosen battles have affected the course of history, much of his attention falling upon the personalities of the protagonists. As such, the book echoes the pattern of many Victorian novels: the focus is on how the lives and personal qualities of individuals connect with and contribute to the life of a nation. The individual is seen in an historical context, but is also seen as the shaper of history.

Creasy's book struck the right note for its time, and indeed for much of the Victorian period, with 38 reprints by 1894.[3] It is a book about war produced in a time of peace, and permeated by an awareness that for the moment, possibly for the foreseeable future, the threat of a major war is not on the agenda. The chapter on Waterloo begins with the fact that 'England has now been blest with thirty-seven years of peace', and he celebrates the advances in 'science, commerce and civilisation' that have been made possible by the absence of conflict.[4] This buoyant feeling of progress is apparent throughout the book: war is something to be regretted; what matters is 'the great cause of the general promotion of the industry and welfare of mankind'.[5] What is unusual about Creasy's work is that he combines an interest in military history with the non-militaristic instincts of his time. Many of his contemporaries seem simply indifferent to military matters. This is particularly apparent in attitudes towards heroism. The realistic novel all but dismisses heroism; its concern is with the non-heroic, ordinary business of life, although a concept of heroism is, of course, necessary to define the non-heroic. In George Eliot's *Middlemarch* (1871–2), for example, there are references to the story of Cincinnatus, a hero of the early Roman republic. In 458 BC he left his work on the land in order to deliver the consul Minucius from imminent disaster at the hands of the Aequi. As soon as his task was accomplished, however, he returned to his farm. In *Middlemarch* this is a story that Mrs Garth, an admirable mother-figure, has taught her children; the emphasis falls upon the fact that Cincinnatus has done his duty, but Mrs Garth's fondness for this story, as against other possible illustrations of dutifulness, is presumably due to the fact that it privileges domestic life above all other forms of existence.[6]

It is possible that Eliot is mocking Mrs Garth's provincial reading of classical history, and to some extent this is the case, but it is also clear that Eliot thinks in the same way. For example, the Duke of Wellington is referred to in the context of an auction:

> Here is an engraving of the Duke of Wellington surrounded by his staff on the Field of Waterloo; and not withstanding recent events which have, as it were, enveloped our great Hero in a cloud . . . .[7]

The reference is to Wellington's support of the Dissenters in the repeal of the Test Acts in 1828 and his support for Catholic emancipation in 1829. The significant point is that Eliot seems more interested in these local 'events' than in the achievements of the

'Hero'. As with the reference to Cincinnatus, a hero is acknow-
ledged, but it is domestic concerns that really matter. These
military references in *Middlemarch* are very minor threads in the
text, but their slightness provides the clearest evidence of all of
how those occupying the middle-ground in mid-Victorian Britain
had little time for military matters. The concept of heroism is not
only neglected but even dismissed as faintly absurd.

Eliot speaks for the majority, but there are a number of early to
mid-Victorian writers who retain a traditional enthusiasm for heroism, and, indeed, for everything connected with a military culture.
The mid-Victorian romantic novelist Ouida is particularly interesting in this respect, as she creates the most extravagant heroes. Her
novels might be far-fetched and even silly, yet it is possible to feel
that, in the invention of her military heroes, Ouida touches upon
needs that a novelist such as Eliot is unaware of; it could even be
argued that Ouida exposes the smugness of Eliot's ironic vision.
Ouida's three best-known novels, *Held in Bondage* (1863), *Strathmore*
(1865) and *Under Two Flags* (1867), all feature worldly guardsmen,
the most memorable being Bertie Cecil of the Life Guards in *Under
Two Flags*. Bertie fakes his own death and leaves London in order to
protect the reputation of a lady and the honour of his younger
brother. Enlisting in the *Chasseurs d'Afrique*, under the name Louis
Victor (like Sergeant Troy, he can adopt a new identity when he
wishes to), he fights heroically against Arab rebels in Algeria. At
the same time, Cigarette, a beautiful camp follower, falls in love
with him. Bertie strikes his commanding officer, and is sentenced
to death at a court martial. Cigarette, aware of his real identity,
wins a reprieve for Bertie, but arriving at the very moment when
Bertie is facing the firing squad, she hurls herself in front of him
and dies in the fusillade of bullets.

Bertie may be the kind of aristocratic military hero that had
largely disappeared from fiction by the 1860s, but it seems that
men a little like Bertie continued to exist in real life. Particularly in
a period of peace, the life of an army officer was that of a country
gentleman, spending an immense amount of time hunting and
shooting. Moreover, as the world changed, this officer class with-
drew into a defensive cocoon, cultivating a superior and languid
style. As John Sutherland suggests in relation to *Under Two
Flags*, 'Young officers must have read the novel not just as a
flattering looking-glass, but as a manual in which they might pick
up tips as to how they should comport themselves'.[8] It is in

the 1860s, therefore, that two opposed positions are most clearly in evidence: on the one hand, there is a widespread indifference to everything relating to the army, but, on the other, in the same decade the officer class is at its most 'swell', cultivating a swagger in defiance of the world as it is. The circle in which Ouida moved (which included, perhaps surprisingly, Philip Meadows Taylor, the author of *Seeta*) provides an illustration of a military 'set' occupying a rarefied position in English society.[9] It is true that a substantial number of members of parliament had served in the army at some stage in their lives, but in a time of peace military expenditure was so far down the list of priorities that it would be wrong to regard them as a military lobby close to the heart of power. In a sense, the army was invisible, either serving overseas or in garrison towns. Against such a background, Ouida is almost on her own in carrying the torch for a certain kind of soldier hero.

By the end of the century, however, the aristocratic military hero is beginning to reappear in literature. Alongside the new, empire-building heroes of G.A. Henty and Rider Haggard, a dandified hero appears in Anthony Hope's *The Prisoner of Zenda* (1894) and in the Brigadier Gerard stories of Sir Arthur Conan Doyle (1896 and 1903).[10] Doyle's hero is a French cavalry officer fighting for Napoleon. It is an interesting reversal of earlier attitudes. A follower of Napoleon is no longer seen as a dangerous insurrectionary but as a gentleman living in accordance with a code of honour. Doyle's stance indicates a nostalgic fondness for an old aristomilitary culture; it is part of a widespread romantic reconsideration of the Napoleonic era in popular art at the end of the century, representing, as all such escapes into the past do, a refuge from the modern world.[11] Ouida's hero, Bertie, also belongs in a world where honour is everything; there is, however, no place for such a man in Britain, so Bertie has to seek the life of a soldier elsewhere. What makes *Under Two Flags* work so well is the panache with which it conceives the aristocratic hauteur of its hero. John Sutherland defines this: 'The essence of winning is to do so effortlessly, without having to try. And, at the end of the day, winning is not everything; *style* is everything'.[12] We can set this against the life of Sir Henry Havelock, which, as presented by his contemporary biographers, was a story of duty and effort finally being rewarded.[13] In *Under Two Flags* there is contempt for such middle-class application. Ouida might seem an entirely frivolous novelist, but her works represent another voice, possibly a significant voice of opposition, in the cultural consensus of the 1860s.

An essential aspect of Bertie's style is languor, an aristocratic listlessness. It is again John Sutherland who provides a gloss on this: he comments that the stance was something Sir Walter Scott noted in the young English officers after Waterloo, partly in imitation of the *sang-froid* of Wellington. The idea of the hyper-cultivated English officer appears most elegantly in Mrs Gore's 1841 novel, *Cecil*. The assumption is that the apparently indifferent officer has an inner strength that will be called upon in moments of crisis: 'Until that emergency, the hero exists in a condition of latency – or "ennui" – relieved only by beautiful women, gaming, and peacock-like decoration of his own person'.[14] Where this style persisted into the 1860s, it was cultivated with an even greater degree of self-consciousness, as an act of defiance against the spirit of the age. Bertie Cecil is the most outrageous hero of this kind, yet, in the very process of celebrating his style, Ouida demonstrates his failings, essentially his irrelevance, for in the course of the novel Bertie is both defeated and embarrassed. The resolution of the plot depends upon his being saved by a woman; in a sense, he is emasculated. It is a pattern that is repeated in military fantasies of the mid-Victorian era, particularly in the Muscular Christian novels of Charles Kingsley and G.A. Lawrence. Unlike Ouida's Bertie Cecil, the heroes of their novels are bounding with energy, but with little sense of purpose or direction, and frequently they become dependent upon women.

In *Under Two Flags*, however, the issue goes deeper than this, for one aspect of Bertie is his 'Wildean sexual ambiguity'.[15] This has to be seen in connection with a curious child-like quality about Cigarette. In their relationship, Bertie poses and swaggers, but has nothing more to offer. The masculine energies of the soldier are being questioned. Without a real enemy, he has to confront his peacock-like self and the relationships induced in a world of male camaraderie. And this is the experience of an officer who is at a remove from all the conventions of family life and domesticity. Altogether it is not all that surprising that Bertie has mutated into a sexually ambiguous dandy. Rather similar problems are raised by Thomas Carlyle and Charles Kingsley, both of whom also cultivate the idea of the hero, and both of whom then go on to raise doubts about the nature and purpose of heroism, Carlyle in a sinister way, Kingsley in an unintentionally humorous way. But the issue is more far-reaching than this, for Ouida sets up a pattern of male power being linked with a simultaneous sense of male inadequacy that will persist for the rest of the century.

THOMAS CARLYLE'S *THE FRENCH REVOLUTION* AND CHARLES KINGSLEY'S *HEREWARD THE WAKE*

Like Ouida, both Carlyle and Kingsley are ill at ease with the democratic and domestic temper of their age. In the case of these two writers, however, this expresses itself in a furious energy, even anger, that often lacks purpose or direction. Both are, in rather similar ways, alienated writers in the cultural context of mid-Victorian Britain. Where we begin to see this with Carlyle is that he has a way of looking at the world that has nothing in common with the perspective of Victorian novelists. Whereas the novelist always has the anchor of character, Carlyle works with ideas, and his ideas can appear abstract and alarming. This is the case in *The French Revolution* (1837), the model for which is epic rather than the novel, and which, at its heart, conveys the idea of a cosmic power struggle. The events Carlyle records, he manages to imply, could not be described by a novelist as they are expressive of such deep human drives. In *The French Revolution*, the revolutionary forces are the Titans who are ranged against the Olympian court of Louis:

> It was the Titans warring with Olympus; and they, scarcely crediting it, have *conquered*; prodigy of prodigies; delirious – as it could not but be.[16]

This is an inversion of earlier epics; what we see here is the over-turning of society, France reconstituting itself on a more primitive basis.

Whereas the novelist would focus upon the role of individuals in the conflict, Carlyle works with a different sense of dark forces. The vision is one in which military order becomes essential as the only means of checking and controlling these forces that threaten to destroy society. Indeed, the most marked effect in *The French Revolution* is a sense of chaos that is spiralling out of control. Initially the response to this is measured. As is often pointed out, in the earlier stages of the work there is a light touch, with viewpoints shifting and a variety of voices; control is exercised, but it is a flexible, open control of the narrative. Such detachment proves hard to sustain, however, and as the aura of violence, anarchy and madness develops, Carlyle moves towards the army. As Albert J. LaValley points out:

> As if sickened by the mad whirl of the Terror, he welcomes the order of the army that will halt such chaos[17]

There is, as LaValley notes, some hesitation on Carlyle's part, a recognition that this is a desperate reaction to disorder, but it is clear that in soldiering 'and not elsewhere, lies the first germ of returning Order for France!'[18] It is a state of affairs that leads to the rise of Napoleon, the necessary military leader:

> With the army Carlyle seems to indulge in feelings of sublimity and triumph over all obstacles; man is viewed under the impersonality of force and becomes a force of nature and history, impersonal and inexorable.[19]

The point is obvious but worth repeating, that Carlyle's view has little in common with the liberal commitment to the individual that is at the heart of the thinking of so many of his contemporaries.

Pinning down Carlyle's exact position is, however, rather more difficult than establishing how he differs from other writers of his time. Quite evidently, he adopts a deeply illiberal stance, military order being seen as essential as the only way of checking the anarchy that threatens to consume society. More often than not, though, this threatening force is conceived symbolically, as a kind of metaphoric threat, rather than logically identified and evaluated. It is, consequently, a vision that works by fear, stirring up a nightmare of dark anxieties, and urging military order as the only possible response. In so far as there is a real, rather than symbolic threat, it can be pointed out that Carlyle's view of the French Revolution is inseparable from his fears of new, and potentially anarchic, social energy in the Chartist agitation of the late 1830s and 1840s. It is in the same context, of a critique of democracy, that Carlyle's philosophy of the hero emerges; his belief in individual action is characterised by a belief in the individual actions of the few rather than the many. Most people move in tune with the anonymous forces of nature and history; only a few exceptional individuals constitute a force in themselves. Inevitably, Carlyle's favoured heroes are always military figures; the sequence of heroes in *On Heroes and Hero-Worship, and the Heroic in History* (1841) ends with Cromwell and Napoleon, who appear in the final chapter under the heading 'The Hero as King'.[20] Both are leaders who can establish order in a world where anarchy is imminent.

It might seem absurd to compare Carlyle's militarism with Ouida's, but the comparison is surprisingly illuminating; moreover, it helps define what is so sinister about Carlyle's manner of thinking. Both write at a time when a military culture is a thing of the past (though for Carlyle, in 1837, a very recent past). Ouida's hero, therefore, has to cast around for a war to fight in; fighting as a volunteer in a foreign army, with no commitment to that nation's cause, is a spectacular if futile gesture. Carlyle, by contrast, in the absence of an enemy, resorts to inventing one, essentially an enemy within. There is a force within the state acting against the interest of the nation, and the role of the army, therefore, becomes primarily one of imposing social control at home. Carlyle, it can be argued, anticipates fascism, for, against imagined dark forces, he exalts the state. *The French Revolution* conveys vividly the fervour of change, and the thrill and charge of military activity, but there is always something chilling in Carlyle's vision. It is instructive to compare him with a novelist such as Gaskell, who looks at the role of the army in an industrial dispute; but Gaskell, as with most of her contemporaries, prefers to pull back from confrontation. Carlyle, we can imagine, would revel in social control being established by the intervention of the army. In the context of mid-Victorian Britain, that is the period about twenty years on from the publication of *The French Revolution*, his view seems alarmist, even ridiculous, yet there is also something disturbing about the manner in which Carlyle has anticipated a core of ideas of extreme right-wing thinking that persists to the present day.[21]

Looked at alongside Carlyle, Charles Kingsley appears a cheerful innocent. As with Carlyle, the initial impression is of an aggressive temperament seeking an outlet; in the absence of a war (although Kingsley responded quickly to the Crimean War and all other conflicts), there is, most of the time, no real focus for his aggression. At this point Carlyle invents an enemy, but in Kingsley there is simply an impression of boundless masculine energy for its own sake. Indeed, Kingsley is credited with inventing the 'berserker' hero, a hero who thrashes around violently and destructively but also aimlessly.[22] Given the absurdity of Kingsley's berserker

heroes, it is at first hard to grasp why he is so consistently demonised in modern criticism. His views on race are, admittedly, both
crude and crudely expressed, but he is attacked more often as the
embodiment of aggressive masculinity. It helps that his novels, like
most Victorian historical novels, prove so unreadable today, as this
enables critics to define his position from his public statements
rather than from the impression that is conveyed by his works as
a whole.[23] But it should be noted that modern distaste for Kingsley
was to a large extent shared by George Eliot, who, in a review of
Westward Ho! that is only superficially respectful, deplored his
'fierce antagonism and his perpetual hortative tendency'.[24] When
a hostile attitude towards Kingsley is dropped, however, it
becomes possible to see that he might be always more than half
aware of the preposterousness of advocating the heroic in a non-
heroic age, and of supporting militarism in a society that has
turned its back on militarism. It might be true that his works
begin the formulation of a rhetoric of race and empire that will
become central in literature by the end of the century, but when his
novels are actually read Kingsley's contradictions are far more
evident than his convictions.

The nature of Kingsley's militarism is most evident in *Hereward
the Wake* (1866).[25] Like *Westward Ho!*, it takes a line that distinguishes it from Kingsley's earlier social novels. In *Alton Locke*
(1850) and *Yeast* (1851) the resolutions are achieved through compromise.[26] There are reservations, but in various respects the pattern echoes that of a Gaskell novel in that the members of society
manage to establish terms on which they can live and work
together. In his military novels, however, Kingsley moves in the
opposite direction. This is evident even in a summary of *Hereward
the Wake*: Hereward is outlawed by his God-fearing mother, and,
after a series of adventures, arrives in Flanders, where he marries
Torfrida. In the years after 1066 Hereward returns to Britain and
musters a rebel army to fight the Normans. His resistance is worn
down, however, both by William's army and by the wiles of a
woman, Alftruda, who separates him from his wife. Confronted
in his home by an old enemy, Hereward dies calling Torfrida's
name. He is followed by more peace-loving English leaders, but
clearly we are meant to admire Hereward's primitive energy. It
needs to be accommodated within the discipline of marriage and
domesticity, but Hereward's desperate energy has a value that is
important.

Repeatedly, he refuses to compromise. When Harold is made King of England, he offers to restore Hereward's land. Hereward's wife answers on his behalf:

> 'I was sorely tempted...Surely. To see you rich and proud upon your own lands, an earl, may be – may be, I thought at whiles, a king. But it could not be. It did not stand with honour, my hero, not with honour.'   (p. 155)

It is honour that motivates Hereward; it is more important than personal ambition or domestic happiness. Central to Kingsley's novel is a sense of noble warriors keeping 'alive in their hearts that proud spirit of personal independence...and they kept alive, too, though in abeyance for a while, those free institutions which were without a doubt the germs of our British liberty' (p. 3). *Hereward the Wake* clusters words such as liberty and freedom, always associating them with an idea of Britain, and then stressing that there can be no compromise, that the only possible policy is direct action. The idea is extended by constantly associating Hereward with fire imagery, creating a sense that the world is in need of purging, in need of the fire of destruction and renewal.

Yet, for all the storming energy with which these views are put forward, there are also qualifications. The novel starts with an introductory section on the early history of the people of the fens, where we see 'the germs of our British liberty', but the last four pages of this 'Prelude' focus upon the difficulty of establishing sources, indeed of verifying any evidence at all about the events the novel is going to record. Here, in essence, Kingsley questions the authenticity of his story. And this sets the tone for a novel which is repeatedly sceptical as well as enthusiastic about the warrior code. The novel's scepticism is most vividly established in relation to the question of what Hereward is fighting for: it is soon established that there is no England, only separate states, which if they are to be unified will only be unified by the foreign invader, William. What is confronted is the fact that the English are not a 'pure' race, so undermining the sense of racial superiority that the novel subsequently develops. The whole question of inheritance is also a fraught issue in the novel: Hereward's relationship with his parents is problematic in various ways, and his close friend Martin murders his own father.

The overall impression is that, in the very process of asserting a military code in opposition to the effete values of mid-Victorian

Britain, Kingsley questions the foundations upon which the military code is built. In Carlyle, militarism is brought forward as the only means of establishing order in society, but in Kingsley militarism is murky at its very source. The novel then adds to this negative impression by demonstrating that the consequences of a military dispensation include lawlessness and violence, such as at the battle of Aldreth where thousands drown 'in the dark water, or, more hideous still, in the bottomless slime of peat and mud' (p. 286). The most graphic image, however, is one that haunted the Victorians, an image of cutting off someone's head. It appears in reports of the Indian Mutiny, and is the central image in accounts of the death of General Gordon.[27] In *Hereward the Wake*, it is Hereward who first cuts off the head of an unnamed Norman. The description is brutally abrupt:

> After which he recollected very little, at least in this world. For Hereward cut off his head with his own sword.   (p. 304)

Then Hereward is killed in the same way, his head being set up 'over the hall-door, as a warning to those English churls that their last man is dead' (p. 414). Inherent in the image of decapitation is an idea of savagery defeating rationality, but the fact is that, under the conditions of war, no side can claim ethical superiority over any other. Violent images do, it is true, have a crude appeal in a work such as this, but Kingsley's careful handling of all such images provokes questions about the legitimacy and morality of military conduct.

The two sides of Kingsley – the enthusiast and the sceptic – are most apparent in his presentation of issues pertaining to gender. The noisy, masculine code of the book must imply a disdain for everything feminine. There is, consequently, much in the following tone: 'The Norse trader of those days... was none of the cringing and effeminate chapmen who figure in the stories of the middle ages' (p. 58). But the text also acknowledges that Hereward is a character with a 'boastful self-sufficiency... which bordered on the ludicrous' (p. 133), and, as such, is an embarrassment to his wife, Torfrida. Furthermore, as much as Hereward cultivates the role of the warrior, at significant moments his wife speaks on his behalf, and at the heart of the plot is the fact that he becomes obsessed with Alftruda; he appears, therefore, to be both foolish and dependent upon women. The novel acknowledges his bravery, but never hesitates to point out how inept he is in comparison with the disciplined King William. The effect, as in Ouida's *Under Two Flags*, is that a sense of the soldier's strength is repeatedly linked with a sense of his inadequacy. With a hero who is 'a broken man, querulous, peevish' (p. 399), Kingsley seems totally aware of the shortcomings of his military hero.

A similar sense of ludicrous energy without purpose runs through a number of works by the so-called Muscular Christian novelists. G.A. Lawrence's most popular novel was *Guy Livingstone*.[28] After a brief spell in the Household Brigade, Guy devotes himself to the life of an English squire. He is discovered, however, by Constance Brandon, to whom he is engaged, kissing another woman. Their engagement is terminated, and Guy embarks upon an orgy of dissipation in Paris. Constance and Guy are eventually reconciled as she lies on her deathbed. Guy himself dies when he is injured on the hunting field. As in Kingsley's novels, this is a hero with energy but little else; in the absence of a military conflict, where he would prove useful, he simply wastes his life flirting with, but ultimately depending upon, women. Lawrence, however, is a far simpler author than Kingsley. Lawrence seems to undercut himself without realising that he is doing so, whereas Kingsley has a degree of awareness of the limitations of a masculine code. In *Hereward the Wake*, this results in a novel that constructs both a defence and critique of militarism. But what we also encounter in Kingsley is an embryonic version of the rhetoric of race, empire and nation that will come to occupy a central role in literature by the end of the century.

THE SUDAN

Whereas enthusiasm for military matters is unusual in the liberal orthodoxy of mid-Victorian Britain, in the last twenty years of the century there is a remarkable revival of militarism. The obvious point at which to start considering this new mood is with the appearance of Jingoism in 1877–8. 'By jingo' had been in use since the seventeenth century as a phrase of emphasis, but it acquired its familiar associations in the chorus of music-hall song of 1878 supporting Disraeli's decision to send a British fleet into Turkish waters to deter Russian expansionism:

We don't want to fight, but by Jingo if we do,
We've got the ships, we've got the men, we've got the money too.
We've fought the bear before, and while Britons shall be true,
The Russians shall not have Constantinople.[29]

The significance of the song is indirectly illuminated in a comment by Peter Gay on the nature of the liberal temper:

The liberal temper notes, and does not lament, the many shades of gray that make up human experience. As the last trait to be developed – children, born conservative, are strangers to it – it is also the first to be set aside; not an attitude easily acquired, it is an attitude easily lost.

The liberal temper is so precarious because it is steadily under pressure from more primitive demands – for quick decisions, simple answers, forceful action, above all instant gratification. The threat – for most, the promise – of regression lurks everywhere. Most people find that hitting out, whether calculated or spontaneous, yields greater satisfactions than holding in, at least in the short run; smiting the other's cheek is more delightful than turning one's own.[30]

The words of the music-hall song provide a striking example of the desire for 'quick decisions, simple answers, forceful action, above all instant gratification'. The liberal voice, even in the last twenty years of the century, in fact turns out to be a lot more resilient than we might expect, but it is clear that the mere threat of war is enough to release aggressive impulses of which people may well have been unaware in calmer times.

The same is true during the period of the Crimean War, where we encounter belligerent and nationalistic songs that reveal the mood of the moment; songs such as 'England! Empress of the Sea!', 'England's Queen to England's Heroes', and 'England's patriotic appeal to her sons against the Russian despot, To Arms!'[31] There is, however, a difference between these songs and 'By Jingo'. The Crimean War songs proved ephemeral; they were soon forgotten. The durability of 'By Jingo' suggests that it might reflect a more fundamental cultural shift. Indeed, the song seems to become increasingly important as an expression of the national temper as the century moves towards its conclusion. Confirmation of this is to some extent provided by the fact that the Jingoism of

1878 disappeared as rapidly as it emerged. As Hugh Cunningham writes, 'The 1880 election seemed to put an end to Jingoism. The body politic appeared to have been cured, and until the late eigh-teen-nineties references to Jingoism were rare'.[32] The explanation for the sudden collapse of Jingoism after 1878 would seem to be that there was, in reality, nothing new at that time about the political situation or about the threat posed by the Russians. The Russians had always been a potential threat to India, and the old political order found no difficulty in coping with this possible, rather than real, enemy.

What the first wave of Jingoism seems to represent, therefore, is the emergence of a new attitude from the public, who sought a target for aggressive and nationalistic feelings. The emergence of this attitude indicates a new constituency making its presence felt, a broad section of the public granted a new awareness by the introduction of compulsory education, and who increasingly demanded a culture in tune with popular taste. 'By Jingo' conveys this new, direct and boisterous sentiment. But such thinking requires an enemy, a focus for both hostile and self-congratulatory feelings. The military story of the 1880s and 1890s becomes, there-fore, a story about a search for an enemy. Eventually, and almost preposterously, one is found in the Sudan.

The idea of seeking an enemy is neatly illustrated in an account of the military career of Frederick Burnaby. An 1870s portrait of Bur-naby, of the Horse Guards Blue, shows him reclining on a sofa, with waxed moustache and cigarette in hand; the picture conveys the bored manner of a mid-Victorian army officer.[33] It could serve as a portrait of Ouida's Bertie Cecil. What complicates the picture are some of the details of Burnaby's character. He was reputed to be the strongest man in the British army, and was also remarkably intelli-gent, with an exceptional gift for languages. This, however, only adds to the sense of a man lacking any purpose in his life. Burnaby joined the Blues in 1859, and travelled to the Sudan with General Gordon in 1875, the same winter journeying across the Russian steppes on horseback. In 1876–8 he travelled to Asia Minor and Armenia, producing *On Horseback Through Asia Minor*. In 1882 he crossed the channel to Normandy in a balloon.[34] There is, then, constant activity, but most of the time Burnaby is busy doing nothing. In his travel book, he tries to alert his readers to the danger the Russians represent, in particular drawing attention to their bestiality:

Circassian pregnant women cut to pieces! – does this go for nothing in the eyes of those gentlemen who called out for vengeance on the Circassians in Bulgaria? Circassian children butchered by Russian soldiery![35]

The problem with this, however, is that everything Burnaby says has an air of trying to make a little go a long way, as he uses isolated examples of Cossack brutality to condemn an entire nation. The weakness of his case becomes evident as he breaks into capital letters: 'BARBARITY, THE ATROCIOUS VILLAINY, I will call it, TO MURDER IN COLD BLOOD THE WOUNDED SOLDIERS'.[36] The impression is that Burnaby is desperately trying to create an enemy, an enemy that everyone else refuses to see.

For much of his career, therefore, Burnaby appears to be a gentleman playing a game, coming close to fighting but never actually encountering an enemy. It is the role an army officer is reduced to in a period of peace; he is an insignificant, almost superfluous, figure. Where this changes for Burnaby is with his death, fighting in the Sudan. At this point he becomes a hero, with his death – fighting the Mahdists in the square at Abu Klea – being commemorated in a number of contemporary prints.[37] More notably, it is the death of Burnaby that is referred to in the second verse of Henry Newbolt's 'Vitaï Lampada', a poem that is central in both reflecting and creating the new public attitude towards militarism in the late nineteenth century:

The sand of the desert is sodden red, –
    Red with the wreck of a square that broke; –
The Gatling's jammed and the Colonel dead,
    And the regiment blind with dust and smoke.[38]

Just as the Sudan eventually provided an enemy for Burnaby, it also proved central in establishing the rhetoric of Jingoism, as we see here. This is despite, or perhaps because of, the fact that Britain's involvement in the country was such a protracted and unsatisfactory business.

Following the Battle of Tel el Kebir in 1882, Britain dominated Egypt. The Mahdi Mohammed Ahmed, in the neighbouring Sudan, turned religious ferment into a military cause, initially leading skirmishes against the Egyptians, but then wiping out 10,000 Egyptian troops at El Obeid on 3 November 1883. The following

January, General Charles Gordon was sent by the British to evacuate Khartoum, but was besieged until, a year later, he and his garrison were massacred. Two days too late, a British relief expedition arrived. The Mahdi died in 1885, but the Mahdists maintained control of the country for ten years. In 1896, however, the British and the Egyptians decided to reconquer the Sudan. Under the leadership of General Kitchener, it took an Anglo-Egyptian army over two years to advance up the River Nile before eventually defeating the Sudanese army at Omdurman on 2 September 1898. For nearly two decades, therefore, this is a story of military embarrassments, yet to a remarkable extent these events in the Sudan provided a focus for public feeling in Britain.[39]

Why did the conflict create such a deep impression? The first point is that Britain had found an enemy at last, and an enemy that offered some resistance. Moreover, it was not one of Britain's traditional European enemies, but an enemy that could be regarded as barbaric. The protracted dispute became, therefore, a confrontation between civilisation and savagery, and also a confrontation between Christianity and Islam. Britain's role consequently acquired the overtones of a religious crusade. But what proved even more important was the sense of a situation that could not be controlled, where the English could not achieve their usual swift victory. The Indian Mutiny had also been interpreted in Britain as a confrontation with savagery, but order had been re-established quickly in India. The dispute in the Sudan, by contrast, dragged on, beginning to convey for the first time a sense of a new world order in which Britain was no longer the totally dominant force. The actual events in the Sudan were relatively unimportant for the British (both strategically and in terms of troop deployment), but what matters is the symbolic dimension, the way in which the conflict begins to reveal Britain's self-doubt. The bombast of Jingoism must, at least in part, be seen as a means of concealing a new sense of insecurity.

The sense of a changing order becomes clearer when we consider Gladstone's role in relation to the developments in the Sudan.[40] Gladstone's reluctance to commit troops is characteristic of the Liberals' lack of enthusiasm for imperial expansion. Gordon had been sent to the Sudan as a special representative of Britain; as his situation became desperate, the press and public became outraged at Gladstone's apparent willingness to leave him to his fate. It was August 1884 before a relief expedition was sanctioned. Gladstone's caution can be defended as commendably anti-imperialist, but what is also evident is that international tensions were developing in a way beyond the comprehension of the established liberal dispensation. This faltering of confidence stimulated the desire for new, and easy, answers. It is this desire for answers that leads to the period's need for heroes, for men who can unite the nation, producing a sense of coherence at a time when things are far from coherent. It is also possible to argue, however, that the emergence of heroes such as General Gordon indicates a fundamental ideological shift at the end of the century, something that is evident in the emergence of militarism in a new guise. Alfred Vagts, in his classic work *A History of Militarism*, published in 1937, describes a change at this time from the idea of an elite class as the functioning principle of militarism to a doctrine of race.[41] What gives the war in the Sudan its particular significance is that this conflict more than any other established this new version of militarism, together with its accompanying rhetoric of race, empire and nation.

We can see the emergence of this new stance in contemporary accounts of events in the Sudan. What is also clear, however, is that a liberal voice continues to be heard, even if it becomes progressively more muted as we approach the end of the century.[42] The persistence of a liberal view is one of the most notable features of E.A. De Cosson's *Days and Nights of Service with Sir Gerald Graham's Field Force at Suakin*, first published in 1886. In recent years this has been republished as *Fighting the Fuzzy-Wuzzy*, a title that is totally at odds with the tone of the work. One surprising thing about De Cosson's book is the respect he shows for his enemy, who are not represented as savage in any way. The sense that dominates is of a professional soldier respecting other soldiers, who are different but not inferior. De Cosson's stance is, however, most revealingly evident in his citation of George Eliot, who provides him with a philosophical perspective upon war:

'My mind', wrote one of our most thoughtful women-writers – George Eliot – 'is in this anomalous condition, of hating war and loving its discipline, which has been an incalculable contribution to the sentiment of duty.' And again, speaking of the men – 'the devotion of the common soldier to his leader – the sign for him of hard duty – is the type of all higher devotedness, and is full of promise to other and better generations.' Some such feeling of hatred for the horrors of war, and admiration for the qualities it brings out, must have struck every man who has seen a battle or a battlefield.[43]

The reflective thoughtfulness of De Cosson's memoir is not only striking in itself, but is also markedly different from the characteristically coarse accounts of events in the Sudan that were published in the 1890s.

The kind of steadying observation De Cosson offers is jettisoned in favour of a more aggressive political view. It is R. Slatin Pasha's *Fire and Sword in the Sudan* that provides the most intriguing illustration of this development, for this is a memoir where an overt political interpretation has been grafted on to the original manuscript.[44] Sir Rudolf Slatin, an Austrian by birth, had been kept in captivity in the Sudan, eventually escaping in 1895. His book is an account of his experiences. It had, however, been translated into English by F.R. Wingate, who worked from Slatin's notes.[45] Wingate was also the author of Father Don Joseph Ohrwalder's *Ten Years' Captivity in the Mahdi's Camp*, published in 1892: 'Having supervised the composition of Ohrwalder's German manuscript, he rewrote it in "narrative form" from a rough English translation made by a Syrian clerk'.[46] In addition to these works, under his own name Wingate published *Mahdism and the Egyptian Sudan* in 1891. As head of the Egyptian Intelligence Department, Wingate's primary concern in producing these works was to propagate a particular view of the events in the Sudan with the aim of maintaining British involvement. One aspect of this is that Wingate can be credited with inventing the story of the circumstances of General Gordon's death, in which Gordon was 'struck down unresisting by a wild but determined band of the followers of the Sudanese Mahdi . . . and that he met his fate resolutely and calmly, displaying to the end his moral superiority over his enemies'.[47]

More significant than the story itself, however, are the assumptions that inform Wingate's framing of the narrative, and which are pervasive in his translation of Slatin's book. Centrally, Gordon is presented as 'a symbol of the rightness and righteousness of imperialism',[48] a stance that demands that military action must be conceived in terms of a discourse of race:

> In the Sudan we have before us a terrible example of nascent and somewhat crude civilisation suddenly shattered by wild, ignorant, and almost savage tribes, who have built over the scattered

remnants a form of government based to some extent on the lines
they found existing, but from which they have eradicated almost
every symbol of right, justice, and morality, and for which they
have substituted a rule of injustice, ruthless barbarity, and
immorality.[49]

It could be argued that the initial responses to the Indian Mutiny
are expressed in the same terms, but whereas commentators at that
time groped towards an expression of their sense of outrage, in
Wingate's transformation of Slatin's notes an interpretation exists
quite independently of the events themselves, and is imposed upon
them.

The terms in which Wingate discusses his material makes the
concept of a superior civilisation absolutely central. The inevitable
consequence of introducing an analysis couched in these terms is
that, step by step, it becomes more openly abusive. This is evident
in G.W. Steevens's *With Kitchener to Khartum*, published at the end
of the century.[50] Steevens, who worked for the *Daily Mail*, and died
during the siege of Ladysmith, was a classical scholar. It is, however, hard to reconcile the view of Steevens as a man 'whose
literary talent and wit elevated the standard of writing'[51] with
remarks in his work such as, 'The way those niggers cried!', 'a
black can never be made to understand that a horse needs to be
groomed and fed', 'However old the black may be, he has the
curious faculty of always looking about eighteen', and 'They love
their soldiering, do the blacks'.[52] Racist language is, of course, used
in accounts of the Indian Mutiny, but what is different in Steevens's
work is the relentless consistency of this tone, something that is
integral to an analysis based upon race, empire and nation in which
every element seems to have been reduced to Jingo simplicity:
'Now that the long struggle is crowned with victory, we may
look back on those fourteen indomitable years as one of the highest
achievements of our race'.[53] What adds to the offensiveness is the
fact that this is written after the hostilities; a degree of excess might
be expected at a time of national tension, but Steevens maintains
his analysis even after the provocation has been removed.

In Steevens's work all the features of late nineteenth-century
imperialist militarism are in place: 'The Sudan must be ruled by
military law strong enough to be feared, administered by British
officers just enough to be respected'.[54] In just over twenty years,
therefore, the country has reconstituted the terms in which it

discusses military matters, the language of negotiation and compromise yielding to a discourse of confrontation and domination.
Quite simply, the politics of nationalism seem to have displaced the
politics of liberalism. Yet the issue is not as clear-cut as this. In the
next chapter, which focuses on Kipling, I examine the complexity
of the new militarism, and how it seems to disintegrate in the very
process of being put together. At this point, however, I want to look
at the problems involved in elevating Gordon to the role of military
and imperial hero.

GENERAL CHARLES GORDON

The liberal tradition is anti-heroic. By contrast, supporters of Jingoism are always seeking heroes who can provide an instant answer
to difficult problems, or, failing that, who at least die gloriously in
the attempt. In the last twenty years of the nineteenth century,
military leaders such as Gordon, Wolseley, Roberts, Kitchener
and Baden-Powell capture the imagination in an unprecedented
way. In part this can be related to the demand for popular reading
matter from a newly educated public, but it also arises from the
shift to a new politics of empire, race and nation; the new heroes
are, of course, heroes of the empire.[55] The most obvious literary
expression of this new enthusiasm for heroism is the huge expansion of juvenile literature from the 1870s onwards, in particular
adventure fiction for boys. As is the case in G.A. Henty's novels,
these stories are often set in the empire, making use of real incidents and celebrating the achievements of real military leaders.[56]
There was also a new emphasis to the history taught in schools; as
Graham Dawson points out, 'history was "brightened up" by
narratives of great men and women, with pride of place going to
war stories'.[57] Accounts of heroism appealed equally to an adult
audience, however, as can be seen in the virtual canonisation of
Gordon as the hero of the Sudan.

Charles George Gordon was born in 1833, the son of a lieutenant-
general in the Royal Artillery. He was commissioned into the Royal
Engineers in 1852, and subsequently saw service in the Crimea. In
1860 he took part in the Second Opium War in China, and was then
asked to head the 'Ever Victorious Army', a multi-national force
that helped dissolve the Taiping Rebellion. Back in England,
'Chinese' Gordon was appointed to supervise fort construction at

Gravesend. In the 1870s he was appointed Governor-General of the Sudan. Deeply religious, he considered his major task to be to wage a crusade against the slave trade. After resigning his Sudanese position in 1879, in quick succession he accepted posts in India, Mauritius, South Africa and the Congo. In 1884, however, he was persuaded to return to the Sudan. His mission was to evacuate Khartoum, but it was here that he was to die. Gordon's exploits in China had already made him famous, but it was the circumstances of his death in Khartoum that transformed him into a genuine national hero.[58]

A contemporary biography, Eva Hope's *Life of General Gordon*, published in 1885, begins to tell us about the late-Victorian image of the hero. Hope draws a moral lesson from Gordon's life:

> We may get from him, as from all good men and women, light to guide us in the formation of our characters, and the direction of our actions. To the young especially, who desired to make the best of their lives, an account of Gordon and his work cannot be other than useful; and if they stop to ask what has made him great, they will be able to discover in him the qualities out of which all heroes are made.[59]

For Hope, the qualities that all heroes share have a religious dimension: the Christian must accept the tasks that are assigned to him. Conveniently, the rhetoric of a religious crusade coincides with the idea of an imperial mission, enabling Hope to offer a moral justification of colonialism. There is, none the less, a sense of strain in her comment, something that is most evident in her desire to connect the exceptional individual and people in general. Essentially, she wants Gordon's exploits abroad to provide an example to those at home. It is a wish to connect domestic experience and military experience that is first given prominence in accounts of the life of Havelock, the hero of the Indian Mutiny, where, because of his social and religious background, the connection seems plausible. But in general, as we see in the conception of Ouida's Bertie Cecil, in Carlyle's vision of a hero, and Kingsley's picture of Hereward the Wake, the qualities associated with heroism are directly in opposition to the qualities prized in domestic life.

In the case of Gordon, the gap between domestic life and his life as a soldier is so extreme that even his contemporaries found it hard to ignore the awkward details in the heroic image. In recent years, as we might expect, attention has been paid to Gordon's sexual orientation, specifically his fondness for the company of young boys. Other imperial heroes from this period, in particular Cecil Rhodes and Baden-Powell, have been discussed in similar terms.[60] Speculation in this area is, however, generally fairly tedious. Sex at home and within marriage is sanctioned yet private; the majority who have chosen this option inevitably speculate about the sexual arrangements of the minority who have chosen a less secure course in life, particularly when these lives have become a form of public property. This is just one aspect of a late nine-teenth-century separation between the sphere of the home and the sphere of military activity. In a society where a liberal discourse of home is dominant, the individual who desires a life of adventure is seen to place himself outside this discourse of family, marriage and a domestic existence. It is, to a degree, a tension that is in evidence throughout the Victorian period. In the 1880s and 1890s, however, as the new discourse of empire becomes established, it seems more necessary to make a choice between these alternative approaches to life. The construction of Havelock's double-image, as both family man and soldier, a construction that seemed entirely appropriate in the late 1850s and 1860s, no longer seems either plausible or poss-ible at the end of the century. Gordon's career provides an extreme example of an inability to accept domestic security. He was for ever restlessly moving on from one post to another, never establishing roots, and always rejecting all forms of material reward. To some extent such energy is characteristic of the Victorian period as a whole, but it was often channelled into business or public life at home; in Gordon's case, however, his restless energy can find no outlet in Britain.

It could be argued that this is far from unusual, that heroes in general do not have much to do with the societies in which they live but to which they can scarcely be said to belong. But the division seems far more pronounced at the end of the century; there are those who stay at home, and there are those who, like Peter Pan, refuse to grow up, using the empire as their playground. The split reflects a fundamental tension in late nineteenth-century Britain between a liberal discourse, that continued to be of importance, and an opposed discourse of empire. The result is that, although militarism experi-ences a revival at the end of the century, it is an attitude that is consistently contested by those taking a different line.

Lytton Strachey, in his essay on Gordon in *Eminent Victorians*, still provides the best account of these divisions.[61] One feature of Strachey's method is to use other characters as foils to the principal subject of each biographical sketch. In the Gordon essay, the Mahdi is one of the most memorable characters; he is also an almost exact reflection of Gordon. Both men are driven by religion, both men are rebels, and both men are extremists. The leader of the Taiping rebels is presented in similar terms. But these rebel warriors live in societies that have nothing in common with nineteenth-century Britain. This is most obvious in the way that the Mahdi and the Chinese rebel leader can fundamentally affect the lives of their fellow countrymen; Gordon, equally committed to a personal vision, has no real effect upon the lives of the British. He becomes an elusive figure, either travelling the world, or, as in his fort-building at Gravesend, committing himself briefly to a domestic routine that is out of character. But there are also divisions within Gordon's personality; he is torn between his spiritual commitment and his life of action. His religious views are, however, baffling, for this is not a religion based upon humility but a religion of his own invention, the creation of a man with personal vanity and ambition, and a man who, for all his asceticism, is at the mercy of ungovernable passions.

The overall effect in Strachey's essay is that Gordon is presented as a slippery character, who evades capture and definition; just as he refused to be pinned down in one place, in a similar way he cannot be pinned down by his biographer. Gladstone, in the same essay, is presented in rather similar terms, as a character who evades comprehension:

> Did his very essence lie in the confusion of incompatibles? His very essence? It eludes the hand that seems to grasp it. One is baffled, as his political opponents were baffled fifty years ago.[62]

Sir Evelyn Baring, Consul General in Egypt, is almost equally elusive:

> His life's work had in it an element of paradox. It was passed entirely in the East; and the East meant very little to him; he took no interest in it.[63]

In the comment on Baring there is, however, this helpful direct contrast between home and abroad. The contrast brings into focus how the Victorians are caught between the safe and the unsafe, between security and danger. Baring, Gladstone and Gordon all fall into the same pattern of being a product of the contradictions of the Victorian period. It is an era that asks for conformity, duty and reasonableness, but which is also characterised by non-conformity, selfishness and excess. The mid-Victorian years manage to conceal the cultivation of extremes, but in the last twenty years of the century there is an unavoidable clash of conflicting values. As the next chapter will argue, Kipling's initial success was in large measure due to the fact that he managed to synthesise conflicting attitudes in the culture of his time, but even before the end of the century Kipling's synthesis began to disintegrate, as there was no way in which the insularity of liberalism could be genuinely reconciled with imperial aggression.

7

Kipling's Militarism

Rudyard Kipling is, without question, the most important writer on military matters in the Victorian period. Thackeray, his only real rival, might deal just as often with soldiers and soldiering, but Thackeray is always reflecting on a military order that belongs to the past, whereas Kipling writes of the present. There is, however, more to the issue than this, for Kipling's works define a mood for the 1890s; the central aspect of this is his reinvention of militarism. As I have argued in previous chapters, the Victorian period saw the disappearance of the military code of the Wellington era. The army might have continued to cling on to its traditional values, but these values meant little to the country at large.[1] In the 1880s, however, militarism began to re-emerge, but in a manner that was more often strident than coherent; for example, enthusiastic support for the British soldier abroad was not matched by any great enthusiasm for the army at home, or by any great readiness to pay for an effective army. The achievement of Kipling – or, at any rate, the achievement that makes him a key figure in the history of militarism – is that he re-establishes a link between the lives and values of the military and the lives and values of the people as a whole. Indeed, Kipling puts society back at one with the army for the first time since Waterloo.

In this respect, there is a world of difference between Kipling's militarism and the militarism evident in boys' adventure stories from the 1880s and 1890s.[2] G.A. Henty produced a much-repeated novel in which a young boy is involved in stirring military escapades, often in a colonial setting. Starting in 1868, Henty wrote over 100 novels, his contract with his publisher requiring him to produce three books a year. In the context of a tradition of juvenile literature, one of the distinctive qualities of Henty's works is that they abandon the kind of piety that is found in, for example, Thomas Hughes's *Tom Brown's Schooldays*, emphasising practical qualities of resourcefulness and leadership rather than the spiritual qualities of the hero. It is tempting to make a connection between the popularity of Henty's stories and the new emphasis on athleticism in Britain's public schools, and then to move on to the conclusion that the country was consumed by the idea of indoctrinating the young with military values.[3] But Henty catered for a specific audience; the failure of his novels directed at adults should give some indication of how limited his appeal, and real significance, was. He was not speaking to, or in any sense for, the whole country.

In fact, as with Carlyle and Kingsley, Henty is best seen as an oppositional figure, promoting a masculine code against what he would have construed as the effete character of the age. This was certainly the case at the beginning of his career in 1868. Unlike Carlyle and Kingsley, however, he did not remain an isolated voice: by the 1890s his novels constitute one element, along with Jingoism, new uniformed organisations, public parades and the cult of empire in a resurgence of militarism. But Henty's novels were just one aspect of a late-century culture that was pulled in a number of directions. Edward Said makes this point in writing about Kipling, that, in the 1890s, alongside a strain of thinking in which the emphasis was nationalistic and triumphalist, there existed a sombre stance:

> one way of grasping what is unusual about Kipling is to recall briefly who his contemporaries were. We have become so used to seeing him alongside Haggard and Buchan that we have forgotten that as an artist he can justifiably be compared with Hardy, Henry James, Meredith, Gissing, the later George Eliot, George Moore, or Samuel Butler... Yet the works of these writers are essentially novels of disillusion and disenchantment... Almost without exception the protagonist of the late nineteenth-century novel is someone who has realised that his or her life's project ... is mere fancy, illusion, dream.[4]

When we consider this broader picture, it seems inappropriate to talk too glibly about a new spirit of militarism creating a sense of national unity that transcended class, party and factional interests. Henty, in particular, seems a very small voice in a very big debate.

A sense of the confusion in values in this period is provided, perhaps surprisingly, by George du Maurier's best-seller from

1894, *Trilby*.[5] Like many popular novels, it captures the mood of its time by touching upon deep-seated anxieties. The plot concerns three British art students – Taffy, Sandy and Little Billee – and their life in Paris where they come in contact with Svengali who, through his hypnotic powers, has transformed the beautiful but tone-deaf Trilby into a famous singer. The novel explores a bohemian, and alien, world: Little Billee, in love with Trilby, is so shocked when she models naked that he leaves Paris. Svengali is, of course, a sinister foreigner with thoroughly unBritish powers. What is really odd in *Trilby*, however, is that the three British students who encounter this world are thoroughly old-fashioned; they appear as three gentlemen out of their depth. Taffy is an ex-soldier: for three years he had

> borne Her Majesty's commission, and had been through the Crimean campaign without a scratch. He would have been one of the famous six hundred in the famous charge at Balaklava but for a sprained ankle (caught playing leap-frog in the trenches), which kept him in hospital on that momentous day.   (p. 5)

This, we are meant to believe, is a character who discovers that he has 'an irresistible vocation for art' (p. 5). In Paris, however, a typical 'afternoon was healthily spent in athletic and gymnastic exercises till dinner-time' (p. 21).

The impression, inevitably, is of three silly public schoolboys caught up in the decadent 'nineties; their caricatured values do not seem to equip them for the world as it actually exists. The implications of this are taken further when the novel touches on the subject of Jingoism. Little Billee visits a music-hall in London where a song, sung with 'a good rolling jingo bass', reflects the 'manly British pluck that found expression in these noble sentiments'. In the next sentence, however, the impression is of 'swaggering, blatant and idiotically aggressive vulgarity!' (pp. 142–3). The ambiguity of the response reflects a general uncertainty that permeates the novel. It is as if, both at home and abroad, the characters find themselves in situations where traditional points of reference have disappeared; consequently, they cling on to the manly image of the British character. In the music-hall, however, Billee encounters an attitude that in some ways overlaps with his own sense of national identity, but which also seems frighteningly unfamiliar.

The extraordinary achievement of Kipling in the 1890s is that he unites such divergent strands, bringing them together in a vision of militarism that, for a brief moment, seemed to appeal to the whole country. Kipling for a short period, and even though there were hostile critics, seems to speak in a national voice and for the nation. This is, however, an illusion, for the splintering of culture towards the end of the century is absolute. Even by the end of the 1890s, Kipling's voice sounds narrow and factional. But for a brief moment at the start of the decade he seems to offer a coherent vision that can displace the old liberal consensus. Joseph Bristow writes about Kipling's awareness of 'the considerable inconsistencies in British national identity', and how it was Kipling's 'lifetime labour to devise narrative strategies both to observe and resolve these differences in order to create a strong imperial culture'.[6] It is the importance of Kipling's version of militarism in resolving, by obscuring, these inconsistencies in the national identity that I consider in this chapter.

KIPLING'S SOLDIERS

At the heart of Kipling's early stories – those tales that first appeared in England towards the end of the 1880s – is his reinvention of an aristocratic military code for a democratic age. Essentially, he takes the aristocratic code, puts it in the mouths of working-class soldiers, and sells the illusion to a middle-class audience. There has never been a clearer case of the right author with the right material at the right time. A great deal of Victorian literature implicitly rejects chivalric standards, heroic endeavour and the culture of the soldier. It can even be argued that such a rejection of a military code is inevitable in novels, given that the genre focuses upon individuals in conflict with society rather than one society in conflict with another. It is certainly the case that when John Ruskin criticises Cervantes, he focuses upon a way of looking that is determined by the form as much as by the individual author. Cervantes, as a novelist:

> most helped forward the terrible changes in the soldiers of Europe, from the spirit of Bayard to the spirit of Bonaparte, helped to change loyalty into licence, protection into plunder, truth into treachery, chivalry into selfishness.[7]

Ruskin himself is a representative of a contradictory strand in Victorian thinking, the strand that revered, and sought to revive, an old chivalric order. Mark Girouard has explored this aspect of Victorianism in *The Return to Camelot*, but it must be stressed that such thinking had very little to do with the real world of the nineteenth century, representing no more than a desire to escape from the present.[8] Kipling, however, engages in a far more complex reconsideration of the aristocratic military code, adapting and repositioning traditional values to make them relevant to the modern age.

At the centre of the aristocratic military code is the duel. It is a duel, or form of duel, that features in one of Kipling's most effective stories, 'His Private Honour'. This is one of a number of stories featuring three regular soldiers: Mulvaney, Ortheris and Learoyd. 'His Private Honour', from Kipling's fourth collection, *Many Inventions* (1893), focuses upon the events that ensue after Ortheris is struck on parade by a young officer, Ouless.[9] Ortheris broods over his lost honour as a soldier. The problem is resolved when Ouless suggests that, out of the public eye, they settle the matter with a fist fight. This is a traditional duelling story in that an affront to a man's reputation can only be settled by a private confrontation. It is an untraditional story in that Ortheris is only a private soldier: a duel should take place between social equals. But the essence of the story is that Ortheris has absorbed the military code of his social superiors. This is the pattern of all the stories about the three soldiers: they always act in accordance with the values of the traditional military code. Even in Thackeray this code is seen as belonging to the past, but in Kipling it is revived. We can see this in the way that 'His Private Honour' excludes other means of resolving the argument. When Thackeray presents a duel, he always makes it clear that it is a dispute about nothing or a dispute that could be settled in another manner. But in 'His Private Honour' there is no alternative solution:

> I was speculating whether Ouless had sent money to Ortheris, which would have been bad, or had apologised to him in private, which would have been worse, or had decided to let the whole affair slide, which would have been worst of all   (p. 121)

It is clear that Kipling's story has been constructed in support of an idea of honour that makes all three of these reasonable options seem unreasonable.

There is, in fact, another possibility open to Ortheris, which would be to report Ouless for misconduct. Indeed, the point of the story could be that Ortheris, by not reporting the officer, shows himself to be the better man. But that would be to move the story into an area where the decision is made by the individual, rather than the individual acting in accordance with a code. Kipling makes it plain that Ortheris has rights when he is struck (Ouless, if charged, would lose his commission), but, in refusing to report Ouless, Ortheris shows his indifference to the kind of contractual relationship that had developed in the Victorian period. The military code of honour is preferable. The effect is to revitalise this code, extending it beyond the military elite. It becomes a scheme of values relevant to all ranks. In addition, the code not only seems appropriate in the army, but also, by implication, comes to be seen as a straightforward code that is relevant in civilian life. In order to make the tale work as he wants, however, Kipling has to indulge in some strategic engineering: as unlikely as it may seem, the young officer is made the victor in the fight. The story is, therefore, both democratic and conservative: the common soldier takes on board the values of those who remain his superiors.

In a story such as this, Kipling clearly strikes a chord with the society of his day, appealing to a resurgent conservative spirit, but his unique ability is to gauge a mood and then take it a step further, converting a feeling into a coherent philosophy. The resurgent conservatism of late-Victorian Britain is largely based upon a sense of threat, both an external threat and a perceived internal threat from an expanding working class. Part of the project of the soldier stories becomes, therefore, to calm such fears, particularly fears about disturbance from below. The shrewdest, and politically most significant, move in the stories about Mulvaney, Ortheris and Learoyd is to take three potentially awkward characters – an Irishman, a Cockney, and a northerner – and then make them spokesmen for a set of shared national values. This is happening shortly after uniformed organisations (specifically, the Salvation Army, the Church Army and the Boys' Brigade) had been established.[10] As against an emphasis on individual choice, in Kipling's stories and in the new uniformed organisations, people are offered a rigid structure that only permits freedom of action in ways that are centrally sanctioned. Essentially, the rights of the individual are sacrificed in favour of the standards established in the received military code.

This is apparent when the three soldiers speak. As an Irishman, a Cockney and a northerner, their language might exhibit genuine variety; a polyphonic medley of accents could express points of view that are at odds with or dissent from any notion of a norm. The reality, however, is that the voices of the three soldiers are orchestrated; they speak in a way that Kipling controls rigidly, saying what they are required to say. Indeed, Kipling's control over class and regional divergence is overwhelming. And not just control of their speech. The three soldiers are allowed moments of madness, days when they get drunk or break the rules, but there is a far greater stress on their loyalty. A central point is made over and over again: 'A recruit must learn first that he is not a man but a thing, which in time, and by the mercy of Heaven, may develop into a soldier of the Queen if it takes care and attends to good advice' (p. 110). Such incidental comments contribute to Kipling's overall social philosophy, in which military values are shown to be relevant in every area of life. Every element of the stories contributes to this end, but the cleverest stroke is undoubtedly the way in which Kipling puts words into the mouths of his common soldiers so that they become spokesmen for the military code as an expression of common-sense values.

The extent of the impact of this becomes evident in the way that life began to imitate art. Sir George Younghusband drew attention to the way in which, in his youth, he had never heard the words and expressions used by Kipling's soldiers, but several years later, 'the soldiers thought, and talked, and expressed themselves exactly like Rudyard Kipling had taught them in his stories'.[11] This is not just the adoption of a manner of speech; it is an internalisation of the values implicit in this way of speaking. It seems to be around this time that the ordinary soldier took on board, rather than just giving lip service to, a positive idea of his role, and this in turn led to a change in the public perception of the soldier, who ceased to be a rogue in uniform and became a figure to be admired. It can, of course, be argued that such changes would have taken place even if Kipling had never written a word, or that Kipling himself is merely a symptom of, rather than an instigator of, change, but the overwhelming impression is that Kipling is not only the spokesman for but also, in large measure, the creator of these new attitudes. Music-hall songs might have lavished praise on the common soldier, but that is not the same thing as Kipling's success in making military values seem like core values for the nation as a whole.

Remarkably, he did not have to work out this stance; it is a position that is instinctively grasped from the moment the tales began to appear, the three soldiers making their first appearance in 'The Three Musketeers' in *Plain Tales from the Hills* in 1888.[12] The soldier stories in this volume are, however, fairly simple.

By contrast, in *Soldiers Three*, his second collection, which also appeared in 1888, a comprehensive social agenda seems to be wrapped up in the stories.[13] The opening story, 'The God From the Machine', takes place at a regimental ball in India, a ball that in some ways echoes the famous ball on the eve of Waterloo that is featured in *Vanity Fair*, raising similar questions about military and social discipline. On this occasion, however, the focus is on the ordinary soldiers who are permitted to attend. Mulvaney tells a story about a colonel's daughter and her relationship with a disreputable captain; their plan to elope was foiled by Mulvaney. As always, the incident is trivial, the effectiveness of the story lying entirely in the manner of the narration. Initially this appears embarrassing, because of Kipling's handling of a regional accent. The effect can seem like a caricature, and in a sense it is. Yet, at the same time, the essence of the story is that the central proposition, about maintaining good order, is reflected in Mulvaney's actions but even more so in the words he uses. The surface mannerisms of his speech might differ from standard English, but at a deeper level, particularly in his sensitivity to questions of reputation, he shares the same values as his officers. Indeed, he is superior to some officers, such as the disreputable captain, in his respect for a code of conduct.

Another way in which Kipling demonstrates the idea of officers and the men sharing values is in his handling of episodes that involve alcohol. The soldiers at the ball, with their flutes of champagne, resemble their commanding officers. They can also maintain a gentleman's standard of behaviour; they get drunk at times, but are always capable of sobering up when required to do so. It is through such gestures that Kipling by-passes class tensions. The soldiers might appear rough, and their speech might sound rough, but the differences are only on the surface. In terms of rank, the soldiers are approximately the equivalent of Sergeant Troy, in Hardy's *Far From the Madding Crowd*, but they would be the first to find fault with him. All these points are evident in 'The Big Drunk Draf'', another story in which Mulvaney supports the existing order.[14] A group of soldiers about to return home from India is drunk and undisciplined. It is an unusual situation, where the soldiers' usual standard of self-discipline has lapsed, and, as a result, their young officer has little idea how to handle them. At the behest of Mulvaney, an insubordinate soldier is punished; another soldier, who protests that the punishment breaks army regulations, is then also punished. At this point the rest of the soldiers fall into line, and the young officer will have no further problems, either now or later in his career.

Mulvaney in this story is, in fact, no longer a soldier, but back in India as a civilian. He has, however, retained his fondness for good order, and appreciates that a distinction needs to be drawn between what is stated in regulations and what people know about an unwritten code; regulations defend the rights of the individual, but the military code Mulvaney has absorbed is more important in maintaining a general standard of discipline in life. By making the Irishman Mulvaney the spokesman for, and enforcer of, this code, we are led to believe that social values are not imposed from above but are a matter of enlightened self- interest. The illusion Kipling creates is that these values emanate from ordinary people because they are so thoroughly embedded in the everyday language of the rank and file of the army, or those who have been shaped by the army.

The effect is all the more powerful because the stories seem to provide a solution to the sense of sombre disillusion that is so widespread in the 1890s. These early stories from Kipling offer a military structure with implications for society as a whole, as they offer an alternative to an excessive, even self-pitying, emphasis upon the self. When Mulvaney leaves the army, there is a feeling of emptiness in his life. This is the natural reaction of anyone who has spent his entire working life in uniform, but Kipling manages to convince us not only of the security provided by a military structure but also its relevance even for those who have never been in the army. Part of the secret is that Kipling pays consider- able attention to the complex personalities of his three soldiers; they are introspective and alienated men, as introspective and alienated as any of the characters in late-Victorian fiction. Any other military writer might simply propose the army as the remedy for such malaise, but Kipling understands the continuing sense of alienation of his soldiers; these are men with dark, bitter or resigned feelings who, more by accident than design, have found themselves in the army. The army provides them with a sense of security and identity, but this co-exists with continuing anxieties about their lives and identities. The stories, as such, provide far more than a straightforward conservative social message; they offer a complex response to the questions about the self that are so central in the literature of the time.

We can see this in 'On Greenhow Hill', from *Life's Handicap* (1891).[15] Learoyd, the soldier from Yorkshire, recalls the time when he joined the Primitive Methodists because of his love of a young woman. His rival in love was the minister, a man Learoyd was tempted to murder. The young woman marries neither of them, however, for she goes into a decline and dies. Learoyd's despair leads to his decision to enlist. The story is told to Mulvaney and Ortheris as they lie in wait for a native deserter who, at the end of the story, Ortheris shoots. It would be wrong to impose too formulaic an interpretation on this multi-faceted story, but it is illuminating to consider its ending, and what this suggests about the relationship between work and private life:

> 'That's a clean shot, little man,' said Mulvaney.
> Learoyd thoughtfully watched the smoke clear away. 'Happen there was a lass tewed up wi' him, too,' said he.
> Ortheris did not reply. He was staring across the valley, with the smile of the artist who looks on the completed work. (p. 84)

The way in which Kipling employs a frame story to surround the central anecdote always creates a tension between the outer structure and the story within. Each story, consequently, becomes an investigation of the ways in which the language and structure of a literary text work to control chaos. In 'On Greenhow Hill', the final lines of the story elevate 'work' above all other considerations; provocatively, Kipling talks about the artistry of killing, as if work can thrive quite independently of human considerations. The inner story and the frame story together, however, explore the gulf between the structure provided by the army and the presence of personal feelings. The frame, in which Learoyd speaks intimately to his two friends, conveys the sense of comradeship and a common purpose that is found in the army, but this cannot erase continuing individual feelings of pain, loss and isolation.

We see this again in all the stories which, while conveying the vigour of Mulvaney's story-telling, also indicate his black moods. The army provides a kind of answer to depression, but depression never goes away, and Kipling returns to it repeatedly. In most adventure stories, the hero has an Achilles' heel, one area in which he is vulnerable, but this is usually precisely defined and limited in significance. In Kipling it is a much more pervasive sense of psychological unease. It is the presence of such elements that makes for the plausibility and complexity of Kipling's new vision of militarism. If Thackeray's novels indicate how difficult it was for his generation to abandon the precepts of a military culture, Kipling's stories illustrate the range of considerations involved in reconstructing militarism. Kipling has to formulate a position that responds to, rather than just providing an alternative to, all the tensions of the 1890s. In the case of most authors, it would be an exaggeration to say that their ideas made a profound impression on their contemporary audience; with Kipling, however, it is different. This was the most popular author since Dickens, making an immediate impact in a way that even Dickens could not match. There were, from the beginning, dissenting voices, but the over-whelming sense at the start of the 'nineties is that Kipling, with his reinvented militarism that makes a coherent whole out a mixture of anxieties, is saying something really important to his first audience.[16]

KIPLING'S MEN AND WOMEN

There is something touching about the details of the school Kipling attended. The United Services College had been established in 1878, primarily 'to get the sons, including a high proportion of the less bright or the more refractory sons, of retired officers into the military academies of Sandhurst or Woolwich'.[17] It was located in a terrace of seaside houses at Westward Ho! Kipling started as a pupil in 1882, and throughout his life valued what he had learned there:

> he saw it as an institution which had taught him how to live closely with the world of action and still be himself. And he rightly thought that his great distinction from most other (certainly English) writers of genius was this close relation to the world of action. With this high sense of what the United Services College had done for him, he came to draw from what he learned there a general recipe for life, especially for the life of men of action themselves.[18]

Yet the curious thing about the United Services College is that it was an imitation of a public school rather than the real thing, with a very circumscribed view of its function. It appealed to army officers who could not afford the fees of established schools. Unexpectedly, the headmaster, Crom Price, was a man with radical political views, in all probability an anti-imperialist even as he educated young men for a career in the army.

It is facts such as these that first lead one to realise that Kipling's militarism, as powerful and influential as it proved, was a fabrication, a copy of an earlier idea, reworked to give it a new practical relevance, but flawed because of the existence of other points of view even at its very heart. The early stories offer a seductive impression of coherence, reconnecting the army with the public at large, but if one looks a little more closely the stories fall apart. Even India is part of the illusion. India enabled a man to play a role, that of soldier or gentleman, that he could not play at home. Moreover, India (leaving aside the aberration of the Indian Mutiny) was a safe and familiar military location. In the Sudan the British army encountered an enemy that frustrated and thwarted its efforts. In India, however, the established military order could sustain and renew itself, despite the fact that the army was imposed upon India with no real support from the country in which it had located itself.

Given these circumstances, Kipling has to engage in a great deal of tactical manoeuvring to defend his military position. We have already seen how, in relation to the issue of class, he moves to incorporate the ordinary soldier into his military code. He is equally shrewd on matters of race. It is, of course, easy to attack Kipling's racism, but it is more interesting to consider the astuteness with which he acknowledges questions of race, allowing India enough difference to be different, with a culture and identity of its own, while never relinquishing his sense of British superiority or his view that the British military presence in India is essential. It is, therefore, the case that Kipling has covered the most obvious lines of attack: the ways in which his military philosophy is vulnerable on matters of class and race. His unprotected flank, however, is gender. The central difficulty he faces is defending the male culture of the army in a society that has moved in new directions, a society that sees men in uniform as the exception, and which is heavily committed to the domestic order of home and family. The answer an author such as G.A. Henty arrives at is to ignore the existence of women (with the exception of mothers), but Kipling is more than a mere writer of adventure stories. He appeals to a broader constituency than Henty, and has to offer a more ambitious set of ideas.[19] But it is always the case that when women appear in Kipling's stories there is a sense of strain; similarly, there are numerous moments where the characteristics of a male culture appear alarming.

I started the previous section with 'His Private Honour', which is nearly entirely coherent as a story. One reason for this is that it almost totally excludes women characters: the only reference is a brief comment about Ouless's mother. The story, as such, has a self-enclosed quality, with values operating as they should in a closed male environment. There is, however, one awkward aspect to the story, when Ortheris takes out his anger on another soldier:

> Samuelson, whom Ortheris bullied disgracefully. If the Jew opened his mouth in the most casual remark Ortheris would plunge down it with all arms and accoutrements, while the barrack-room stared and wondered. (p. 121)

This is the institutionalised racism of all uniformed organisations, where the sense of shared identity and shared values is maintained by identifying certain members of the group as less than full members. In a self-enclosed world there is a generalised contempt for all outsiders, but there is also a need to find targets closer to home. Yet there is a sense in which it is not so much a racial issue here as a gender issue, that a soldier can only assert his masculine identity through aggression.

The difficult question, however, is how we respond to Kipling's inclusion of this detail in the story. Up to a point, Kipling is obviously characterising Ortheris's behaviour as disgraceful. The scene can, therefore, be read as a critique of a masculine culture; that the complement of an honest fight is toleration of bullying and violence. More generally, it is often the case in the stories that Kipling's promotion of a military culture has a nervous edge, in that he sees the limitations of a code built upon aggression. Yet, at the same time, Kipling seems to present scenes such as Ortheris's bullying of Samuelson provocatively, with an air of 'this is how life is, and only sentimental liberals would quarrel with the facts'. He even seems to enjoy bullying, seeing it as an intrinsic aspect of maleness; he certainly delights in overstepping the mark, offering incidents that challenge the more delicate feelings his audience could be expected to have. All of these issues are apparent in 'The Incarnation of Krishna Mulvaney', another story about the 'three men who loved each other so greatly that neither man nor woman could come between them'.[20] The plot involves Mulvaney impersonating, and being taken for, the God Krishna. At first it might seem difficult to establish a connection between this esoteric story and the references to the bond between the three men. The connection, however, would seem to be a matter of questions of ritual, contest and unusual rites.

The story starts with a fight, but a fair fight, between Mulvaney and Dearsley, a white man who has been exploiting coolies. On leave, Mulvaney visits Dearsley; Dearsley gets him drunk and puts him on a train in order that Mulvaney will be punished as a deserter. This strange behaviour – fighting, a drinking contest, cruel pranks, indifference to the fate of the victim – is offered to us as typical of soldiers' lives. The rituals of male behaviour seem, in fact, to amount to little more than friends and enemies, and fighting and drink. It appears, however, that Kipling approves of all this: it overlaps with the world of the school, the world of secret societies, and organisations such as the Freemasons, all of them the kind of closed male societies that Kipling loved. This behaviour is contrasted with the kind of superstitious belief that can mistake Mulvaney for a god. The effect is disturbing: the sense of a difference between east and west, between advanced and primitive societies, breaks down. Indeed, it is the west that seems to have the stranger rituals and to be more primitive. This creates an ambivalent impression, both here and in other stories: Kipling has an instinctive grasp of the deep structure of army life, the aggression that binds men together in friendship, but this military culture is both defended and derided.

Sometimes Kipling did not get the balance right, and at such times self-censorship was brought into play. Some of his Indian stories were never published in Britain, including 'his most gratuitously brutal story, "The Likes of Us", a tale of self-righteous army bullying'.[21] Other stories, however, are nicely poised between pride in and embarrassment at the convictions that inform the life of a soldier. This is the unique quality of Kipling: other novelists might write about the army, but Kipling understands the army at a different level. We might balk at the way in which, late in the nineteenth century, Kipling lauds something primitive, but the shrewdness lies in his grasp of the psychology of being a soldier. As repellent as the stories are to the majority of modern readers, they all reveal an understanding of the thought processes of men of action in a way that is very unusual in English literature. In Kipling, we seem to get inside the minds of people who would rather act than put their feelings into words. The unfamiliarity of this stance, however, together with Kipling's awareness of how it is contentious, invests all the stories with a strange, appalling yet enticing, quality.

The tensions are always most apparent when women are given a prominent role. It is easy to understand why: it is in such stories that masculinity is put on trial, tested, and found wanting. Sometimes this testing assumes a bizarre form. In 'His Wedded Wife', a subaltern newly arrived from England achieves revenge on a senior subaltern, who bullies him, by disguising himself as a woman and passing himself off as the abandoned wife of the senior subaltern, who is engaged to be married. When his triumph is complete, the young subaltern reveals his true identity.[22] It is a comic story, but it raises serious issues; in particular, the subaltern's bullying is seen to be entirely consistent with his sexual predatoriness. This aggressive, careless and selfish version of maleness is undermined by the cross-dressing subaltern, who, through mockery, questions the assumptions behind accepted forms of behaviour. Indeed, there comes a point at which the male feels more threatened by women than by the enemy or other men. The soldier's life is built upon conflict and conquest, but the woman (and, even more obviously, the man dressed as a woman) does not observe the established rules of conflict.

Kipling returns to the role of women in 'The Courting of Dinah Shadd', where Mulvaney speaks of his relationship with Dinah.[23] It is a relationship that is almost wrecked by his folly in flirting with another woman. Dinah, however, forgives Mulvaney. The complication is that the other woman's mother curses Mulvaney and Dinah. Mulvaney feels that the curse has been cruelly effective in that they have lost their only child. 'The Courting of Dinah Shadd' is a story in which we see the central male character as exposed and vulnerable, dependent upon women, and incapable of reconciling a male code of conquest with the demands of domestic existence. Unlike a story such as 'The Madness of Private Ortheris', where a depressed Ortheris is talked out of his decision to desert by his two friends, in 'The Courting of Dinah Shadd' male support

counts for nothing.[24] The story does, it is true, begin with several
pages of male camaraderie, but as Mulvaney starts to tell his story
Ortheris leaves and Learoyd falls asleep. The narrator is listening,
but essentially it is a story told in isolation. And, at the end,
Mulvaney is totally alone: 'lonely as Prometheus on his rock, with
I know not what vultures tearing his liver' (p. 65). During the
course of the story, the code of the soldier is exposed as inadequate,
a fact that is evident in just about every detail. For example,
Mulvaney has fought another man for Dinah's favours, but this is
no different from the aggressive concept of conquest that leads him
to flirt with, with a view to conquering, the other young woman in
the story. It is also very apparent that when his child dies, the
fraternal support of his colleagues counts for nothing.

Kipling returns to his questioning of the military code in 'Love-
o'-Women', where Mulvaney tells the story of Tighe, an unscrupul-
ous seducer.[25] He serves in the ranks even though he is a gentleman, but a gentleman who heartlessly abandons the women he has
seduced. He finally begins to feel remorse, but by this time knows
that he is dying. He encounters an old woman friend again and
discovers that, after he had abandoned her, she turned to prostitu-
tion. He dies in her arms and she kills herself. This is another story
about how the soldier's need for military conquest runs in tandem
with a need for sexual conquest. As such, it reveals an unpalatable
truth, the dark secret that a soldier might prove a dangerous misfit
in society. Tighe, as a gentleman-ranker, has lost contact with the
disciplines and restraints of the social group to which he belongs.
In their place, the army not only provides him with an opportunity
to indulge himself but also, because of its code of conflict and
conquest, actively encourages such behaviour. There is, of course,
a strict code of discipline in the army, but it operates on a selective
basis, demanding uniformity but turning a blind eye to excesses
that would be unacceptable in civilian life. All these issues are
present in 'Love-o'-Women', but what makes it so impressive as a
story is that it never appears to know which way to turn: it wavers
between being moral, being sentimental, and facing up to the issue
of sexuality. In particular, the story is permeated by an awareness
of behaviour that defies the limits of military order, but which is
given an unique opportunity to flourish within the distinctive
atmosphere of army life. What is true of this story is true generally
of the early stories: in the very act of constructing military life as a
model for society as a whole, Kipling is simultaneously aware that

the aggressive assumptions about life that underlie militarism are totally at odds with the standards that apply in civilian life. At the start of the 'nineties he is able to control the contradiction, but as the decade develops a sense of strain becomes more and more evident in his work.

KIPLING AND THE NOVEL

In 1859, the Scottish historian and literary critic David Masson produced a study of English prose fiction, *British Novelists and Their Styles*. In his final chapter he classifies the novels of his own time. He identifies 'thirteen distinct varieties of the British novel', including, as types nine and ten, the Military Novel and the Naval Novel:

> the first represented in such stories of military life and adventure as those of Mr Gleig, Mr Maxwell, Mr Lever, and, more incidentally, in parts of Thackeray's fictions; the second in the sea-stories of Captain Marryat, Captain Chamier, Mr James Hannay, Mr Cupples, and others.[26]

Masson then goes on to write, however, about the fact that the most typical novel of his time is an education novel, a novel about 'the formation of character and the progress of an individual mind through doubt and error'.[27] One version of this, according to Masson, is the kind of novel where the hero or heroine finally arrives at Christian certainty, but increasingly there are novels that do not offer an answer, novels that 'confine themselves merely to a statement of the question. The perpetual knocking at the unopened door – such is their image of human life'.[28]

Masson is writing about the change I have discussed in the earlier chapters of this book, the shift from traditional forms such as the military novel towards fiction that privileges the experience of individuals. Indeed, it can even be argued that some time in the 1850s it ceased to be possible to write a credible military novel because ideas about the individual and his or her relationship to society had changed so much. It is, therefore, hard to conceive how, later in the century, there could be a revival of military fiction; a novel reflects the dominant forms of thinking and feeling within society, and from about 1850 onwards the new forms of thinking and feeling were incompatible with the assumptions that inform military fiction. Quite simply, therefore, how could a credible military novel re-emerge in late nineteenth-century Britain? Adventure stories, such as those by Henty, serve only to draw attention to the problem. Henty does not venture beyond providing a fantasy for a specific audience, whereas a genuine military novel would have to appeal to a far wider audience.

It is arguable that we have to wait until the twentieth century for the military novel, or the war novel as it comes to be known, to be revitalised. The First World War, and the experience of conscription and mass mobilisation, created a situation where people had to consider how they were pulled between the demands of military service and the different values of civilian life; characteristically, the twentieth-century war novel is most likely to feature civilians who find themselves in uniform for the first time. If anyone in the late nineteenth century could, however, have been expected to revive the military novel it should have been Kipling. But Kipling found it difficult to make the move from stories to a novel. There is no way of ignoring the fact that his first novel, arguably his only attempt at a mainstream novel, *The Light That Failed* (1891), is disappointing.[29] It concerns Dick Heldar and Maisie, middle-class orphans boarded out with a Mrs Jennett. Strong-willed characters, they forge a lifelong bond. As a man, Dick becomes a war artist, recording the campaign in the Sudan. Returning to London, he becomes a successful painter, and lodges with a fellow war reporter, Torpenhow. The carefree life of the two young men is interrupted when Dick meets Maisie again. She too is now an artist, although Dick has little respect for her work. They renew their relationship, but at her insistence it remains a purely professional connection. An old battle wound causes Dick gradually to lose his sight; to win Maisie, he creates an ambitious painting, but it is destroyed by the jealous model who sat for it. Dick offers the canvas – now just a mess of paint, although he is unaware of this – to Maisie, but she leaves his life for ever. Discovering what has happened, Dick makes his way to Egypt, where he is shot by an enemy sniper and dies in Torpenhow's arms.

The sense of strain evident in *The Light That Failed* reflects the fundamental difficulty Kipling has in trying to reconcile his military vision with other elements in late nineteenth-century life. The problem is, in part, one of form. Whereas in a short story it is possible to create a finely poised tension, in a protracted work the weight of detail is likely to overwhelm any sense of a central proposition. As we saw in the previous section of this chapter, Kipling in his stories can maintain the case for militarism at the same time as he exposes the shortcomings of militarism. *The Light That Failed* tackles the same tensions that appear in the stories, but it cannot maintain their fine focus. The basic division in the novel is that a man who is involved in a life of action is also considered in a domestic context, as the suitor of Maisie. Dick is, however, only a pseudo-soldier, a war artist not an active participant, and his relationship with Maisie is also less than the real thing.

It is tempting to see something of Kipling himself here, an artist parasitically dependent upon the lives of soldiers, who, despite the fact that he is only an observer, is so committed to this male culture that he is never at ease with domesticity, in particular always in awe of women. The early short stories are capable of creating a feeling of synthesis – that military and civilian life echo each other – but in *The Light That Failed* there is only a feeling of being in limbo, of being fatally caught between two extremes. In the short stories the female characters question the assumptions of the military culture, but in the brief compass of a short story this can be strictly controlled. Maisie, by contrast, who is generally agreed to be an example of the 'new woman' of the late-Victorian period, has a substantial role in the novel and, in becoming more than a pawn in a tightly regulated exercise, offers a real challenge to male hegemony.[30] This need not be a problem. It could, indeed, be the making of the novel: *The Light That Failed* could examine the gulf between two aspects of late nineteenth-century life. It could, in fact in many ways it does, raise questions about the relationship between the male culture of war and imperial expansion and a female culture of the home and domestic concerns. The problem, however, is that Maisie cannot be contained; in terms of her personal ambition, her success in her chosen career, and her wish to preserve her independence she challenges the male on his own territory. But when he sets a new vision of female militancy against the male preserve of the military, Kipling seems to unnerve himself with the character he has created: the novel lapses into a torrent of abuse against women.

The shortcomings of Kipling's first novel add to our sense of how the early stories work. The small canvas of a short story permits an extraordinary degree of authorial control; opposed positions can be expressed, but ultimately everything is part of an overall pattern. This formal discipline is echoed in the content of the stories. They are set in India which, for the British, is a closed society. Challenges from the indigenous population can be introduced into the stories, but the controlling authority is always strong enough to subdue all disruptive elements. *The Light That Failed*, as a novel, cannot maintain the same tight control. In particular, Kipling does not seem capable of controlling Maisie, the character he has created. Consequently, the novel abuses women, and also offers a quite absurd representation of the importance of male friendship. Emotional attachments are seen as a distraction from work, which is the real business of life. As against the dangers associated with forming a relationship with a woman, the companionship of men is restorative:

> Torpenhow came into the studio at dusk, and looked at Dick with his eyes full of the austere love that springs up between men who have tugged at the same oar together and are yoked by custom and use and the intimacies of toil. This is a good love, and since it allows, and even encourages strife, recrimination, and the most brutal sincerity, does not die, but increases, and is proof against any absence and evil conduct.   (p. 58)

On the basis of such passages it is, of course, easy to ridicule *The Light That Failed*, but what such passages really point to is the presence of a crisis of masculinity that is implicit in the very process of their assertion of masculinity.

The novel in all these respects reflects a deep division in late nineteenth-century thinking, something that is perhaps most apparent in the fact that the era of Kipling is also the era of Oscar Wilde, Aubrey Beardsley, *The Yellow Book* and *The Savoy*.[31] And also the era of the new woman. At this point we can begin to see how the new developments of the 1890s increasingly resist narrative containment and control. This is the issue that I turn to in the next chapter, the way in which the Boer War cannot be contained within old narrative frames, in particular the narrative form of the novel as the Victorians understood it. But what is also apparent, even in the years leading up to the Boer War, is that Kipling finds it more and more difficult to construct even a short story that really convinces. The poise of the early tales disappears; the military position starts to be represented as embattled and beleaguered, with Kipling increasingly becoming the 'recruiting sergeant' of popular imagination. It is a problem that affects his work for much of the 1890s, but when the Boer War arrives his stories seem to collapse under the strain. This is, in some ways, very odd. Here is the greatest military writer of the Victorian period, but the moment he is confronted by a real war he appears to have nothing of any interest to say about it. There are three Boer War stories in *Traffics and Discoveries* (1904), and all three are disappointing.[32]

'A Sahibs' War' is a monologue spoken by an elderly Sikh who has accompanied his master, an English cavalry officer, to South Africa.[33] The officer has been killed as a result of Boer treachery. Rather than exploring the conflict between the British and the Boers, Kipling simply demonises the Boers. Attention is transferred to the loyalty of the narrator, the elderly Indian demonstrating the right kind of deference in the colonial relationship. Implicit in the story is a sense that everything about India, including the relationship between the governors and the governed, is a story that is well known, whereas in South Africa the story is running out of control. The use of the Sikh servant as narrator, therefore, becomes a retreat into what is familiar and reassuring. As I emphasised in relation to the earlier short stories, Kipling is quite happy to acknowledge the existence of opposing voices, but only if he can contain and control them. The Boers, however, are an ungovernable threat, and as a result Kipling turns on them aggressively. The form this takes, as in Dickens's Indian Mutiny story, is a desire for revenge: the Boers must be punished.[34] The impression the reader of the story receives, however, is that a sequence of events is developing in South Africa that resists Kipling's narrative control. Unable to adjust the form of the short story in order to cope with this new state of affairs, Kipling resorts to the simplest of all narrative patterns, a fantasy of revenge.

In 'The Captive', Kipling is less openly hostile to the Boers. The narrator of this tale is an American who is being held prisoner by the British. He tells a story about a Boer commandant and a British general, and how, as professional soldiers, they have a deep respect for each other. It is difficult to detect any real level of complication in this story.[35] In the early stories the anecdote that is at the heart of the work always seems to incorporate several layers of meaning, but 'The Captive' does not venture very far at all in exploring any real question about the war. Indeed, it seems to do little more than assert the common bond between soldiers, even if they are on opposing sides, as if the mere existence of such honest values is a sufficient touchstone. The sense that really comes across from the story, however, is a sense that is not actually present in the story at all: the sense that Kipling is so baffled by the war in South Africa that he clings on to his old values, but in a way that has become crude and rather desperate.

The dilemma in which Kipling finds himself is provoked by the Boer War and the shock it rendered to British self-confidence. The colonial situation has suddenly and dangerously strayed beyond the control of the British. The only one of the three war stories that comes anywhere near exploring the issues behind this develop-ment is 'The Comprehension of Private Copper'.[36] The tale features an encounter between a British soldier and an English-speaking settler fighting for the Boers. Private Copper is captured by this man, but then turns the tables, taking the other man prisoner. The story is more substantial than 'A Sahibs' War' or 'A Captive', primarily because it recognises the existence of another voice, another position. Just for a moment it echoes the pattern of the earlier stories, the stories where British military rule is simultan-eously defended and questioned. In 'The Comprehension of Private Copper' there is a recognition of why the other man has chosen to identify with the Boers and their cause, even though his first loyalty might seem to be to the British. This level of perception is, however, rather negated by the reversal in the story, whereby the captor becomes the captured. This is the kind of plot device that features in Henty's novels, and here, as in Henty, the mechanics of the plot resolve the problem, eliminating the cause of unrest.

Angus Wilson sums up the problem with such stories: the prob-lem is 'a complex world that would not arrange itself according to his simplistic vision'.[37] The weakness of the Boer War stories does, however, serve to draw attention again to the extraordinary nature of Kipling's achievement in the early 1890s in reinventing militar-ism: whereas Jingoism is little more than a matter of nationalistic platitudes, Kipling constructs a position that has real depth and substance. The nature of that achievement is evident in, for ex-ample, 'Black Jack', one of the stories in *Soldiers Three*.[38] Mulvaney overhears, and then outwits, a plot to steal his rifle and to kill an unpopular officer with it, so that the blame will fall upon him. It is apparent that underhand dealings are just as common in the army as in any other walk of life; indeed, such conduct is always rather more alarming in the army because of the availability of weapons. What is asserted against such lawlessness is Mulvaney's resourcefulness, one of the military virtues that Kipling repeatedly returns to. But what the story really offers is an impression of poised control, that the military virtues are equal to, and can even overcome, all threats to good order. In this respect, military virtues become exemplary values for the whole of society. In summary, of course, a story such as 'Black Jack' seems formulaic, but, when one reads it, the measure of Kipling's achievement at the start of the 'nineties becomes plain, that he convinces us of the plausibility, and value, of his version of militarism.

8

The Boer War

In every war there are incidents that take hold of, and remain in, the public imagination. They are usually few in number, and sometimes not all that important in themselves, but in a significant way they focus contemporary feelings and define the image of the war for subsequent generations. Most commonly, they mingle a sense of reassurance with a sense of anxiety, frequently combining an illustration of courage with questions about whether courage alone is sufficient; as such, these incidents are likely to express the contradictions that lie at the heart of a nation's involvement in a conflict. Not surprisingly, these are the episodes that appear most often in novels, poems and plays (and, with the passing of time, in history books and films) about the war in question. It is easy to identify the significant events of this nature in the Victorian era. In the Crimean War, the incident that made the greatest impact was the Charge of the Light Brigade: a triumph of glory over strategy, of bravery over pragmatism, for many it defined the inadequacies of an aristocratic military leadership. The image of Florence Nightingale at Scutari is, of course, equally evocative, with everything that it suggests about the roles the Victorians assigned to women, but also what it tells us about a shift of attention at this time from the moment of military confrontation to the human consequences of war. The significance of Nightingale is most apparent if we consider how difficult it would be to associate any such image with the Wellington era.

After the Crimean War, however, another image becomes central: the most characteristic military event that affected the public imagination for the rest of the Victorian period was the siege. In the Indian Mutiny, for example, the events that made the biggest impact were the siege of, and subsequent massacre at, Cawnpore, and the siege of Lucknow. At Cawnpore, the siege lasted three weeks, with the British contingent of about 300 soldiers and about 500 non-combatants, most of them women and children, surrounded and constantly under fire from 3,000 British-trained sepoys. About 250 died during the siege, with many more being killed after the false promise of safe passage down the Ganges to Allahabad. The surviving men and women were murdered when it became known that Sir Henry Havelock was on his way to relieve Cawnpore. The siege at Lucknow lasted four and a half months; after three months, Havelock and Sir James Outram fought their way in and reinforced the garrison, but the siege was then resumed until Sir Colin Campbell arrived with a stronger force six weeks later. Nearly thirty years later, in the Sudan, the death of General Charles Gordon at the conclusion of the siege of Khartoum made an even deeper impression on the public imagination.[1] It is, in part, the circumstances of colonial warfare that dictate the centrality of the siege in the Victorian period; only when a country is occupied by an invading force is a small group of soldiers, located in a handful of locations, going to attempt to control large areas of that country. The colonial force is always surrounded and out-numbered; it only takes a minor provocation to trigger a situation where the occupying force is under siege.[2]

This is not the pattern of all siege warfare. In Europe, most characteristically, the invading force besieges the city that is the seat of power. For the Victorians, however, the threat was always from the indigenous population. It is this that explains why sieges attracted so much attention. What is of primary importance is that a siege pits a British community – in Cawnpore, as in most sieges, there was a great deal of emphasis upon the presence of women and children – against a barbarous foe. Here is a small British enclave defending not just itself but the very idea of the English way against everything that is unEnglish; the idea of a British community maintaining values that are designated more narrowly as English is, of course, standard thinking at the time. Sieges appealed, and still appeal, to novelists, for here is a microcosm of the British social order, with each rank knowing its place and playing its part, defending civilised life as it meets a challenge from an uncivilised enemy. Although far from home, the domestic values of Britain are put on trial, and, as we might expect, discov-ered to be the qualities that matter. The siege becomes a definition and defence of the social order of Britain.[3]

It comes as no surprise, therefore, that not just one but three sieges are central to the Boer War. This was the longest, the bloodiest and the most expensive war fought by the Victorian army, and, as such, the most difficult for the public to come to terms with; the three sieges fall into place as the basis upon which the Victorian public could construct its explanation of the war. By the Boer War, I mean the conflict that took place between the British and the South African Boers between 1899 and 1902. There had been an earlier Boer War, in 1881, which I return to later in this chapter in a brief discussion of Rider Haggard's novel *Jess*.[4] The second Boer War was, however, a much more extreme conflict, differing in a number of respects from all earlier wars the Victorians had fought. For a start, on this occasion the British were not confronting ill-equipped and ill-trained 'native' armies. Like the Crimean War, therefore, it was a substantial engagement in which, for the first time since the Crimea, the enemy was of European descent. But the numbers involved were far higher than in the Crimea, and technically and strategically it was a new kind of war, moving beyond the era of the cavalry charge. There was a new level of mechanisation, but also guerrilla tactics that bore no resemblance to the three-act drama of the set-piece battle. With new weapons, accurate over long distances, the enemy was at times even invisible. It was the new aspects of this war, particularly as it became obvious that the British were not going to achieve their usual quick victory, that led the public to grasp the sieges of Mafeking, Kimberley and Lady-smith as a way of making sense of what was going on; even if the war as a whole broke with earlier patterns, the siege was a familiar predicament that could be interpreted with confidence.

The background to the war was resentment at British rule, tensions increasing dramatically with the discovery of huge mineral deposits in South Africa. In 1899 Paul Kruger, President of the Transvaal Republic, issued an ultimatum demanding an end to British suzerainty, and on 11 October Boer troops invaded Cape Colony and Natal. It was a strategic mistake on the part of the Boers that they failed to follow up their initial advantage; instead of pressing forward, they laid siege simultaneously to Mafeking, Kimberley and Ladysmith.[5] At Mafeking, Baden-Powell and 1,000 men held out against 8,000 Boers. The stand-off is a narrative with all the usual implications about British bravery under pressure, but developed a character of its own because of the boy-scout resourcefulness that Baden-Powell brought to the defence of the town; the image is of a grown-up schoolboy, behaving like the hero of a G.A. Henty novel, endlessly contriving dodges to outwit the enemy. This is not a retrospective reading, constructed to tally with

Baden-Powell's later vocation in life, but one stressed in contemporary reports. Mafeking was eventually relieved on 17 May 1900, after 217 days, when a relief column arrived. What everyone knows about the relief of Mafeking is that there was an unprecedented level of celebration when the news arrived in London, the word 'mafficking' being coined to characterise a certain kind of Jingoistic fervour. But the exaggerated nature of the celebration suggests a tension: on the one hand there is relief that the usual narrative of a siege has arrived at a satisfactory resolution, but there is also an awareness that the story as it unfolded threatened to defy preconceptions.

This is a pattern that repeats itself in responses to the Boer War. A desire to accommodate the war within old frames (the common characterisation of the conflict as 'the last of the gentlemen's wars' attempts to make the war familiar and manageable) has to be set against an awareness that the narrative is falling apart. It is a point that is apparent in the response of Kipling; less than ten years earlier, his stories set in India are faultless, but, as I argued in the previous chapter, his Boer War stories are feeble. Just as a tension is apparent in the response to the relief of Mafeking, the same tension is present in the responses to the sieges of Kimberley and Ladysmith. Kimberley was relieved on 15 February 1900, but the satisfactory resolution of the siege could not eradicate the awareness that Methuen had suffered heavy losses and a number of reversals in his attempt to relieve the town. It was only after Roberts and Kitchener arrived in South Africa, that John French and his 5,000 men relieved Kimberley by mounting a fast and unexpected attack on the Boers.

The relief of Ladysmith was even more bloody in terms of loss of life. Buller, in his advance on the town, was beaten at Colenso, Spion Kop and Val Krary. It was again the arrival of more troops from Britain, and a reorganisation of the army by Kitchener, that paved the way for the eventual relief of Ladysmith at the end of February 1900. The battle of Spion Kop was another military event that caught the public imagination: Buller's reputation could not survive the revelation of his inadequacies in the field, and his tactical blunder at Spion Kop in occupying what seemed a commanding position only to discover as the darkness lifted that they were in a pitifully exposed position. As against the Boer losses of 300, Buller in retreat left behind 1,750 men killed, wounded and captured.[6] What we see in Britain are attempts to make sense of the disaster. There were those who criticised the conduct of the generals, a criticism that resembles complaints from the Crimean period. But others saw the defeat as symptomatic of imperial decline and national disintegration.[7] It is against this background that the public, encouraged by politicians and the press, chose to impose a more positive reading when Mafeking, the remaining siege town, was eventually relieved.

The three sieges of the Boer War might seem to be natural material for novelists: here is a small group of brave Britons, men of all ranks working together, and accompanied by wives and children. A domestic order can, therefore, be identified that tallies with the military order.[8] And it is certainly the case that the public responded to the sieges, particularly the siege of Mafeking, as if they were works of fiction. Here was a group of named characters, with identifiable leaders, in a named place, and, moreover, with a clear purpose to their lives as they confronted an enemy that could be represented in equally unambiguous terms. Despite the military setbacks, therefore, there were enough of the reassuring elements of a siege narrative present to construct a positive story. The fact is, however, that the three sieges did not find their way into fiction as quickly as one might expect. G.A. Henty deals with the relief of Ladysmith in *With Buller in Natal*, but this is something of an exception.[9] Indeed, the short-comings of Henty's novel indicate the nature of the problem for novelists in general. Henty writes as if there is no threat in the war that the British hero cannot cope with. Beyond Henty, however, what we see is that the bewildering events in South Africa disrupt the sense-making potential of the narrative models available to British novelists.

THE BOER WAR IN FICTION

Surprisingly few Boer War novels were published during the con-flict or in the years that followed. G.A. Henty was quick to respond with *With Buller in Natal* (1901) and *With Roberts to Pretoria* (1902), and F.S. Brereton, another prolific writer of adventure stories, published *One of the Fighting Scouts: A Tale of Guerrilla Warfare in South Africa* (1903). Other authors who entered the fray were E. Harcourt Burrage with *Carbineer and Scout* (1901), Bertram Mitford with *Aletta: A Tale of the Boer Invasion* (1900), Herbert Hayens with

Scouting for Buller (1902), Arthur Laycock with *Steve the Outlander: A Romance of South Africa* (1900), and Bracebridge Hemyng with *Jack Harkaway in the Transvaal; or Fighting for the Flag* (1902) and *Jack Harkaway's War Scouts Among Boer Guerrillas* (1902).[10] The list might seem substantial, but the majority of these are boys' adventure stories. In some ways there is nothing unusual about the fact that the Boer War did not provoke substantial novels; it had, after all, been the case throughout the Victorian period that most novelists showed little interest in war.

When we consider, however, the crop of Indian Mutiny novels that appeared in the 1890s, together with a renewed interest in the Napoleonic era and the Crimean War, we might reasonably expect a rush of novels dealing with the current conflict. Indeed, van Wyk Smith, in his excellent book on the poetry of the Boer War, draws attention to a

> remarkable literary feature of the war: it proved a rich new source of exciting narrative material for the enormous popular press of magazine and story, and for the Victorian genres of parlour poem and public recitation. Everything soldiers could produce was seized upon, and where they failed the professional ballad writer filled the breach.[11]

This torrent of words, however, always stops short at a certain point: the novel, the favourite genre of the Victorians, is almost irrelevant in considerations of the war. The reason would seem to be that the events and circumstances of the conflict increasingly strayed outside received narrative patterns. Implicit in the structure of a Victorian novel is a containment of experience; except in the hands of the most assured novelists, the form strains if it attempts to confront events that are unfamiliar. In the Boer War, it was only novelists such as G.A. Henty who could write with confidence, but they did so only because they ignored all the awkward facts of the dispute.

Some aspects of the standard pattern of a South African war/ adventure novel are evident in Rider Haggard's *Jess*, a novel about the first Boer War published in 1887.[12] Its hero, Captain John Niel, is the typical public-school type that emerges in late Victorian fiction. In South Africa, this gentleman hero is ranged against a Boer enemy, Franz Muller, who is the antithesis of everything an Englishman stands for. Muller beats and whips native servants, 'would betray his own father if he thought it in his interest to do so', is 'a liar and a traitor', and thoroughly despicable in his conduct during the war (p. 58). Niel, by contrast, obviously shines forth as an exemplary hero. There is, however, a level of complication in Haggard's novel, a level of complication that is never allowed to appear in the works of Henty and his followers. *Jess* as a novel can only conclude when Jess herself, the heroine, kills Muller:

> He was awake, but fear paralysed him, he could not speak or move.
> He was awake and she could hesitate no more...
> He must have seen the flash of the falling steel, and – (p. 321)

The pattern is, in fact, a familiar one in Victorian fiction; the assertively masculine hero, in Haggard's novel Niel, is revealed to be dependent upon a woman.

It represents an interesting undermining of male hegemony, but Haggard is working in fairly conventional territory. This extends to his description of the female character:

> John stood opposite to her and looked at her, and the old curiosity took possession of him to understand this feminine enigma. Many a man before him has been the victim of a like desire, and lived to regret that he did not leave it ungratified.   (p. 45)

A sense of the woman as spirited mixes, as is so often the case, with a view of the woman as an enigmatic temptress. What emerges in the Boer War, however, are new threats to the power of the British male, including an enemy that is more cunning and resourceful than the British. The response of Henty, and his imitators, is to deny the existence of any problem. There is an extraordinary lack of tension in *With Buller in Natal*. The hero, Chris King, is a schoolboy who, along with his young friends, does his bit in fighting the Boers. He participates in the Battle of Colenso, the Battle of Spion Kop, and the relief of Ladysmith, but there is no sense that any of these has proved at all troublesome to the British. As in a child's game, the hero, almost single-handedly, thrashes an unbelievable number of the enemy:

> They cantered along in high glee; not one had received a scratch, while some twelve of the first party of Boers had fallen, and fully

fifteen of the second, and it was certain that at least as many more must have been wounded. (p. 147)

This is typical of Henty's method; at no stage is there any real opposition. What we might particularly note in *With Buller in Natal* is that there is not a word of acknowledgement that Buller's leadership qualities and strategy had been widely questioned during the course of the war. Henty simply ignores all threats, problems and difficulties.

Most Boer War novels operate at the same undemanding level. A few writers, however, are more ambitious. Bertram Mitford lived mostly in South Africa from 1873, producing numerous adventure novels. His Boer War novel, *Aletta*, is fundamentally pro-British, but at the same time tries to be fair to the Boers. *Aletta* is set in the farming district of the Cape just before the war starts. The hero, Colvin Kershaw, has a Boer family as his neighbours on one side, and a staunchly imperialist family as his neighbours on the other. Kershaw falls in love with Aletta, the daughter of the Boer family, and promises her that he will not enlist. He visits the war zone as an observer, however, watching the action from the Boer positions, but is then arrested for allegedly helping a British prisoner to escape. Aletta and her family intervene to save his life. It is clear that Mitford's novel belongs to a liberal tradition: at one level it is a plea for dialogue rather than confrontation. Yet there is at the same time a bias to the text, Mitford making it quite obvious that the British are in the right and that the Boers are usually rogues. This is the standard limitation of the liberal vision in a war novel, that toleration cannot dislodge self-interest, understandable, perhaps, when self-interest might mean self-preservation. What *Aletta*, which admittedly is a very early Boer War novel, published in 1900, does not take on board, however, are the new complications in the war; it tries to maintain a liberal perspective without considering the ways in which things have changed. Erhard Reckwitz has written about the literary procedures involved in Boer War novels; he makes the point that we 'explain new occurrences in terms of past experience, and accordingly new stories with new thematic arrangements can be best interpreted by having recourse to the various presentational models traditionally available to a culture'.[13] As the war proceeded, and events became increasingly disturbing, the kind of liberal model that Mitford employs became more and more strained. In particular, even writers of adult fiction increasingly demonised the Boer.

This is perhaps most apparent in Douglas Blackburn's satirical novel *A Burgher Quixote*, published in 1903.[14] Sarel Erasmus relates his participation in various events of the Boer War, it soon becoming apparent that he is an utter rascal. The model for Blackburn's novel is the kind of picaresque Thackeray employs in *Barry Lyndon*, where the 'hero' is a self-serving rogue. Erasmus, while professing to be hardy and honest, is a typical untrustworthy Boer. His only interest is material gain, and this, Blackburn suggests, is true of all his countrymen, who use religion in a way that suits them, but are always betrayed by their fondness for drink. Blackburn was a British war correspondent, so to some extent must have been aware of how he was imposing a reading upon the Boers. At the same time there is evidence of deeper anxieties in *A Burgher Quixote*, anxieties that English fiction could not tackle directly. The Boers are, for example, condemned for their lack of military discipline, but what this actually amounts to is a self-reliance and inventiveness that constantly embarrasses the British. The Boers are not gentlemen, but, much though Blackburn might disparage them, their actions put in question the character qualities the British value so highly.

As the war continues, it becomes even more clear that an old order is collapsing and that the English war novel cannot respond to this change. The popularity of Indian Mutiny novels in the 1890s underlines this impression. A positive message is found in an event that is sufficiently far in the past to be no longer troubling; the Indian Mutiny even provides a diversion from the concerns of the present. After the conclusion of the Boer War, however, we might expect things to change. In particular, from the perspective of the First World War the Boer War might seem to make sense as the foreshadowing of a new and more dangerous level of conflict. But this is not really the case. As the First World War looms, novelists turning their attentions to South Africa are engaged in a quite different enterprise. In Francis Bancroft's *The Veldt Dwellers* (1912), for example, the idea that dominates is the need to reconcile the antagonists in the Boer War; what is stressed is their common cause against new enemies, particularly the Germans.[15] Michael Rice makes the point that a woman increasingly becomes the central character in novels referring back to the Boer War, because of the way in which a woman can more easily be used to symbolise reconciliation and the redemptive power of love.[16] In the lead-up to the First World War, therefore, the Boer War novel does move into a new pattern, in a sense jumping a stage; failing to come to terms with the deeper problems inherent in the conflict, the Boer War novel now invokes a spirit of colonial mutuality, of newly discovered common interests and shared values.

NEW RESPONSES

The Boer War is often referred to as 'the last of the gentlemen's wars', the phrase being used by J.F.C. Fuller in 1937 as the title of his war journal.[17] Especially in the early stages of the war, the British were immensely attracted by anecdotes that suggested a gentlemanly bond with the Afrikaners. For example, van Wyk Smith describes an occurrence at Ladysmith after the Battle of Wagon Hill: 'As the British were carrying their wounded off the field and burying the dead, a party of Boers arrived who helped care for the suffering and prayed over the graves of their enemies'.[18] The concept of gentlemen soldiers extended further than this, however, even being apparent in the grasp of tactics. In particular, the siege strategy that dominated the early part of the war conveys the impression that both sides were, initially, constrained by traditional, even chivalric, military thinking. Yet the most distinctive feature of the Boer War was that the rules of engagement had changed. It took some time for this fact to sink in. As the conflict started, nobody could foresee that this was going to be a war on a major scale involving large numbers of volunteers. Nor was it possible to see that this war was going to affect the lives of the civilian populations of the countries involved to a far greater extent than had been the case in the past. And, as it developed into a guerrilla war, it increasingly lacked the comprehensibility of past wars. It was at this point that the Boer began to be demonised, rather than respected, as an enemy. As the war dragged on, the idea of 'the last of the gentlemen's wars' seems more and more like wishful thinking, a desire to accommodate a new conflict within an old interpretative frame.

There was, however, one war that provided a precedent. The American Civil War had involved large numbers of the civilian population, technologically sophisticated weaponry and innovatory tactics.[19] It is interesting to consider one of the literary products of this conflict. Stephen Crane had never been involved in a battle, and *The Red Badge of Courage* was published, in 1895, some thirty years after the war had ended, but it is a novel that does justice to the changing nature of war in a way that no English novel of the Victorian or Edwardian years does.[20] The difference is that it focuses on the terror of a single soldier. Henry Fleming enrols with the Union army; he is anxious to participate in the glory of the fight, but this soon disintegrates into a mass retreat in which he receives a superficial head wound. He is proud of his bravery, but in a second encounter with the enemy he flees into the forest. He comes across the body of a dying soldier, and feels enraged at the injustice of war. Eventually he returns to battle, picking up the regiment's colours when they fall from another's hands, but he no longer feels heroic. He is filled with guilt, and with thoughts of the 'tattered' soldier, a wounded man who was abandoned on the field. The sense that dominates is a feeling of bewilderment. It is a feeling that probably becomes more common in modern warfare, but it is a feeling that the English novel cannot seem to express before the First World War.[21]

This is apparent in the way that the majority of Boer War novels simply maintain the chivalric code in its late-century 'public schoolboy as hero' guise. Popular histories of the war were constructed along rather similar lines. The impression is of British heroes confronting an enemy that is initially respected, but which is soon exposed as a bunch of vicious scoundrels. Such thinking is evident in Conan Doyle's *The Great Boer War* (1903), Donald MacDonald's *How We Kept the Flag Flying* (1900) and G.W. Steevens's *From Cape Town to Ladysmith* (1900).[22] These works are to some extent informed by a crisis of confidence, but the authors work hard to restore a sense of purpose and direction. Van Wyk Smith comments on the 'vivid narrative competence of these writers', a comment that is interesting in that it suggests how literary form can be exploited to create a sense of coherence and direction even where none exists.[23]

Given that the supporters of the war all seem to speak with one voice, we need to turn to the other side in Britain to see what kind of response they were offering. For the most part, the impression is disappointing. George Bernard Shaw's *Arms and the Man* was produced some years before the Boer War, in 1894, but is so directly engaged with the issue of militarism that it demands to be considered.[24] Even in 1894, however, it seems an oddly old-fashioned play. The hero of the play, Bluntschli, a Swiss mercenary, encounters a young woman when he takes refuge in her bedroom; he proceeds to disabuse her of her ideas about the glamour of war, Bluntschli maintaining that military heroism is a civilian fiction. The play works brilliantly on the stage, but does not appear to deal at all with the new kind of Jingoistic and imperialist militarism emerging in the 1890s. One might have expected a play that was in some manner a riposte to Kipling, but Shaw only seems interested in challenging a concept of militarism that Kipling has by this time overhauled and renewed. Consequently, the impression *Arms and the Man* produces is that, while mocking those who are caught in the grip of traditional views, Shaw himself thinks in traditional terms, mounting a standard liberal critique of aristomilitary culture. All in all, the play looks more like a response to the world evoked in an Anthony Hope novel, such as *The Prisoner of Zenda*, rather than being a play that tackles attitudes that actually existed in the 1890s.

What *Arms and the Man* seems to indicate is that opponents of militarism had, for the most part, no new view to offer; they were tied to the liberal assumptions of the mid-century. Indeed, it is clear in the 1890s that it is the conservatives in Britain who are setting the pace, incorporating new ideas that bolster their inherited convictions. One aspect of this is Social Darwinism, which can be characterised as the wedding of evolutionary theory to a conservative political philosophy, seeing the inevitable defeat of the unfit, the inefficient and the incompetent.[25] Supporters of the British cause in South Africa could claim that imperialism simply bore out the views of Darwin, that the stronger race would defeat the weaker, and that this was an inexorable law of nature. Kipling is the author who did most to revitalise militarism, but the context in which he was working was one in which a variety of elements, such as Social Darwinism, were all moving in the same direction.

The flaw in Social Darwinism was the fact that it was only a pseudo-science, a facile stringing together of platitudes in order to justify a desired state of affairs. The conservative attitude towards the Boer War might have been bullish, but the war itself turned out to be sufficiently shocking to expose the flimsy intellectual justification of imperialism. This becomes particularly evident if we consider how even the notion of 'imperialism' was one of the new ideas of the 1890s. As Patrick Brantlinger argues:

Imperialism itself, as an ideology or political faith, functioned as a partial substitute for declining or fallen Christianity and for declining faith in Britain's future.[26]

Brantlinger then examines how a cluster of new, yet conservative, ideas finds expression in the typical romances of the 1890s, the works by Stevenson, Haggard, Kipling, Doyle and Bram Stoker, which he labels as 'imperial Gothic'. These *fin de siècle* colonial fantasies do not, however, overlap all that much with the military novels inspired by the Boer War. The military novels tend to emphasise a sense of duty and order rather than probing behind the surface. Indeed, a novel that in any way resembled *The Red Badge of Courage*, that is to say a novel probing the anxieties of the individual soldier, might be seen as conceding a loss of confidence at the very heart of the army.

Alongside Social Darwinism, another new idea in late nineteenth-century social thinking was the concept of 'degeneration'. In the specific context of the Boer War, questions needed to be asked about the failure of the British to achieve the kind of quick victory the country was used to. The outcome was two official enquiries, in 1903 and 1905. William Greenslade has commented on their significance:

Behind these investigations lies a prevailing sense that the nation's military incompetence is a symptom of a pervasive degeneracy at the heart of Empire at the century's turn. In the immediate aftermath of the war the military question attracted to it all the wider fears about national degeneration: fears provoked by the existence of under-bred, physically inefficient recruits, and old-fashioned amateurish and outmoded military commanders.[27]

The idea of 'degeneracy' confronts an understandable, even if unsubstantiated, worry at the time, but, in relation to the army and war, the argument then moves on to the importance of military discipline as a means of restoring the race. Indeed, rather than stressing degeneration, the emphasis in a number of military novels is on regeneration. *The Dop Doctor*, by Richard Dehan, published in 1910, is constructed around the siege of Mafeking.[28] A young doctor, falsely accused of performing an abortion, leaves for South Africa, where he acquires a reputation as a drunkard.

Under siege, however, he becomes a different man, battling against alcoholism and winning the love of a young woman in the town (a young woman who has been raped by a renegade Englishman). It is her love that secures his redemption. *The Dop Doctor* confronts anxieties about nationality, addiction and sex, but outflanks them to restore a vision of the British hero with supportive female partner; as such, it might be a novel influenced by the degeneration debate, but in the end it turns out to be a simple romance.

With *The Dop Doctor*, however, we move into the Edwardian era, where a whole new range of issues become apparent. In the 1890s, what is most clear is the strength of the conservative political position; ideas about nationhood, imperialism, militarism, Social Darwinism, degeneracy and race, together with some traditional ideas about the role of a gentleman, interconnect to produce a plausible explanation of the international situation. The problematic nature of the Boer War, however, challenges the authority of this new social and political analysis. It also leads to a significant revival and reassertion of the liberal voice. This is most obvious in the organised campaigning against the war, a stance of opposition to the nation's military effort that has no precedent in the Victorian period. A number of Liberal newspapers aligned themselves with Lord Rosebery and the Liberal Imperialists, but *The Morning Leader*, *The Star* and, most significantly, *The Manchester Guardian* endorsed the pro-Boer sympathies of Liberals such as Sir William Harcourt, John Morley and David Lloyd George. Their views were shared, and taken even further, by organisations such as the Stop the War Committee.[29]

Most interestingly, however, an ambitious form of cultural critique of imperialism begins to take shape at this time.[30] In the views of J.A. Hobson, developed in three books published during the Boer War, Victorian liberalism moves beyond its somewhat myopic focus upon domestic concerns. In *The War in South Africa* (1900), *The Psychology of Jingoism* (1901) and *Imperialism: A Study* (1902), Hobson takes the strands of thinking that had been exploited by the conservatives, but then takes a step back to offer a far more rigorous intellectual analysis of current developments: he constructs a comprehensive theory about the connections between imperialism, militarism, war, race, class and capitalism.[31] Hobson's thinking does have roots in earlier critiques; in particular, his economic humanism owes a certain amount to the social concern of John Ruskin. Ruskin, however, retained a chivalric conception of war, whereas Hobson condemns the manner in which industrial capitalism generates war; one aspect of this is the annexation of preindustrial countries. The militarism of the late nineteenth century is seen, therefore, as a direct consequence of the economic structure of western society, and, furthermore, seen as damaging to an older pattern of democracy. The future prospect is an era of ruinous wars. The present is characterised by the collapse within the west of traditional principles in politics, religion and morality. In their wake, cruder and coarser values have emerged, which include Social Darwinism, Jingoistic militarism, racism and xenophobia. All these factors contribute to the modern, barbaric war spirit.

With the views of Hobson, we have moved on a long way from the liberalism of Elizabeth Gaskell's era. Hobson offers a vision of a society that has regressed, that has reverted to a stage of primitivism; the emergence of militarism is the most direct manifestation of this. Part of the strength of Hobson's analysis is that, whereas conservative thinkers in the period are participants in the system of beliefs they appear to be discussing, Hobson seems to withdraw himself, as if he can explain the resurgence of militarism from a position of detached understanding. His comprehensive analysis seems to connect all the social, political and cultural movements of the late nineteenth century, and the tremendous impact of his ideas, for example on Lenin, cannot be overestimated. Edward Said, however, makes the point that, for all his hostility towards the heartless economics of imperialism and his understanding of the facade of well-meaning 'civilising' pretexts, Hobson retains the idea of a superior race and an inferior race.[32] In addition, when Hobson draws upon the work that had been done in evolutionary and degenerationist theory, it is evident that he shares the anxieties of his contemporaries, accepting the same myths about degeneration.[33] The difference is that he uses these ideas to construct a critique rather than a justification of imperialism. He does so, however, in three magisterial works that, in an almost imperial manner, annexe and control vast areas of knowledge, and vast areas of the world, in order to construct an all-embracing theory. The completeness of the picture consequently becomes another expression of imperialism, as Hobson constructs a world view in which the preindustrial countries function and exist in relation to Britain at the centre. Indeed, the great appeal of Hobson's work is that he can provide an explanation of what is happening at the time. Novelists cannot seem to move beyond old narrative patterns, whereas Hobson, despite reservations about the comprehensiveness, coherence and Anglo-centrism of his works, clearly does produce a new narrative.

THE POETRY OF THE BOER WAR

Hobson describes a society where traditional religious, political and moral convictions have disappeared, and where people embrace a new militarist, imperialist philosophy. The Boer War, however, begins to undermine the strength of these new convictions: the narrative of the war as it unfolds is at odds with the expected story of yet another triumph for the empire, race and nation. As we have seen, novelists at the time cannot meet the challenge of responding to this new state of affairs. In poetry, however, the picture is different, perhaps in part due to the fact that the brevity of a poetic lyric is well suited to the task of expressing a sense of bewilderment, of being lost in a world that no longer makes sense. But whatever the reason, the fact is that, whereas Boer War novels are without exception disappointing, a great deal of the poetry prompted by the war is not only impressive but often startling and genuinely new. Not all of it, of course; the war produced a vast amount of crudely nationalistic verse. Swinburne, for example, with a poem such as 'Strike, England, and Strike Home', has declined into one of the muses of imperialism.[34] There was, obviously, a lot of poetry that struck this note. A taste for patriotic verse was, in fact, in evidence before the war, an anthology such as *Lyra Heroica*, in 1892, laying a trail for the resurgent militarism of the 1890s, but when the war broke out it is noticeable, even in the immediate response, that there is a move away from blatant celebrations of heroism and rather more on the ethics of war and personal reactions to the conflict.[35]

Where a new attitude is most apparent, however, is in Thomas Hardy's Boer War poems. Van Wyk Smith draws attention to a review of Hardy's *Poems of the Past and Present* (1902), where the reviewer comments on:

a sheaf of War Poems, which differ from the serviceable Kiplingisms and Begbie-isms of the hour most notably in this, that they dwell not on the glory, but on the piteousness of the struggle.

Like other Gods, in Mr Hardy's view, the God of Battles has had his day.[36]

It is a perceptive comment, but it is possible to define more precisely the effects that are achieved in these war poems of Hardy's. The starting point has to be that Hardy inverts the chivalric tradition. Rather than focusing on a hero who can turn the course of events, Hardy, as in his novels, focuses upon a small, powerless, defeated (or even dead) individual in an enormous universe. In doing this, Hardy overturns the chivalric tradition, but he also challenges the liberal tradition which puts the individual at the centre, focusing upon the individual's ability to change the world through negotiation and compromise. In a typical Hardy war poem, by contrast, there is a sense of bafflement, with a small character encountering a world that not only defies control but also defies comprehension. In this respect we can see a further difference between Hardy and Hobson. Hobson draws all aspects of contemporary life together into a grand theory, but Hardy has no such sense of a large pattern; there is only a fragmented sense of loss, confusion, uncertainty and pain.

'Drummer Hodge' establishes Hardy's approach:

They throw in Drummer Hodge, to rest
　　Uncoffined – just as found:
His landmark is a kopje-crest
　　That breaks the veldt around;
And foreign constellations west
　　Each night above his mound.

Young Hodge the Drummer never knew –
　　Fresh from his Wessex home –
The meaning of the broad Karoo,
　　The Bush, the dusty loam,
And why uprose to nightly view
　　Strange stars amid the gloam.

Yet portion of that unknown plain
　　Will Hodge for ever be;
His homely Northern breast and brain
　　Grow to some Southern tree,
And strange-eyed constellations reign
　　His stars eternally.[37]

Pity might be the dominant emotion, but what really suggests the wretchedness of the fate of the almost-anonymous soldier ('Hodge' being the generic, somewhat insulting, name for a farm labourer) is the way in which the poem dismantles a sense of security. The movement in the first verse is from the soldier, by way of unfamiliar, and therefore unnerving, words (specifically 'kopje-crest' and 'veldt'), through to images of a vast cosmos. The soldier, consequently, is rendered as a speck in the universe, but he is in fact just as lost in a South African landscape that is so strange that only an alien language can describe it. And this is the experience of a man who would have had an intimate knowledge of, and intimacy with, the English landscape. There is an equally impressive economy of effect in the unexpected appearance of the word 'uncoffined' in the second line, which conveys far more than just the fact of the disposal of the soldier's body; it suggests a world where the necessary reassuring rituals of death have been abandoned. It becomes more poignant because the victim is not a career soldier but an agricultural labourer in a place where he does not belong.

The pattern of the second verse is almost identical: the soldier's name (with the addition of the adjective 'Young', which adds to the pathos), unfamiliar South African words, then the sense of a huge cosmos (the poetic inversion of the last two lines underlining the way in which a connection has been lost with the usual order of existence). The third verse changes direction slightly to offer a tribute to the soldier, the poem becoming the memorial that they failed to construct over the grave, or ditch, where he was buried. By making the poem a memorial to an unknown warrior, Hardy shows his compassion, but compassion alone would be a trite response; at the heart of the poem is Hardy's remarkable evocation of a bewildering world. As against the usual gestures of imperialism, in which Britain establishes order and control, in this poem the empire retaliates, the alien landscape contributing to an undermining of all convictions.

Hardy's ability to convey human suffering, and then to transcend even that achievement as he demolishes any sense of security, is again apparent in 'The Man He Killed':

> 'Had he and I but met
> By some old ancient inn,
> We should have sat us down to wet
> Right many a nipperkin!

> 'But ranged as infantry,
>   And staring face to face,
> I shot at him as he at me,
>   And killed him in his place.
>
>   'I shot him dead because –
>   Because he was my foe,
> Just so: my foe of course he was;
>   That's clear enough; although
>
>   'He thought he'd 'list, perhaps,
>   Off-hand like – just as I –
> Was out of work – had sold his traps –
>   No other reason why.
>
>   'Yes; quaint and curious war is!
>   You shoot a fellow down
> You'd treat if met where any bar is,
>   Or help to half-a-crown.' [38]

This might appear such a simple poem as to defy analysis, a poem where the idea is everything. But the simple questions Hardy poses lead on to complex issues, for there is clearly no connection between the code of generosity that operates in private life and the brutal code that operates in war. At the heart of the chivalric code is the idea that a gentleman in private life also behaves as a gentleman in battle, but here we have only an anonymous killing. We might also refer to the way in which in Henty's novels the morality of the public school is carried over into battle, but where have such ethical guidelines disappeared to in the war that Hardy describes? In Hardy's poem there is no connection between the rules of civilian life and the rules of war. The dilemma is added to by the fact that the opponent here is clearly recognised as an equal; the poem exploits a sense of shared identity, and even shared values, that would not have been relevant in earlier colonial wars.

The tension in 'The Man He Killed' is established by the initial juxtaposition of the somewhat rarefied language and phrasing of the first verse with the more brutal and direct second verse, a verse where we have left the past for a present of infantry exchanges. Then in a simple but stunning move forward, the sentences almost disintegrate in verse three; there are gestures towards reasoning and explanation, as the narrator tries to rationalise killing, but the verse fumbles and words are repeated as the idea is too difficult for language to comprehend, let alone control. Stanza three, as with the poem as a whole, could be more melodramatic and extreme, but it works so well because it underplays its effects. The technique is astonishingly simple; for example, the middle verse is the only one that does not end with a full stop, the thought limping over untidily and awkwardly into the next verse. The fourth verse is little more than a collection of stray phrases; they combine to convey information, to stress the similarity between the two men, but the piecemeal construction of the verse pulls in the opposite direction, creating a sense of disquiet, something that is underlined by the fact that both men are rejected and alienated, robbed of employment and their possessions. It is small details such as these that establish the connection between the economic and class structure of Britain and the existence of a colonial war. The effect is that we can understand the human consequences of the conflict, and also grasp something of the economic picture behind it, but, none the less, language has run into difficulties in trying to comprehend war. This is underlined by the lameness of the phrase 'quaint and curious' in the last verse. But what words would be more fitting? Words such as 'horrific' and 'inhuman' would sound equally empty and contrived, for words inevitably crumble in attempting to confront war.

The essence of both these poems is that they fail to make sense of the conflict. Seemingly trivial poems, apparently focusing on nothing more than the pathos of the experiences described, they are, in fact, engaged in an ambitious dismantling of the premises of traditional war poetry. The reader is, of course, most aware of the feelings of the people at the centre of the poems, but this is because this is all that is left after Hardy has finished his demolition of the usual myths. This point is particularly evident in 'A Wife in London':

I

She sits in the tawny vapour
    That the Thames-side lanes have uprolled,
    Behind whose webby fold on fold
Like a waning taper
    The street-lamp glimmers cold.

A messenger's knock cracks smartly,
    Flashed news is in her hand

Of meaning it dazes to understand
Though shaped so shortly:
　　He – has fallen – in the far South Land . . .

II

'Tis the morrow; the fog hangs thicker,
　　The postman nears and goes:
　　A letter is brought whose lines disclose
By the firelight flicker
　　His hand, whom the worm now knows:

Fresh – firm – penned in highest feather –
　　Page-full of his hoped return,
　　And of home-planned jaunts by brake and burn
In the summer weather,
　　And of new love that they would learn. [39]

As with 'The Man He Killed', initially this poem might appear to amount to little more than the anecdote on which it is based, but what the poem manages to do is to juxtapose the human with the inhuman, the knowable with the unknowable; as against the human contact of the letter, there is the anonymity of the telegram, euphemistically evading the word 'death'. The poem runs the risk of being trite or sentimental, but avoids being so because of its awareness of the implications of its small story. The husband's story builds a fiction, constructing a narrative in confident sentences in the last verse of the poem, but the war, as the other verses have already told us through their imagery and phrasing, is about the collapse of all fictions.

It might seem unlikely that a similar sense of confusion could exist in Kipling's poems from the Boer War, but this is the case. It could even be argued that the impression is more striking in Kipling than in Hardy, because Kipling starts with a coherent philosophy of England's mission, but a philosophy that falls apart as the conflict develops. *The Seven Seas*, published before the Boer War in 1896, is 'redolent with a spirit of imperial activism and racial mission'.[40] Yet in a poem such as 'Hymn Before Action' the tone becomes sombre, Kipling anticipating a cautionary note that is at the centre of 'Recessional' and 'The White Man's Burden'. These are anxious poems calling for self-sacrifice in the service of the

empire. The Boer War adds to Kipling's doubts about the purpose
and viability of the imperial cause. In *The Five Nations*, published in
1903, there are a number of poems that continue 'the quest for a
viable vision of empire', but there are other poems in which a sense
of bewilderment is dominant.[41]

The two strains in Kipling's poetry can be appreciated if we
compare 'Bridge-Guard in the Karroo' with 'The Dykes'. The first
poem deals with a foot patrol, concluding:

> So we return to our places,
>   As out on the bridge she rolls;
> And the darkness covers our faces,
>   And the darkness re-enters our souls.
>
> More than a little lonely
>   Where the lessening tail-lights shine.
> No – not combatants – only
>   Details guarding the line! [42]

The line about 'darkness' entering their 'souls' might suggest that
this is a gloomy and oppressive poem, but the sentiments, as with
the rhythm, are stirring. At the heart of the poem is a sense of
belonging, a sense of fellow-feeling with one's colleagues, who are
a group of men with a task to perform. Guarding the bridge might
be the most insignificant of duties, but the men know that, as a part
of the total picture, they are indispensable to the war effort. This is
Kipling's democratised version of the chivalric code, in which the
lowliest soldier shares the ideals of the elite.

In 'The Dykes', by comparison, there is no sense of belonging, no
sense of being able to relate to a larger idea:

> At the bridge of the lower saltings the cattle gather and blare,
> Roused by the feet of running men, dazed by the lantern-glare.
> Unbar and let them away for their lives – the levels drown as
>   they stand,
> Where the flood-wash forces the sluices aback and the ditches
>   deliver inland.
>
> Ninefold deep to the top of the dykes the galloping breakers
>   stride,
> And their overcarried spray is a sea – a sea on the landward side.

> Coming, like stallions they paw with their hooves, going they
>   snatch with their teeth,
> Till the bents and the furze and sand are dragged out, and the
>   old-time hurdles beneath.[43]

The central image is of the flimsiness of the dykes, and, by extension, the flimsiness of the structures – of belief, of civilisation, of
empire – that the British have constructed in defence of their land.
What is also likely to strike the reader is the extraordinary structure
of every line of the poem, the lines, as in this extract, all seeming
overcrowded, as if, like the dykes, they are close to being overwhelmed. Any sense of the glory of war has been abandoned; there
is only a sense of the collapse of everything that Britain has endea-
voured to build.

In drawing attention to the Boer War poems of Hardy and
Kipling, perhaps all I am demonstrating is that the best writers in
any period can express a sense of doubt in a way that lesser writers
cannot. It follows that if good novelists had turned their hands to
Boer War novels, they might have had something interesting to
say. But the fact is that even Kipling found it difficult to write
effective stories about the Boer War, and this might suggest that
poetry could convey a new mood that fiction was incapable of
articulating. The sense of the greater flexibility of poetry at this
time is borne out by the fact that Hardy and Kipling were not alone
in producing a new kind of poem; a sense of bewilderment and
confusion is present in a lot of Boer War verse. It is, for example,
the feeling that is at the centre of A.E. Housman's 'Astronomy'.[44]
As with Hardy's poems, it offers pathos, but also a feeling of
cosmic vastness and a sense of old structures that have collapsed.
The testimony of a poem such as Housman's is disconcerting: at
the height of the imperialist phase of British history, the country
embarks upon its only really testing colonial war, but everything
that the country is fighting for seems to be doubted.

What happens in life and what happens in art are two quite
different things. In practical terms, the Boer War benefited Britain
militarily in that it helped the country prepare for the First World
War.[45] In literature, however, the picture is more muddled. It
might seem odd to end this book with a few short poems expressing a sense of confusion, but it is appropriate. The pattern of the
first half of the nineteenth century is easy to discern: the militarism
of the Wellington era yields to liberal anti-militarism. But when

militarism begins to re-emerge at the end of the 1870s, the picture is more complex. The combination of militarism and imperialism provides the country with a sense of a mission, but the voice of the imperialists seems too noisy, as if a lot of shouting is concealing a certain emptiness. There is, however, no possibility of simply retreating into domestic concerns; Britain is unavoidably a player on the world stage, and a central aspect of this, according to contemporary analysts such as Hobson, is the increasing likelihood of major wars. The novel and even the short story find it hard to control this expanding picture, but, almost paradoxically, the tiny poem can offer just the right sense of being a speck in an increasingly insecure world.

Notes

1 The Army in Victorian Literature and Life

1. Elizabeth Gaskell, *North and South* (Harmondsworth: Penguin, 1970), p. 38.
2. For a consideration of how the 'Liberal optimism and pacificism of the nineteenth century... were made possible by victory over Napoleon', see Correlli Barnett, *Britain and Her Army* (Harmondsworth: Penguin, 1970), p. xviii.
3. See, for example, J.A. Mangan and James Walvin (eds), *Manliness and Morality: Middle-Class Masculinity in Britain and America, 1800–1940* (Manchester: Manchester University Press, 1987), Graham Dawson, *Soldier Heroes* (London and New York: Routledge, 1994), and Donald Hall (ed.), *Muscular Christianity: Embodying the Victorian Age* (Cambridge: Cambridge University Press, 1994).
4. For hostile views of Kingsley, see the essays by C.J.W. Wee and Laura Fasick in Hall, *Muscular Christianity*, pp. 66–88 and 91–113.
5. There is a useful descriptive account of Lever's career as a writer in John Sutherland, *The Longman Companion to Victorian Fiction* (Harlow: Longman, 1988), pp. 372–4. Throughout this chapter, and indeed throughout this book, I have made extensive use of Sutherland's guide, which to my mind is the indispensable reference work for anyone interested in the Victorian novel. Terry Eagleton writes about Lever in *Heathcliff and the Great Hunger: Studies in Irish Culture* (London: Verso, 1995), pp. 214, 224 and 254–6.
6. Military fiction was, in fact, always far less prominent than nautical fiction, reflecting the fact that Britain has always regarded itself as primarily a naval power. The leading writer was Captain Frederick Marryat, but mention can also be made of M.H. Barker, Captain Chamier, Captain Glascock, and Edward Howard. See Sutherland, *op. cit.*, pp. 455–6, for information on the Victorian nautical novel.
7. See Sutherland, *op. cit.*, pp. 423–4.
8. See *ibid.*, pp. 249–50.
9. See *ibid.*, pp. 258–9.
10. Linda Colley, *Britons: Forging the Nation 1707–1837* (New Haven and London: Yale University Press, 1992), p. 7.
11. On the idea of an aristomilitary culture, see in particular Andrew Rutherford's 'Introduction' to *The Literature of War: Five Studies in Heroic Virtue* (London: Macmillan, 1978), pp. 1–10.
12. James M. Cahalan, in *The Irish Novel: A Critical History* (Dublin: Gill & Macmillan, 1988), discusses the way in which Lever 'made fun of Irishmen' (p. 65), but also suggests that the accusation is rather unfair.

13. Sheila Smith and Peter Denman, 'Mid-Victorian Novelists', in Arthur Pollard (ed.), *The Penguin History of Literature: Vol. 6: The Victorians* (London: Penguin, 1993), p. 281.
14. *Ibid.*, p. 281.
15. Charles Lever, *Jack Hinton, The Guardsman* (London, Edinburgh and New York: Thomas Nelson, 1903), p. 23. All references are to this edition.
16. Charles Lever, *Charles O'Malley, The Irish Dragoon* (London: Walter Scott, n.d.), p. 459. All references are to this edition.
17. There are usually a number of duels in a Lever novel. Duels are, as I discuss in Chapter 3, equally central in Thackeray, but in Thackeray the duel becomes the focus for a debate about old and new ways of resolving disputes, old and new ideas about the conduct expected of a man. In Lever the duels are nothing more than routine events in the life of an officer.
18. See John Sutherland's 'Introduction' to Ouida, *Under Two Flags* (Oxford and New York: Oxford University Press, 1995) for a discussion of a 'kind of Wildean sexual ambiguity' (p. xx) about her officer hero.
19. See Alison Adburgham, *Silver Fork Society: Fashionable Life and Literature from 1814 to 1840* (London: Constable, 1983).
20. For an account of the changes in patterns of discipline and punishment in the Victorian army, see Alan Ramsay Skelley, *The Victorian Army at Home: The Recruitment and Terms and Conditions of the British Regular, 1859–1899* (London: Croom Helm, Montreal: McGill-Queen's University Press, 1977), pp. 125–79.
21. Charles Lever, *Lord Kilgobbin* (Belfast: Appletree, 1992; first published 1872), p. 77.
22. Patricia Morton, 'Army', in Sally Mitchell (ed.), *Victorian Britain: An Encyclopedia* (Chicago and London: St James, 1988), p. 39.
23. Colley, *op. cit.*, p. 191.
24. See Neville Thompson, 'The Uses of Adversity', in Norman Gash (ed.), *Wellington: Studies in the Military and Political Career of the First Duke of Wellington* (Manchester: Manchester University Press, 1990), for an account of Wellington's conservative views, including his fear that 'the Crystal Palace Exhibition would provide the signal for a general insurrection' (p. 3). On the 'cult of heroism', see Colley, *op. cit.*, pp. 257–8.
25. Hew Strachan, in *Wellington's Legacy: The Reform of the British Army, 1830–54* (Manchester: Manchester University Press, 1984), takes a different line, arguing that the army did change substantially in the years before the Crimean War, and that there has been too great a readiness to accept the Victorian middle-class view of aristocratic incompetence.
26. It is difficult always to state with confidence where and when a colonial dispute becomes a war, but, none the less, it is fairly widely agreed that there were about 75 small wars fought against non-European enemies during Victoria's reign.
27. Brian Bond (ed.), *Victorian Military Campaigns* (London: Tom Donovan, 1994; first published 1967), p. 11.

28. See Peter Burroughs, 'An Unreformed Army? 1815–1868', in David Chandler (ed.), *The Oxford Illustrated History of the British Army* (Oxford: Oxford University Press, 1994), p. 161.

29. See *ibid.*, p. 169.

30. See Bond, *op. cit.*, pp. 11–12, for an account of the harsh conditions in the army that helped make it such an unattractive proposition for anyone in a position to choose and pursue alternative employment.

31. The manner in which Kipling reconciles an aristocratic military code, middle-class readers and working-class soldiers, making it seem that they all share the same values, is discussed in Chapter 7.

32. Bond, *op. cit.*, p. 13.

33. Burroughs, *op. cit.*, p. 184.

34. *Ibid.*, p. 185.

35. Barnett, *op. cit.*, p. 273.

36. On invasion scares, see Bernard Bergonzi, *Heroes' Twilight: A Study of the Literature of the Great War* (London: Macmillan, 1980), pp. 23–4.

37. Byron Farwell, *Queen Victoria's Little Wars* (Harmondsworth: Allen Lane, 1973), p. 1.

38. On the Maori Wars, see James Belich, *The Victorian Interpretation of Racial Conflict: The Maori, the British, and the New Zealand Wars* (Montreal and Kingston: McGill-Queen's University Press, 1989).

39. Patricia Morton, 'Wars and Military Engagements', in Sally Mitchell (ed.), *op. cit.*, p. 845.

40. Burroughs, *op. cit.*, p. 186.

41. Bond, *op. cit.*, p. 16.

42. A hymn such as 'Onward Christian Soldiers' is often regarded as evidence of an increasing impact of militarism on all areas of Victorian life, but it can equally be seen as an example of the way in which military metaphors could be borrowed for other areas of life at a time when they were not being used all that much in their original context. See Chapter 4 for a discussion of Christian militarism.

43. Edward M. Spiers, *The Late Victorian Army, 1868–1902* (Manchester and New York: Manchester University Press, 1992), p. 60.

44. One of the complications of Jingoism, apparent in Kipling's works, is that the middle-classes might seem to be putting words and thoughts into the mouths and minds of working-class people. It is a problem addressed in Richard Price's *An Imperial War and the British Working Class: Working-Class Attitudes and Reactions to the Boer War 1899–1902* (London: Routledge & Kegan Paul, Toronto: University of Toronto Press, 1972).

45. Colin Ford and Brian Harrison, *A Hundred Years Ago: Britain in the 1880s in Words and Photographs* (London: Bloomsbury, 1994), p. 243.

46. Arthur Waugh, *Tradition and Change* (London: Chapman & Hall, 1919), p. 150.

47. Wilfred Owen, 'Dulce et Decorum Est', in M.H. Abrams (ed.), *The Norton Anthology of English Literature: Vol. 2* (New York and London: Norton, 1986), p. 1913.

48. Christopher Ricks (ed.), *Tennyson: A Selected Edition* (Harlow: Longman, 1989), p. 511.

49. Bergonzi, *op. cit.*, p. 16.
50. M. van Wyk Smith, *Drummer Hodge: The Poetry of the Anglo-Boer War (1899–1902)*, (Oxford: Clarendon, 1978), p. 12.
51. For a discussion of a number of Crimean War poems, see Joseph Bristow, 'Nation, Class and Gender: Tennyson's *Maud* and War', in *Genders*, no. 9 (1990), 93–111.
52. Van Wyk Smith, *op. cit.*, p. 5.
53. *Ibid.*, p. 17.
54. A comment on the horror of war is, in fact, a fairly routine gesture even in orthodoxly heroic poetry. Van Wyk Smith cites Thackeray's 'The Due of the Dead' as a poem that is truthful about the slaughter of war:

> The wounded writhe and groan – the slain
> Lie naked staring to the sky.

But the poem, which is a response to the Crimean War, is, as a whole, very conventional:

> Those noble swords, though drawn afar,
> Are guarding English homesteads still.

> Jon Stallworthy (ed.), *The Oxford Book of War Poetry* (London: Oxford University Press, 1984), pp. 119–20.

55. W.E. Henley, 'Invictus', in in M.H. Abrams (ed.), *The Norton Anthology of English Literature: Vol. 2* (New York and London: Norton, 1986), p. 1657.
56. Isobel Armstrong, 'Victorian Poetry', in Martin Coyle, Peter Garside, Malcolm Kelsall and John Peck (eds), *Encyclopedia of Literature and Criticism* (London: Routledge, 1990), p. 286.
57. Armstrong, *ibid.*, p. 287.
58. Adelaide Anne Procter, 'The Lesson of War', *The Complete Works of Adelaide Anne Procter* (London: Bell, 1905), pp. 141–3. The poem was originally published in Dickens's *Household Words* in February 1855.
59. Bristow, *op. cit.*, p. 104. The Crimean War also saw a wave of patriotic plays, discussed by J.S. Bratton in 'Theatre of War: The Crimea on the London Stage', in David Bradby, Louis James and Bernard Sharratt (eds), *Performance and Politics in Popular Drama: Aspects of Popular Entertainment in Theatre, Film and Television, 1800–1976* (Cambridge: Cambridge University Press, 1980), pp. 119–37. As Bratton's excellent essay indicates, there is a tremendous amount to discuss in popular drama of war in the Victorian period, but in this current study I pay even less attention to drama than to poetry, mainly because my interest is in a response to war, as evidenced by literature from the period, that is more deeply engrained than emotional responses at the height of a crisis.
60. Christopher Ricks (ed.), *Tennyson: A Selected Edition* (Harlow: Longman, 1989), p. 518.
61. *Ibid.*, pp. 581–2. The war was called the Russian War at the time, and was fought on two fronts, hence the reference to the Black and Baltic Seas.

62. Olive Anderson in *A Liberal State at War: English Politics and Economics During the Crimean War* (London: Macmillan and New York: St Martin's, 1967), suggests that initially Tennyson's sentiments were widely shared, the war being welcomed 'as an opportunity for the nation to purge itself of sordid utilitarianism... the war was held to offer tremendous moral opportunities only because it was believed to be a just war and an event of profound significance in the divine scheme of things' (p. 20).

63. Ricks, *op. cit.*, p. 563.

64. Chris R. Vanden Bossche, 'Realism Versus Romance: The War of Cultural Codes in Tennyson's *Maud*', *Victorian Poetry*, XXIV (1986), p. 70.

65. *Ibid.*, pp. 72–3.

66. Goldwin Smith, 'The War Passages in *Maud*', *Saturday Review*, November 1855, reprinted in John D. Jump, *Tennyson: The Critical Heritage* (London: Routledge & Kegan Paul, 1967), p. 189.

2   The Crimean: a Novelists' War

1. Russell's reports, along with those of other correspondents for *The Times*, were first published in book form in two volumes in 1855 and 1856. A selection edited by Russell, *The British Expedition to the Crimea* (London: Routledge), appeared in 1858. Nicholas Bentley's *Russell's Despatches from the Crimea* (London: André Deutsch, 1966) is a selection from this volume. References in this chapter are to Andrew Lambert and Stephen Badsey (eds), *The War Correspondents: The Crimean War* (Stroud: Alan Sutton, 1994).

2. Tennyson's 'The Charge of the Light Brigade' was composed in 1854, after Tennyson had read *The Times*'s account of the battle. *Maud*, as discussed in Chapter 1, also refers to the war, offering an ambivalent sense of the traditional chivalric code: is the speaker in the poem to be admired for his commitment to a higher cause or is he disturbed in seeking consolation in war for the failure of his domestic life? See Robert Bernard Martin, *Tennyson: The Unquiet Heart* (London: Oxford University Press and Faber & Faber, 1980), pp. 381–8, for a discussion of the genesis and reception of both poems. For a broader discussion of a variety of poetic responses to the war see Cynthia Dereli, 'Gender Roles and the Crimean War: Creating Roles for Women', in Christopher Parker (ed.), *Gender Roles and Sexuality in Victorian Literature* (Aldershot: Scolar, 1995), pp. 57–82. On Nightingale, see Mary Poovey, 'A Housewifely Woman: The Social Construction of Florence Nightingale', in *Uneven Developments: The Ideological Work of Gender in Victorian Fiction* (London: Virago, 1989), pp. 164–98.

3. Mary Seacole, *Wonderful Adventures of Mrs. Seacole in Many Lands* (New York and Oxford: Oxford University Press, 1988; first published 1857), and Elizabeth Davis, *The Autobiography of Elizabeth Davis: A Balaclava Nurse*, edited by Jane Williams, 2 vols (London: Hurst & Blackett, 1857). Another woman's view of the war is Mrs

Henry Duberly's *Journal Kept During the Russian War* (London: Long-mans, Green & Roberts, 1856). A very readable account of the war appears in Sir George Bell, *Soldier's Glory: Being 'Rough Notes of an Old Soldier'* (Tunbridge Wells: Spellmount, 1991; first published 1867). A broad selection of accounts of the war can be found in Kellow Chesney, *Crimean War Reader* (London: Frederick Muller, 1960).

4. The Marquess of Anglesey's *One-Leg: The Life and Letters of Henry William Paget, First Marquess of Anglesey* (London: Jonathan Cape, 1961), provides a vivid impression of thinking and writing about war at the time of the Napoleonic Wars. Gillian Russell's *The Theatres of War: Performance, Politics and Society, 1793–1815* (Oxford: Claren-don, 1995) examines the social and cultural ramifications within Britain of this period of major conflict. The best account of how attitudes changed between 1815 and 1855 is to be found in Matthew Paul Lalumia's *Realism and Politics in Victorian Art of the Crimean War* (Ann Arbor: UMI Research Press, 1984); in particular, he deals with how the visual arts of the Crimean period 'abandoned the heroizing modes of traditional battle art' (p. xxi).

5. A.W. Kinglake, *The Invasion of the Crimea: Its Origins and Account of its Progress down to the Death of Lord Raglan*, 8 vols (Edinburgh and London: W. Blackwood, 1863–87).

6. Charles Kingsley, *Westward Ho!* (London: J.M. Dent and New York: E.P. Dutton, 1960).

7. There are numerous histories of the Crimean War, for example A.D. Lambert, *The Crimean War: British Grand Strategy Against Russia, 1853–6* (Manchester: Manchester University Press, 1990). The most interesting in the context of this present book, however, are those that place the war in a British social context: in this respect, of particular significance is Olive Anderson, *A Liberal State at War: English Politics and Economics During the Crimean War* (London: Mac-millan, 1967). Literary, artistic and theatrical responses to the war are discussed in Cynthia Dereli, *op. cit.*, Matthew Paul Lalumia, *op. cit.*, J.W.M. Hichberger, *Images of the Army: The Military in British Art, 1815–1914* (Manchester: Manchester University Press, 1988), pp. 49–58, and J.S. Bratton, 'Theatre of War: The Crimea on the London Stage, 1854–5', in D. Bradby, L. James and B. Sharratt (eds), *Performance and Politics in Popular Drama: Aspects of Popular Entertainment in Theatre, Film and Television, 1800–1976* (Cambridge: Cambridge University Press, 1980), pp. 119–37.

8. For a characteristic reinterpretation of the war see Philip Warner, *The Crimean War: A Reappraisal* (London: Arthur Barker, 1972). A.D. Lambert's history of the war, *op. cit.*, also presents itself as a revison-ist reading. For a critical view of Russell's reports, see Hew Strachan, *Wellington's Legacy: The Reform of the British Army, 1830–54* (Manches-ter: Manchester University Press, 1984).

9. The novel begins: 'Thirty years ago, Marseilles lay burning in the sun one day.' Charles Dickens, *Little Dorrit* (Harmondsworth: Penguin, 1967; first published 1857), p. 39.

10. On *David Copperfield*, see John Peck (ed.), *'David Copperfield' and 'Hard Times'* (London: Macmillan, 1995).

11. This is, of course, the British experience: a belligerent little nation that more often than not has been on the winning side. Repeated defeats could lead to a very different kind of soul-searching and self-examination.

12. See Gillian Russell, *op. cit.*, for a consideration of how war can be seen as a dramatic encounter. The theatricality of war is also examined in Adam Piette, *Imagination at War: British Fiction and Poetry, 1939–45* (London: Papermac, 1995); Piette demonstrates that such thinking was still central in the Second World War. The idea of war as a confrontation between two great generals continues in the sense we have of Montgomery and Rommel confronting each other in the North African desert.

13. Chenery's report from Scutari is reprinted in Lambert and Badsey, *op. cit.*, pp. 78–86.

14. Dickens, *op. cit.*, p. 145.

15. For a consideration of the idea of Wellington as heroic leader, see Lalumia, *op. cit*, pp. 25–6. On Raglan, see John Sweetman, *Raglan: From the Peninsula to the Crimea* (London: Arms & Armour, 1993).

16. For discussions of Nolan and his role in the Charge of the Light Brigade, see Cecil Woodham-Smith, *The Reason Why* (London: Constable, 1953), and Matthew Paul Lalumia, *op. cit.*, pp. 109–10.

17. Mary Seacole, *Wonderful Adventures of Mrs. Seacole in Many Lands* (New York and Oxford: Oxford University Press, 1988), pp. 90–1. All references are to this edition.

18. Elizabeth Davis, *The Autobiography of Elizabeth Davis: A Balaclava Nurse*, edited by Jane Williams, 2 vols (London: Hurst & Blackett, 1857), vol. 2, p. 89. All references are to this edition.

19. *David Copperfield* (Harmondsworth: Penguin, 1966; first published 1850). *The Adventures of Philip*, vol. XVI of *The Oxford Thackeray* (London: Oxford University Press, 1908; first published 1862).

20. The construction of the nurse-mother figure, specifically as associated with Florence Nightingale, is discussed in Dereli, *op. cit.*, p. 67.

21. Daniel Defoe, *Moll Flanders* (Harmondsworth: Penguin, 1967; first published 1722).

22. The book could be said to be the work of its editor, Jane Williams, in that it is put together from conversations with Elizabeth Davis, but it does seem to offer a genuine impression of Davis, and there is always a sense of a gap between the narrator and the editor. For a discussion of the circumstances of the work's composition, see Deirdre Beddoe's 'Introduction' to the only current reprint of Davis: *The Autobiography of Elizabeth Davis* (Cardiff: Honno, 1987), pp. ix–xix.

23. The Crimean War receives little direct treatment in fiction, but novelists did comment and become involved in a variety of ways. Thackeray, for example, produced a series of mock communiqués for *Punch* in the early stages of the war ('Important from the Seat of War! Letters from the East by Our Own Bashi-Bazouk'), but when Russell's reports

began to appear soon became involved in the Administrative Reform Association. See Ann Monsarrat, *Thackeray: An Uneasy Victorian* (London: Cassell, 1989), p. 343. In addition to his invention of the Circumlocution Office in *Little Dorrit*, Dickens wrote 'Prince Bull: A Fairy Tale', an allegory on British inefficiency and humiliation in the war, which appeared in *Household Words*. Novels making reference to the war include George Meredith's *Beauchamp's Career* (1875), Ouida's *Held In Bondage* (1863), Henry Kingsley's *Ravenshoe* (1862), G.A. Lawrence's *Sword and Gown* (1859), and, somewhat surprisingly, George du Maurier's *Trilby* (1894). William Russell also wrote a Crimean novel, *The Adventures of Dr Brady* (1868), the story of an Irish military surgeon who serves both on the battlefields of the Crimea and in the Indian Mutiny. The novel did not prove a success: John Sutherland suggests that this was probably because too long was spent on the hero's youth, the Crimean material only appearing in the third volume (*The Longman Companion to Victorian Fiction* [Harlow: Longman, 1988] p. 548). One novel that does deal with the war is *The Interpreter*, by George Whyte-Melville, published in 1858. Set around the siege of Sevastopol, it draws attention to the incompetence of the British generals and the failings of those at home entrusted with responsibility for the war. Whyte-Melville is an interesting example of the traditional officer type that I refer to a number of times in this book. He is primarily remembered as a hunting novelist, indeed he died on the hunting field; there is a sense, therefore, in which his army life and social life cannot be separated. It is interesting, however, that even someone who seems to be such a typical traditional army officer was shocked by the blunders of the Crimean War (see Sutherland, *op. cit.*, pp. 671–2).

24. Margaret Farrand Thorp, in *Charles Kingsley, 1819–75* (New York, Octagon, 1969; first published 1937), describes *Westward Ho!* as 'a novel of propaganda, a recruiting novel for the Crimean War' (p. 117). Kingsley began to write it in the spring of 1854, shortly after France and England had entered the hostilities.

25. Most critical commentaries on Kingsley are almost totally dismissive, as if he is a writer who needs to be exposed. For a clear illustration of this tendency, see the essays in Donald Hall (ed.), *Muscular Christianity: Embodying the Victorian Age* (Cambridge, Cambridge University Press, 1994), in particular the essay by C.J.W. Wee, 'Christian Manliness and National Identity: the problematic construction of a racially "pure" nation', pp. 66–88, which notes Kingsley's aggressive and didactic intentions, including his formulation of 'a national-imperial high cultural identity' (p. 79), but pays only fleeting attention to levels of self-doubt in the novel.

26. Charles Kingsley, *Westward Ho!* (London: J.M. Dent, and New York: E.P. Dutton, 1960), p. 1. All references are to this edition.

27. The best account of such changes in thinking, specifically as we move from the eighteenth to the nineteenth century, is Nancy Armstrong's *Desire and Domestic Fiction: A Political History of the Novel* (New York and Oxford: Oxford University Press, 1987).

28. One significant aspect of the change, from an old military order to a new set of values in the course of the nineteenth century, is the matter of discipline. Ruthless and extreme punishments might seem acceptable in a warlike society, but during the course of the nineteenth century flogging, etc., started to be seen as unacceptable. See Strachan, *op. cit.*, pp. 79–85.

29. There are many scenes where Amyas encourages his men with cries such as ' "Fire, men! Give it the black villains" ' (p. 381), and a predictably large number of distasteful references to 'savages' (p. 381).

30. A comparison with Tennyson's *Maud* seems appropriate: both works feature heroes who are entangled with old ways of thinking, and at a remove from the assumptions of a middle-class, liberal age. Consequently they both seem deranged; but only from the perspective of a new middle-class sense of what is normal or acceptable.

31. On nineteenth-century aggression, see Peter Gay, *The Cultivation of Hatred* (London: HarperCollins, 1994).

32. George Eliot's review of *Westward Ho!* provides a vivid illustration of the gulf between the two authors in terms of subject matter, sense of character, informing values, and, perhaps most of all, language ('Charles Kingsley's *Westward Ho!*', in George Eliot, *Selected Essays, Poems and Other Writings* (London: Penguin, 1990), pp. 311–19. Although I have only made passing references to *Little Dorrit*, a case could be made that Dickens's novel was profoundly affected by the Crimean War. It is perhaps the first of his novels to abandon any hope of reform and renewal within society, and consequently, in the person of Arthur Clennam, features a hero who is rootless and alienated in the kind of way I have touched on in this chapter. Like *Westward Ho!*, it could be said to offer a vision of how exposed the individual is in a society where the old order has gone and there is very little confidence in the new liberal dispensation, the liberal notion of a productive mutual relationship between the individual and society. The Crimean War may well have provided the trigger for a new and gloomier vision for Dickens, just as it did for Kingsley.

3 Thackeray and the Culture of War

1. *Barry Lyndon*, vol. VI of *The Oxford Thackeray* (London: Oxford University Press, 1908; first published 1856); *Vanity Fair*, vol. XI of *The Oxford Thackeray* (London: Oxford University Press, 1908; first published 1848); *Henry Esmond*, vol. XIII of *The Oxford Thackeray* (London: Oxford University Press, 1908; first published 1852); *The Virginians*, vol. XV of *The Oxford Thackeray* (London: Oxford University Press, 1908; first published 1859). The Seven Years War, 1756–63, was rooted in the rivalry between Austria and Prussia and the imminent colonial struggle between Britain and France in the New World and the Far East. The two opposing power blocs were Austria, France, Russia and Sweden, and Prussia, Britain and Portugal. The Battle of Waterloo, 18 June 1815, resulted in the defeat of

Napoleon, bringing to an end the Napoleonic Wars which had been waged between France and Britain since 1803. Waterloo was a hard-fought battle in which Blücher's Prussian force arrived at the climax to support Wellington's mixed Allied force. The War of the Spanish Succession, 1702–13, fought ostensibly over the throne of Spain, saw the Grand Alliance (Britain, the Holy Roman Empire, and the United Provinces of the Netherlands) ranged against France, under Louis XIV, and Spain. The American War of Independence, the only major war Britain has lost, continued from 1775 to 1883 and established the thirteen American colonies as independent from Britain. Correlli Barnett's *Britain and her Army: 1509–1970* (Harmondsworth: Penguin, 1970) offers a useful overview of Britain's military history. In addition to the wars in the four novels discussed in this chapter, there are a great many soldiers and ex-soldiers in Thackeray's other novels, particularly soldiers who have served in India.

2. Andrew Rutherford, *The Literature of War: Five Studies in Heroic Virtue* (London: Macmillan, 1978), p. 14.

3. *Ibid.*, p. 6.

4. By far the best account of the cultural assumptions about war of different societies at different times in history is John Keegan's *A History of Warfare* (London: Hutchinson, 1993).

5. For a relevant discussion of Sir Walter Scott, see Graham McMaster, *Scott and Society* (Cambridge: Cambridge University Press, 1981).

6. See Mary Poovey, *Uneven Developments: The Ideological Work of Gender in Victorian Fiction* (London: Virago, 1989), and Robin Gilmour, *The Victorian Period: The Intellectual and Cultural Context of English Literature, 1830–1890* (London: Longman, 1993) for two particularly interesting accounts of the process and experience of change in Victorian Britain.

7. The popularity of Charles Lever's novels (see Chapter 1) in the 1840s and 1850s, along with other fictional and non-fictional works looking back to the Waterloo era, suggests a continuing market for war. The most popular work by the military historian and novelist W.R. Gleig, for example, was his *Story of the Battle of Waterloo* (1847), which was Thackeray's main source for his Brussels and Waterloo chapters in *Vanity Fair* (see G. and K. Tillotson, 'Thackeray: Historical Novelist', in Arthur Pollard (ed.), *Thackeray, 'Vanity Fair': A Casebook* (London: Macmillan, 1978, p. 83). But the real evidence for a culture of war is far more widely dispersed than this; it starts with the sense of a new respect for an elite heroism, for an elite military code, that emerged in the 1770s. Britain increasingly defined itself in terms of its ability to fight, and this sense, reinforced by victory at Waterloo, persisted well into the Victorian period (indeed, it never disappears). For the fullest discussion of this sense of British national identity see Linda Colley, *Britons: Forging the Nation, 1707–1837* (New Haven and London: Yale University Press, 1992). As Colley makes clear, there is a code of heroism that has persisted for centuries in Europe, but it was both given fresh life and redefined in the context of Britain's emergence as a leading world power in the late eighteenth and early nineteenth centuries.

8. A contrary view is widely established in Thackeray criticism. In particular, Gordon Ray's central thesis in his justly celebrated biography of Thackeray is that he is a writer who breaks away from old ideas, redefining the idea of the gentleman for a middle-class age: that is to say, Thackeray is helping to define the new social vision of Victorian Britain. See Gordon Ray, *Thackeray: The Uses of Adversity, 1811–1846* (London: Oxford University Press, 1955) and *Thackeray: The Age of Wisdom, 1847–1863* (London: Oxford University Press, 1958). A similar view, argued with impressive subtlety, is offered in Robin Gilmour, *The Idea of the Gentleman in the Victorian Novel* (London: George Allen & Unwin, 1981); Gilmour suggests that Thackeray 'taught his contemporaries to see through their unhealthy preoccupation with the Regency' (p. 82).

9. On duelling and the honour code, see V.G. Kiernan, *The Duel in European History: Honour and the Reign of Aristocracy* (Oxford: Oxford University Press, 1988). Duelling is found in a lot of Victorian novels; it is predictable that works such as Charles Lever's, looking back to the era of Waterloo and focusing on army life, should always feature a number of duels, but it is more surprising that George Meredith's plots often involve a duel.

10. David Gates, 'The Transformation of the Army', in David Chandler (ed.), *The Oxford Illustrated History of the British Army* (Oxford: Oxford University Press, 1994), p. 145.

11. See Colley, *op. cit.*

12. The Marquess of Anglesey, *One-Leg: The Life and Letters of Henry William Paget, First Marquess of Anglesey* (London: Jonathan Cape, 1961), p. 121.

13. *Ibid.*, p. 149.

14. Gillian Russell, *The Theatres of War: Performance, Politics and Society, 1793–1815* (Oxford: Clarendon, 1995), p. 23. Russell's 'Introduction: War and Late Georgian Society', pp. 1–25, provides a good overall sense of the tensions at the start of the nineteenth century.

15. On Napoleon's tactics as a military leader, see C. Hall, *British Strategy in the Napoleonic War, 1803–15* (Manchester: Manchester University Press, 1991).

16. John Scott, *Paris Revisited, in 1815, By Way of Brussels: Including A Walk Over the Field of Battle at Waterloo* (London: Longman, Hurst, Rees, Orme & Brown, 1816), p. 85.

17. *Ibid.*, p. 7.

18. In contrast to the example of John Scott, there are, of course, more radical voices around at the time, voices that challenge government policy, although, as Eric J. Evans points out, in *The Forging of the Modern State: Early Industrial Britain, 1783–1870* (Harlow: Longman, 1983), opposition 'concentrated much more on British economic policy than on the rationale of the war' (p. 82). By the 1850s, disquiet about the conduct of the Crimean War is distinctly middle class in origin; in the case of the Indian Mutiny of 1857 (see Chapter 4), the nation seems to speak with almost one voice.

19. For a discussion of the responses to the Crimean War across the political spectrum of Victorian Britain, including the views of the two leading radicals, John Bright and Richard Cobden, see Paul Adelman, *Victorian Radicalism: The Middle-Class Experience, 1830–1914* (Harlow: Longman, 1984), pp. 29–33.

20. *Barry Lyndon* was first published in *Fraser's Magazine* in 1844. References in this chapter are to vol. VI of *The Oxford Thackeray* (London: Oxford University Press, 1908), which is based on Thackeray's 1856 revision of the novel.

21. On Fielding, see Jill Campbell, 'Fielding and the Novel at Mid-Century', in John Richetti (ed.), *The Columbia History of the British Novel* (New York: Columbia University Press, 1994), pp. 102–26.

22. On the Newgate novel, see Keith Hollingsworth, *The Newgate Novel, 1830–47: Bulwer, Ainsworth, Dickens and Thackeray* (Detroit: Wayne State University Press, 1963).

23. Quoted in Max Hastings (ed.), *The Oxford Book of Military Anecdotes* (Oxford: Oxford University Press, 1985), p. 224.

24. Charles Dickens, *Oliver Twist* (Harmondsworth: Penguin, 1972; first published 1837).

25. A comparison can be made of Barry Lyndon and Amyas Leigh (in *Westward Ho!*, see Chapter 2) as violent characters. In both cases an extreme force is unleashed within society. Amyas is overtly endorsed, however, as his dangerous energies serve the national interest; by contrast, Lyndon's energies suggest a new and destructive force within society.

26. *Vanity Fair*, vol. XI of *The Oxford Thackeray* (London: Oxford University Press, 1908), p. 361. All references are to this edition.

27. For the historical background to *Vanity Fair*, see the notes to the World's Classics' edition, edited by John Sutherland (Oxford: Oxford University Press, 1983), p. 922.

28. *Ibid.*, p. 923.

29. For the connection between war and theatre, see Gillian Russell, *op. cit.*, and Adam Piette, *Imagination at War: British Fiction and Poetry, 1939–45* (London: Macmillan, 1995), particularly pp. 13–22.

30. See Robert M. Polhemus, 'The Comedy of Shifting Perspectives', in Harold Bloom (ed.), *William Makepeace Thackeray's 'Vanity Fair'* (New York: Chelsea House Publishers, 1987), pp. 108–9, for a discussion of the manner in which Thackeray associates and compares Becky and Napoleon.

31. A vivid impression of the prominence of sport in an officer's life is given in Michael Carver (ed.), *Letters of a Victorian Army Officer Edward Wellesley: Major, 73rd Regiment of Foot, 1840–54* (Stroud: Alan Sutton for the Army Records Society, 1995). In these letters to his family, his life, particularly in a posting in South Africa, is fairly leisurely, with regular cricket matches, but, sent to the Crimea, his life becomes busier and more wretched in each letter up to his death, from cholera, in October 1854.

32. See Edward M. Spiers, *The Army and Society, 1815–1914* (London and New York: Longman, 1980), p. 49, for a discussion of how 'unEnglish'

the army was throughout the nineteenth century. There was something of a change during the century, however, as, with the urbanisation of England and Wales, recruits were increasingly drawn from towns rather than the countryside. In 1830, 42.2 per cent of non-commissioned officers and men were Irish; in 1840 the figure was 37.2 per cent; and by 1871 it was 24.5 per cent. It remains a curious aspect of Britain's militarism, however, that the sense of national identity that motivates an army might well not have been fully shared by all the members of that army. As Chapter 4 indicates, however, the English managed to create a sense of serving Britain even among a majority of Indian soldiers at the time of the Indian Mutiny. Figures for recruits from Peter Burroughs, 'An Unreformed Army? 1815–68', in David Chandler (ed.), *The Oxford Illustrated History of the British Army* (Oxford: Oxford University Press, 1994), p. 169.

33. There is a similar stance in *The Book of Snobs*. In a work that is so free in its mockery of all and sundry, there is respect for the British officer class, in particular how the most idle will show their quality as Britons when it matters:

The Duke's dandy regiments fought as well as any (they said better than any, but that is absurd). The great Duke himself was a dandy once, and jobbed on, as Marlborough did before him. But this only proves that dandies are brave as well as other Britons – as all Britons. (*The Book of Snobs* (London: Robin Clark, 1993), p. 40.)

The comment is so trivial that it might seem inappropriate to draw attention to it, but it is interesting that Thackeray should bother to draw attention to the merits of an aristocratic elite; it does serve the broader purpose of *The Book of Snobs*, however, which mocks the pretensions of all social newcomers.

34. For the historical background to the Battle of the Boyne and the War of the Spanish Succession, see Donald Hawes's introductory essay 'Historical Background', in the World's Classics' edition of *Henry Esmond* (Oxford: Oxford University Press, 1991), pp. xxi–xxv.

35. *Henry Esmond*, vol. XIII of *The Oxford Thackeray* (London: Oxford University Press, 1908), p. 37. All references are to this edition.

36. Hawes, *op. cit.*, p. xiii, discusses Thackeray's curious degree of animus towards Marlborough and his corresponding respect and enthusiasm for General Webb.

37. See Kiernan, *op. cit.*, p. 218, for details of 'the last duel'. Kiernan also provides, pp. 246–9, a brief account of duels in Thackeray's novels.

38. Gilmour, 1981, *op. cit.*, p. 30.

39. Kiernan, *op. cit.*, p. 212.

40. For the contemporary response to *The Virginians*, see Robert A. Colby, *Thackeray's Canvass of Humanity: An Author and His Public* (Columbus: Ohio State University Press, 1979), pp. 417–18.

41. For Thackeray's response to the Crimean War (essentially the same as that of all his contemporaries), see Ann Monsarrat, *Thackeray: An Uneasy Victorian* (London: Cassell, 1980), pp. 343–4.
42. *The Virginians*, vol. XV of *The Oxford Thackeray* (London: Oxford University Press, 1908), p. 7. All references are to this edition.
43. On traditional masculine attitudes, see Eve Kosofsky Sedgwick, *Between Men: English Literature and Male Homosocial Desire* (New York: Columbia University Press, 1985).
44. There are in *The Newcomes*, vol. XIV of *The Oxford Thackeray* (London: Oxford University Press, 1908; first published 1855), as in several of Thackeray's novels, three main duels or potential duels. There is a sense throughout the novel that there has to be a confrontation between old and new – between Jack Belsize and Barnes Newcome – but, in fact, the big confrontation between old and new never materialises. There is only one real duel in the novel, and this is between two representatives of the old order, Lord Kew and a French nobleman.

4 The Army Abroad: Fictions of India and the Indian Mutiny

1. The East India Company maintained its own army. After the Mutiny, the European units were transferred to the British army and the Indian units were reduced in numbers. As T.A. Heathcote points out, after the Mutiny 'Indian regiments were no longer regarded as alternatives to British, but as auxiliaries' ('The Army of British India', in David Chandler (ed.), *The Oxford Illustrated History of the British Army* (Oxford: Oxford University Press, 1994), pp. 386–90). The Government of India Act of 1858 abolished the East India Company.
2. For analysis of the Indian Mutiny, see Frances G. Hutchins, *The Illusion of Permanence: British Imperialism in India* (Princeton: Princeton University Press, 1967), pp. 79–100; Thomas R. Metcalf, *The Aftermath of Revolt: India, 1857–70* (Princeton: Princeton University Press, 1964); and Byron Farwell, *Queen Victoria's Little Wars* (London: Allen Lane, 1973), pp. 84–133. For a selection of eye-witness accounts, see Robert Giddings, *Imperial Echoes: Eye-Witness Accounts of Victoria's Little Wars* (London: Leo Cooper, 1996), pp. 29–51. For a broader consideration of Victorian imperialism, see Colin G. Eldridge (ed.), *British Imperialism in the Nineteenth Century* (London: Macmillan, 1984). Edward Said's *Orientalism* (London: Routledge & Kegan Paul, 1978) and *Culture and Imperialism* (London: Chatto & Windus, 1993) are, of course, essential texts for studying the implications of imperialism. On literary responses to the Indian Mutiny, see Patrick Brantlinger, *Rule of Darkness: British Colonial Literature and Imperialism, 1830–1914* (Ithaca: Cornell University Press, 1988), pp. 199–224; Nancy L. Paxton, 'Mobilizing Chivalry: Rape in British Novels About the Indian Uprising of 1857', *Victorian Studies*, XXXVI (1992), 5–30; and Hilda Gregg, 'The Indian Mutiny in Fiction', *Blackwood's Magazine*, CLXI (1897), 218–31. There is a case for

referring to the episode as the 'Indian Uprising' or 'Indian Rebellion', rather than the 'Indian Mutiny', but to alter the received name does seem to labour an obvious point about the connotations of the word 'mutiny'.

3. The relative figures for Indian and British soldiers differ substantially in history books. According to one account, there were 151,000 men in the Bengal army, and only 23,000 British troops, 13,000 of whom were in the Punjab and not immediately available to fight the mutineers (Farwell, *op. cit.*, p. 85). Another set of figures is 40,000 British troops in India in May 1857; they were outnumbered by approximately 300,000 Indians, giving a ratio nearer 8 to 1 (Edward Spiers, *The Army and Society, 1815–1914* (London: Longman, 1980), p. 121). After 1860, at least 60,000 regular British soldiers, or roughly three times the pre-Mutiny numbers, were stationed in India; approximately one British soldier to every two Indian soldiers was maintained as a ratio over the next fifty years (Spiers, *ibid.*, p. 138).

4. For an account of the events at Cawnpore, see Andrew Ward, *Our Bones Are Scattered: The Cawnpore Massacres and the Indian Mutiny of 1857* (London: John Murray, 1996). For an account of the literary response, see Graham Dawson, *Soldier Heroes: British Adventure, Empire and the Imagining of Masculinities* (London: Routledge, 1994), pp. 96–8.

5. Linda Colley, *Britons: Forging the Nation, 1707–1837* (New Haven: Yale University Press, 1992), p. 9.

6. On Christian militarism, see Olive Anderson, 'The Growth of Christian Militarism in Mid-Victorian Britain', *English Historical Review*, LCCCIV (1971), 46–72; on Havelock, see Dawson, *op. cit.*, pp. 79–154.

7. See the final section of this chapter.

8. See Brantlinger, *op. cit.*, and Paxton, *op. cit.*, for surveys of these texts.

9. W.D. Arnold, *Oakfield, or Fellowship in the East* (Leicester: Leicester University Press, 1973). All references are to this edition.

10. Anderson, *op. cit.*, p. 52.

11. *Ibid.*, p. 60.

12. *Ibid.*, p. 66.

13. A more sceptical view of Britain's moral mission was taken by some on the right and left of British politics. Disraeli, for example, spoke with 'considerable sympathy of the Mutiny as a justifiable Indian protest against British harshness' (Hutchins, *op. cit.*, p. 80), and Ernest Jones, the Chartist leader, defended the cause of the Indians. But perhaps the best indication of the anti-Indian feeling that swept the country is the view of Richard Cobden, who might have been expected to take an anti-militaristic line, but who affirmed that 'The only possible course for our authorities to pursue is to put down by any means in their power the murderous rebels who have cut the throats of every white woman and child that has fallen into their hands' (quoted in Spiers, *op. cit.*, p. 126).

14. See 'William Delafield Arnold', in Frances J. Woodward, *The Doctor's Disciples: A Study of Four Pupils of Arnold of Rugby* (London: Geoffrey Cumberlege, Oxford University Press, 1954), pp. 180–228.

15. On the social composition of the officer corps of the British army, see Spiers, *op. cit.*, pp. 1–34.
16. See the discussion of Elizabeth Davis in Chapter 2.
17. Anderson, *op. cit.*, p. 49.
18. Hutchins, *op. cit.*, p. 38.
19. In the case of *Jane Eyre* and *Villette*, one might say that uncertainties about personal identity lead the heroines to fall back upon a sense of their class, national and racial identity. See Penny Boumelha, *Charlotte Brontë* (Hemel Hempstead: Harvester Wheatsheaf, 1990) for a consideration of these aspects of Brontë's novels.
20. *Jane Eyre* (Harmondsworth: Penguin, 1973; first published 1847).
21. See Brantlinger, *op. cit.*.
22. See Woodward, *op. cit.*, p. 215, for a discussion of Arnold's contributions to *Fraser's Magazine*.
23. See Ward, *op. cit.*, pp. 510–18.
24. Brantlinger, *op. cit.*, p. 208.
25. *Ibid.*
26. *Ibid.*, p. 202.
27. *Ibid.*, pp. 202–6.
28. *Ibid.*, p. 207.
29. Peter Ackroyd, *Dickens* (London: Sinclair-Stevenson, 1990), p. 800.
30. Charles Dickens, 'The Perils of Certain English Prisoners', in *Christmas Stories from 'Household Words' and 'All the Year Round'*, vol. 1 (London: Chapman & Hall, 1911), pp. 212–13. All references are to this edition.
31. Quoted in Ackroyd, *op. cit.*, p. 799.
32. For a discussion of the abduction and fate of one young woman, General Wheeler's daughter, see Dawson, *op. cit.*, p. 92.
33. See J.W.M. Hichberger, *Images of the Army: The Military in British Art, 1815–1914* (Manchester: Manchester University Press, 1988), pp. 59–63; and John Hadfield, *Every Picture Tells A Story* (London: Herbert Press, 1985), pp. 100–1.
34. Edward M. Spiers, in *The Army and Society, 1815–1914* (London and New York: Longman, 1980), pp. 125–6, discusses the small number of voices at the time that opposed Britain's actions in relation to the Indian Mutiny. These included some radical newspapers, such as *Reynold's Newspaper*, which attributed the revolt to British perfidy, greed and exploitation. Ernest Jones, the Chartist leader, also defended the Indian cause. But only a handful of people making public statements defied the flood-tide of popular indignation.
35. See Dawson, *op. cit.*, pp. 79–154, and Anderson, *op. cit.*, 49–52.
36. John Clark Marshman, *Memoirs of Major-General Sir Henry Havelock, KCB* (London: Longmans, Green, 1909; first published 1860).
37. Dawson, *op. cit.*, p. 127.
38. *Ibid.*
39. *Ibid.*, p. 83, p. 149.
40. Shailendra Dhari Singh, *Novels of the Indian Mutiny* (New Delhi: Arnold Heinemann, 1973), pp. 230–2. A longer list, of 50 Indian Mutiny novels published in the Victorian period, is included in

Brijen Kishore Gupta, *India in English Fiction, 1800–1970: An Annotated Bibliography* (Metuchen, NJ: Scarecrow, 1973).

41. James Grant, *First Love, Last Love* (London: Routledge, 1868).

42. See Brantlinger, *op. cit.*, and Paxton, *op. cit.*

43. Henry Kingsley, *Stretton* (London: Tinsley, 1869).

44. G.A. Lawrence, *Maurice Dering* (London: Tinsley, 1864).

45. Philip Meadows Taylor, *Seeta* (London: Kegan Paul, 1880; first published 1872).

46. Brantlinger, *op. cit.*, p. 216.

47. Paxton, *op. cit.*, p. 16.

48. Before the Mutiny, it is Thackeray among English novelists who refers most frequently to India, but his Anglo-Indian military characters seem, for the most part, to belong to a world that has disappeared. In *Pendennis*, Major Pendennis is an elderly bachelor officer on half pay. In *The Newcomes*, the contrast between Colonel Newcome, newly returned from India, and the social world of Victorian London is extreme. He possesses an old-fashioned integrity that is entirely alien to his relative Barnes Newcome; yet, before the collapse of the Bundelcund Bank, India has been a source of easy money. In Dickens's *Dombey and Son*, Major Joseph Bagstock is a retired soldier who leeches off Dombey. Bagstock keeps an Indian servant, known as the Native, supposed to be a Prince in his own country, but the butt of all the Major's ill-humoured brutality.

49. Wilkie Collins, *The Moonstone* (Oxford: Oxford University Press, 1976). The ways in which *The Moonstone* might be considered to be an Indian Mutiny novel are discussed in John R. Reed, 'English Imperialism and the Unacknowledged Crime of *The Moonstone*', *Clio*, II (1973), 281–90.

  In relation to the siege, Arthur Wellesley, later the Duke of Wellington, who was a participant, wrote:

> Scarcely a house in the town was left unplundered, and I understand that in the camp jewels of the greatest value, bars of gold, etc., etc., have been offered for sale in the bazaars of the army by our soldiers, sepoys and foreigners. I came in to take command of the 5th, and by the greatest exertion, by hanging, flogging, etc., etc., in the course of that day I restored order among the troops, and I hope I have gained the confidence of the people. They are returning to their houses, and beginning again to follow their occupations, but the property of every one is gone. (quoted in Giddings, *op. cit.*, p. 5)

  Dickens, in his essay 'Dullborough Town', in *The Uncommercial Traveller*, recalls childhood games of the taking of Seringapatam.

5 The Army at Home: from Disraeli to Hardy

1. On Peterloo, see Joyce Marlow, *The Peterloo Massacre* (London: Rapp & Whiting, 1969).

2. See Edward M. Spiers, *The Late Victorian Army, 1868–1902* (Manchester and New York: Manchester University Press, 1992), pp. 210 and 213–14.

3. Elizabeth Gaskell, *North and South* (London: Penguin Godfrey Cave, 1994; first published 1855), p. 207. All references are to this edition.

4. On the role of the yeomanry, see Glenn A. Steppler, *Britons to Arms: The Story of the British Volunteer Soldier* (Stroud: Alan Sutton, 1992), pp. 26–31.

5. Ian Beckett, *The Amateur Military Tradition, 1558–1945* (Manchester and New York: Manchester University Press, 1991), p. 127. See the rest of Beckett's chapter, pp. 126–95, for a full discussion of volunteer soldiering in the Victorian period, including the establishment of the Rifle Volunteer Force.

6. See Spiers, *op. cit.*, pp. 210–11, for an account of the conditions under which the army performed its domestic duties.

7. See Spiers, *op. cit.*, pp. 212–13, for the views of Arthur Balfour on such matters.

8. See Beckett, *op. cit.*, p. 127.

9. George Eliot, *Felix Holt, the Radical* (Oxford: Oxford University Press, 1988), p. 257. All references are to this edition.

10. Benjamin Disraeli, *Sybil; or, The Two Nations* (Harmondsworth: Penguin, 1980), p. 489. All references are to this edition.

11. See Chapter 6 for a discussion of the persistence of an aggressive streak throughout the nineteenth century, something that is central in the works of Thomas Carlyle and Charles Kingsley.

12. One aspect of Brontë's lack of concern for the poor is her suggestion that the employees are not really minded to revolt, that they have been misled by 'bankrupts, men always in debt and often in drink – men who had nothing to lose, and much – in the way of character, cash and cleanliness – to gain' (p. 370). This is, essentially, a denial that there is any problem facing the country other than that occasioned by the country being at war. By the end of the novel, and thanks to Wellington (greatly admired by Brontë) there has been a peace conference and trade has revived.

13. Charlotte Brontë, *Shirley* (Harmondsworth: Penguin, 1974; first published 1849), p. 337. All references are to this edition.

14. The discussion of Brontë's political stance in the 'Introduction' to the Penguin edition, *ibid.*, pp. 30–1, by Andrew and Judith Hook, presents a classic liberal humanist view of the writer.

15. See Penny Boumelha, *Charlotte Brontë* (Hemel Hempstead: Harvester Wheatsheaf, 1990), p. 98.

16. Charles Dickens, *Bleak House* (Harmondsworth, Penguin, 1971; first published 1853), p. 540. All references are to this edition.

17. See Spiers, *op. cit.* pp. 153–78, on civil–military relations.

18. Martin Green, *Dreams of Adventure, Deeds of Empire* (London and Henley: Routledge & Kegan Paul, 1980), p. 207, discusses how the Victorians set the image of the engineer against the image of the soldier, the engineer being seen as 'the hero of peace, constructiveness and the modern system'.

19. See the previous chapter for evidence of the aggressive attitude Dickens was quick to take up during a time of crisis.
20. Charles Dickens, *Great Expectations* (Oxford: Oxford University Press, 1994; first published 1860–1), pp. 30–1. Richard Mullen, with James Munson, in *The Penguin Companion to Trollope* (London: Penguin, 1996), pp. 317–18, lists the military men in Trollope, pointing out that although they 'seem to abound', 'these turn out to be retired officers still using their titles'. He suggests that, 'Trollope had very little knowledge of military matters because, like many Victorians – especially Liberals – he had little interest in or affection for the military'.
21. See Spiers, *op. cit.*, pp. 153–78.
22. For the difference the Franco-Prussian War made, see the chapter 'The Wake of 1870', in Daniel Pick, *War Machine: The Rationalisation of Slaughter in the Modern Age* (New Haven and London: Yale University Press, 1993), pp. 88–114.
23. Thomas Hardy, *Far From the Madding Crowd* (London: Macmillan, 1974), p. 143. All references are to this edition.
24. Thomas Hardy, *The Trumpet-Major* (Harmondsworth: Penguin, 1984), p. 43. All references are to this edition.
25. On the social mix of the British army, see Edward Spiers, 'The Late Victorian Army, 1868–1914', in David Chandler (ed.), *The Oxford Illustrated History of the British Army* (Oxford: Oxford University Press, 1994), pp. 189–214.
26. Roger Ebbatson, *Hardy: The Margin of the Unexpressed* (Sheffield: Sheffield Academic, 1993), p. 50.

6 Heroes

1. Sir Edward Creasy, *The Fifteen Decisive Battles of the World* (London: Oracle, 1996), p. vii.
2. *Ibid.*, p. viii.
3. See Martin Green, *Dreams of Adventure, Deeds of Empire* (London: Routledge & Kegan Paul, 1980), p. 294.
4. Creasy, *op. cit.*, pp. 522–3.
5. *Ibid.*, p. 620.
6. George Eliot, *Middlemarch* (London: Penguin, 1994), pp. 245–6.
7. *Ibid.*, p. 607.
8. John Sutherland, 'Introduction' to Ouida's *Under Two Flags* (Oxford: Oxford University Press, 1995), p. xix.
9. Sutherland, *ibid.*, pp. xv–xvi.
10. The Brigadier Gerard stories have been collected together in Arthur Conan Doyle, *The Complete Brigadier Gerard* (Edinburgh: Canongate, 1995).
11. J.W.M. Hichberger, in *Images of the Army: The Military in British Art, 1815–1914* (Manchester: Manchester University Press, 1988), p. 104, points out that in paintings of military matters in the 1890s 'representations of the battles of the Napoleonic era outnumbered contemporary incidents by two to one'.

12. Sutherland, *op. cit.*, p. xx.
13. For how Havelock was seen by his contemporaries, see Chapter 4 of this book, and also Graham Dawson, *Soldier Heroes* (London and New York: Routledge, 1994), pp. 79–116.
14. Sutherland, *op. cit.*, p. xix.
15. Sutherland, *op. cit.*, p. xx.
16. Thomas Carlyle, *The French Revolution* (Oxford: Oxford University Press, 1989; first published 1837), vol. 1, p. 206.
17. Albert J. LaValley, 'The French Revolution': Change and Historical Consciousness', in Harold Bloom (ed.), *Thomas Carlyle: Modern Critical Views* (New York: Chelsea House, 1986), p. 52.
18. Carlyle, *op. cit.*, vol. 2, p. 177.
19. LaValley, *op. cit.*, p. 46.
20. Thomas Carlyle, *On Heroes and Hero-Worship, and the Heroic in History* (Berkeley: University of California Press, 1993; first published 1841).
21. On Carlyle's political views, see Raymond Williams, *Culture and Society, 1780–1950* (London: Chatto & Windus, 1958), pp. 85–98. On the French Revolution, see also Mark Cumming, *A Disimprisoned Epic: Form and Vision in Carlyle's 'French Revolution'* (Philadelphia: University of Pennsylvania Press, 1988).
22. On the 'berserker' hero, see John Sutherland, *The Longman Companion to Victorian Fiction* (Harlow: Longman, 1988), p. 293.
23. For hostile views of Kingsley, see most of the references in Donald E. Hall (ed.), *Muscular Christianity: Embodying the Victorian Age* (Cambridge: Cambridge University Press, 1994).
24. George Eliot, 'Charles Kingsley's *Westward Ho!*', in *Selected Essays, Poems and Other Writings* (London: Penguin, 1990), p. 312.
25. Charles Kingsley, *Hereward the Wake* (London: Dent, 1964; first published 1866).
26. On Kingsley's social-problem novels, see Josephine M. Guy, *The Victorian Social-Problem Novel* (London: Macmillan, 1996), pp. 173–80.
27. For an account of the death of Gordon that more or less accepts the myth, see John Pollock, *Gordon: The Man Behind the Legend* (London: Constable, 1993), pp. 316–17. For a dissection of the account see Douglas H. Johnson, 'The Death of Gordon: A Victor-ian Myth', *Journal of Imperial and Commonwealth History*, X (1982), 285–310.
28. G.A. Lawrence, *Guy Livingstone* (London: Elkin Mathews & Marrot, 1928; first published 1857).
29. See Hugh Cunningham, 'Jingoism in 1877–8', *Victorian Studies*, XIV (1970), 429–53.
30. Peter Gay, *The Cultivation of Hatred* (London: HarperCollins, 1994), p. 526.
31. See Derek Scott, *The Singing Bourgeois* (Milton Keynes: Open University Press, 1989), p. 172.
32. Hugh Cunningham, *op. cit.*, p. 430.
33. The picture is reproduced in Ian Knight, *Go To Your God Like A Soldier: The British Soldier Fighting for Empire, 1837–1902* (London: Greenhill, 1996), p. 22.

34. For biographical information on Burnaby, see Peter Hopkirk's 'Preface' to Frederick Burnaby, *On Horseback Through Asia Minor* (Oxford: Oxford University Press, 1996), pp. v–viii.
35. Burnaby, *ibid.*, p. 307.
36. *Ibid.*, p. 308.
37. See Knight, *op. cit.*, p. 105, and John Duncan and John Walton, *Heroes for Victoria* (Tunbridge Wells: Spellmount, 1991), p. 140.
38. Henry Newbolt, 'Vitaï Lampada', in Kenneth Baker (ed.), *The Faber Book of War Poetry* (London: Faber & Faber, 1996), p. 118.
39. On the dispute in the Sudan, see John Marlowe, *Mission to Khartum: The Apotheosis of General Gordon* (London: Victor Gollancz, 1969).
40. On Gladstone's role, see Edward M. Spiers, *The Late Victorian Army* (Manchester: Manchester University Press, 1992), p. 183, and Johnson, *op. cit.*, p. 301.
41. Alfred Vagts, *A History of Militarism*, revised edition (New York: Free Press, 1959; first published 1937), p. 157.
42. In the final chapter of this book, I consider J.A. Hobson's vigorous renewal of a liberal social and economic analysis, perhaps the strongest evidence not only of the continuing vitality but also the revival of the liberal temper.
43. E.A. De Cosson, *Fighting the Fuzzy-Wuzzy* (London: Greenhill, 1990), p. 104.
44. For the circumstances of the writing and publication of Slatin's memoir, see Johnson, *op. cit.*, p. 288.
45. On Wingate, see Philip J. Haythornwaite, *The Colonial Wars Source Book* (London: Arms and Armour, 1995), p. 171.
46. Johnson, *op. cit.*, p. 288.
47. *Ibid.*, p. 285.
48. *Ibid.*, p. 301.
49. R. Slatin Pasha, *Fire and Sword in the Sudan: Fighting and Serving the Dervishes, 1879–1895* (London: Greenhill, 1990), p. 404.
50. G.W. Steevens, *With Kitchener to Khartum* (London: Thomas Nelson, n.d.; first published 1899).
51. Haythornwaite, *op. cit.*, p. 332.
52. Steevens, *op. cit.*, pp. 23, 30 and 113.
53. *Ibid.*, p. 37.
54. *Ibid.*, p. 379.
55. See Dawson, *op. cit.*, on the creation of imperial soldier heroes.
56. See the discussion of Henty's *With Buller to Natal* in the final chapter of this book.
57. Dawson, *op. cit.*, p. 147.
58. On Gordon, see Pollock, *op. cit.*
59. Eva Hope, *Life of General Gordon* (London: Walter Scott, 1885), p. 362.
60. See, for example, Dennis Judd's discussion of such matters in *Empire: The British Imperial Experience, From 1765 to the Present* (London: HarperCollins, 1996), pp. 174–8.
61. Lytton Strachey, *Eminent Victorians* (Harmondsworth: Penguin, 1975; first published 1918).

62. *Ibid.*, p. 235.
63. *Ibid.*, p. 239.

7 Kipling's Militarism

1. Gwyn Harries-Jenkins, in *The Army in Victorian Society* (London: Routledge & Kegan Paul, 1977), p. 3, suggests that the army preserved its traditional ideas as late as the period of the Boer War.
2. On boys' adventure stories, see Joseph Bristow, *Empire Boys: Adventures in a Man's World* (London: HarperCollins, 1991).
3. See Geoffrey Best, 'Militarism and the Victorian Public School', in Brian Simon and Ian Bradley (eds), *The Victorian Public School* (Dublin: Gill & Macmillan, 1975), pp. 129–46.
4. Edward M. Said, *Culture and Imperialism* (London: Chatto & Windus, 1993), p. 188.
5. George du Maurier, *Trilby* (London: Penguin, 1994; first published 1894).
6. Bristow, *op. cit.*, p. 223.
7. See Andrew Rutherford, *The Literature of War: Five Studies in Heroic Virtue* (London: Macmillan, 1978), p. 5.
8. Mark Girouard, *The Return to Camelot: Chivalry and the English Gentleman* (New Haven and London: Yale University Press, 1981).
9. Rudyard Kipling, 'His Private Honour', *Many Inventions* (London: Macmillan, 1964; first published 1893), pp. 109–27.
10. The Salvation Army, the Church Army and the Boys' Brigade were established between 1878 and 1883.
11. See Edward M. Spiers, *The Late Victorian Army, 1868–1902* (Manchester and New York: Manchester University Press, 1992), p. 201.
12. Rudyard Kipling, *Plain Tales from the Hills* (London: Macmillan, 1964; first published 1888).
13. Rudyard Kipling, *Soldiers Three* (London: Macmillan, 1964; first published 1888).
14. Kipling, 'The Big Drunk Draf'', in *Soldiers Three*, pp. 28–38.
15. Rudyard Kipling, 'On Greenhow Hill', *Life's Handicap* (London: Macmillan, 1964; first published 1891), pp. 65–84.
16. For contemporary responses, see Roger Lancelyn Green, *Kipling: The Critical Heritage* (London: Routledge & Kegan Paul, 1971).
17. Angus Wilson, *The Strange Ride of Rudyard Kipling: His Life and Works* (London: Secker & Warburg, 1977), p. 38.
18. *Ibid*, p. 39.
19. In the novels of Rider Haggard (see Chapter 8) the hero is often unnerved or upstaged by a strong woman character.
20. Kipling, 'The Incarnation of Krishna Mulvaney', *Life's Handicap*, p. 15.
21. Wilson, *op. cit.*, p. 113.
22. Kipling, 'His Wedded Wife', *Plain Tales from the Hills*, pp. 124–9.
23. Kipling, 'The Courting of Dinah Shadd', *Life's Handicap*, pp. 41–65.
24. Kipling, 'The Madness of Private Ortheris', *Plain Tales from the Hills*, pp. 218–26.

25.   Kipling, 'Love-o'-Women', *Many Inventions*, pp. 199–222.
26.   David Masson, *British Novelists and Their Styles; Being a Critical Sketch of the History of British Prose Fiction* (London: Macmillan, 1859), pp. 227 and 223.
27.   *Ibid.*, p. 279.
28.   *Ibid.*, p. 290.
29.   Rudyard Kipling, *The Light That Failed* (London: Penguin, 1992; first published 1891).
30.   On Maisie as 'new woman', see Norman Page, *A Kipling Companion* (London: Macmillan, 1984), p. 143.
31.   On the *fin de siècle*, see Sally Ledger and Scott McCracken, *Cultural Politics at the Fin de Siècle* (Cambridge: Cambridge University Press, 1995).
32.   Rudyard Kipling, *Traffics and Discoveries* (London: Macmillan, 1949; first published 1904).
33.   Kipling, 'A Sahibs' War', *Traffics and Discoveries*, pp. 77–102.
34.   See Chapter 4 for a consideration of Dickens's short story 'The Perils of Certain English Prisoners', a story prompted by the Indian Mutiny.
35.   Kipling, 'The Captive', *Traffics and Discoveries*, pp. 3–36.
36.   Kipling, 'The Comprehension of Private Copper', *Traffics and Discoveries*, pp. 159–74.
37.   Wilson, *op. cit.*, p. 220.
38.   Kipling, 'Black Jack', in *Soldiers Three*, pp. 77–95.

8   The Boer War

1.   On the Crimean War, the Indian Mutiny, and the Sudan, see Chapters 2, 4 and 6.
2.   On siege warfare, see John Keegan, *A History of Warfare* (London: Hutchinson, 1993), pp. 150–1 and 326–7.
3.   It could be argued that very similar impulses are at the heart of present-day historical novels dealing with sieges, for example J.G. Farrell's *The Siege of Krishnapur* (London: Weidenfeld & Nicolson, 1973).
4.   Rider Haggard, *Jess* (London: Smith, Elder, 1888; first published 1887).
5.   On the Boer War, see Thomas Pakenham, *The Boer War* (Weidenfeld & Nicolson, 1979); Eversley Belfield, *The Boer War* (London: Leo Cooper, 1993; first published 1975); and P. Warwick (ed.), *The South African War: The Anglo-Boer War, 1899–1902* (London: Longman, 1980).
6.   On the relief of Ladysmith, see Kenneth Griffith, *Thank God We Kept the Flag Flying: The Siege and Relief of Ladysmith, 1899–1900* (London: Hutchinson, 1974).
7.   On imperial decline, see Aaron L. Friedberg, *The Weary Titan: Britain and the Experience of Relative Decline, 1895–1905* (Princeton: Princeton University Press, 1988), and J.A. Gallagher, *The Decline, Revival and Fall of the British Empire* (Cambridge: Cambridge University Press, 1982).

8.   It was, of course, the case throughout the Boer War that the presence of the black population of South Africa was almost entirely overlooked; the contest was between the British and the Boers, with no recognition that a third party might have a stake in the country.

9.   On Boer War novels, see R.W.F. Droogleever, 'Boer War Fiction', *Soldiers of the Queen*, LII (1988), 19–20, and Michael Rice, 'The Hero in Boer War Fiction', *English in Africa*, XII (1985), 63–81.

10. G.A Henty, *With Buller in Natal; or, A Born Leader* (London: Blackie, 1901) and *With Roberts to Pretoria* (London: Blackie, 1902); F.S. Brereton, *One of the Fighting Scouts: A Tale of Guerrilla Warfare in South Africa* (London: Blackie, 1903); E. Harcourt Burrage, *Carbineer and Scout* (London: Blackie, 1901); Bertram Mitford, *Aletta: A Tale of the Boer Invasion* (London: F.V. White, 1900); Herbert Hayens, *Scouting for Buller* (London: Thomas Nelson, 1902); Arthur Laycock, *Steve the Outlander: A Romance of South Africa* (London: Digby, Long, 1900); and Bracebridge Hemyng, *Jack Harkaway in the Transvaal; or Fighting for the Flag* (London: Edwin J. Brett, 1902) and *Jack Harkaway's War Scouts Among Boer Guerrillas* (London: Edwin J. Brett, 1902).

11. Malvern van Wyk Smith, *Drummer Hodge: The Poetry of the Anglo-Boer War (1899–1902)* (Oxford: Clarendon, 1978), p. 158.

12. For a discussion of Haggard and Henty together, see Joseph Bristow, *Empire Boys: Adventures in a Man's World* (London: HarperCollins, 1991), pp. 127–53.

13. Erhard Reckwitz, 'History as Romance, Narrative and Farce: Narrative Versions of the Anglo-Boer War', E. Lehmann and B. Lenz (eds), *Telling Stories* (Amsterdam and Philadelphia: B.R. Grüner, 1992), p. 167.

14. Douglas Blackburn, *A Burgher Quixote* (Edinburgh and London: Blackwood, 1903).

15. Francis Bancroft, *The Veldt Dwellers* (London: Hutchinson, 1912).

16. Rice, *op. cit.*, p. 64.

17. J.F.C. Fuller, *The Last of the Gentlemen's Wars: A Subaltern's Journal of the War in South Africa 1899–1902* (London: Faber, 1937).

18. Van Wyk Smith, *op. cit.*, p. 165.

19. See Williamson A. Murray, 'The Industrialization of War', in Geoffrey Parker (ed.), *The Cambridge Illustrated History of Warfare: The Triumph of the West* (Cambridge: Cambridge University Press, 1995), pp. 220–33.

20. Stephen Crane, *The Red Badge of Courage* (New York: New American Library, 1960; first published 1895).

21. In France, a particularly impressive war novel appeared in 1892, Emile Zola's *La Débâcle*, which is set at the time of the Franco-Prussian War, following the fortunes of two French soldiers, Jean Macquart and Maurice Levasseur. The novel, while examining the hold of a romantic, chivalric tradition of war, moves, as one might expect from Zola, to a confrontation with the brutal reality of war.

22. Arthur Conan Doyle, *The Great Boer War* (London: Nelson, 1903); Donald MacDonald, *How We Kept the Flag Flying: The Story of the*

Siege of Ladysmith, (London: Ward Lock, 1900); and G.W. Steevens, *From Cape Town to Ladysmith* (Edinburgh: Blackwood, 1900).

23. Van Wyk Smith, *op. cit.*, p. 162.
24. George Bernard Shaw, *Arms and the Man,* in *Plays Pleasant* (Harmondsworth: Penguin, 1968; *Plays Pleasant* first published 1898).
25. On Social Darwinism, see R.C. Bannister, *Social Darwinism: Science and Myth in Anglo-American Social Thought* (Philadelphia: Temple University Press, 1979) and Greta Jones, *Social Darwinism and English Thought* (Atlantic Highlands: Humanities, 1980).
26. Patrick Brantlinger, *Rule of Darkness: British Literature and Imperialism, 1830–1914* (Ithaca and London: Cornell University Press, 1988), p. 228.
27. William Greenslade, *Degeneration, Culture and the Novel* (Cambridge: Cambridge University Press, 1994), p. 191.
28. Richard Dehan, *The Dop Doctor* (London: Heinemann, 1910).
29. See Edward M. Spiers, *The Late Victorian Army, 1868–1902* (Manchester and New York: Manchester University Press, 1992), pp. 306–8.
30. There was also a turn of the century impulse to forecast the future, as in the writings of the Polish financier Ivan Bloch, who, in a book translated by W.T. Stead, *Is War Now Impossible?* (London: Grant Richards, 1899), anticipated how technological advances in weaponry would lead to situations of stalemate, loss of life on a huge scale, and the involvement of entire populations in wars.
31. J.A. Hobson, *The War in South Africa* (London: James Nisbet, 1900), *The Psychology of Jingoism* (London: Grant Richards, 1901), and *Imperialism: A Study*, 3rd edn (London: Allen & Unwin, 1938; first published 1902).
32. Edward M. Said, *Culture and Imperialism* (London: Chatto & Windus, 1993, pp. 290–1.
33. See Daniel Pick, *War Machine: The Rationalisation of Slaughter in the Modern Age* (New Haven and London: Yale University Press, 1993), p. 112.
34. See van Wyk Smith, *op. cit.*, p. 25.
35. See van Wyk Smith, *op. cit.*, p. 34.
36. Van Wyk Smith, *op. cit.*, pp. 34–5.
37. Thomas Hardy, 'Drummer Hodge', in Jon Stallworthy (ed.), *The Oxford Book of War Poetry* (London: Oxford University Press, 1984), p. 149.
38. Thomas Hardy, 'The Man He Killed', in Stallworthy, *op. cit.*, pp. 150–1.
39. Thomas Hardy, 'A Wife in London', in Stallworthy, *op. cit.*, p. 150.
40. Van Wyk Smith, *op. cit.*, p. 101.
41. Van Wyk Smith, *op. cit.*, p. 105.
42. Rudyard Kipling, 'Bridge-Guard in the Karroo', in Stallworthy, *op. cit.*, p. 158.
43. Rudyard Kipling, 'The Dykes', in Stallworthy, *op. cit.*, p. 159.
44. A.E. Housman, 'Astronomy', in Stallworthy, *op. cit.*, p. 154.
45. See Spiers, *op. cit.*, pp. 306–33.

Index